YESTERDAY

The Hampton, McCracken, Longwith, Mabry, and Wells Families

Diana L. Mellen

HERITAGE BOOKS
2014

HERITAGE BOOKS
AN IMPRINT OF HERITAGE BOOKS, INC.

Books, CDs, and more—Worldwide

For our listing of thousands of titles see our website
at
www.HeritageBooks.com

Published 2014 by
HERITAGE BOOKS, INC.
Publishing Division
5810 Ruatan Street
Berwyn Heights, Md. 20740

International Standard Book Numbers
Paperbound: 978-1-55613-505-7
Clothbound: 978-0-7884-6013-5

...to the memory of

Betty Jo McCracken Brown

ACKNOWLEDGEMENT

Cover: Kinesthetic line drawing by Deborah L. Riley.
Design by W. David Mellen.

Technical assistance given by Jean McCarthy and Thomas Etherington.

Gerald N. Mellen provided encouragement, criticism, underwriting, and many other ingredients that contributed to the compilation and writing of this book.

INTRODUCTION

This book began with my mother's efforts. As a young woman she came to Washington D.C. from her home in Charleston, Tennessee to begin work at the Census Bureau when the 1930 census was underway. By the 1950s she started her family research in the records of the National Archives. From that time until her death in 1975 she traveled many times to the Archives and made copious notes tracing her family lines of McCracken, Hampton, Longwith, Mabry and others.

After her death, as executor of her estate, I came into possession of her notes. They just seemed to represent so many long hours and such a large part of her life I could not discard them. She had spent hundreds of hours and traveled in all kinds of weather riding public transportation in the ice, snow and summers heat, tenaciously clinging to her task as Washington changed from a civilized city to a criminal jungle during the 1960s and 70s. During the last two years of her life she was assualted by criminals on five different occasions. The result of these attacks, shaken and robbed she would be on the streets of D.C. with no money and no way home. I pleaded with her to give it up "stay out of there." It was many years before I would realize the importance of these trips to her and one for which she would take such risks.

All of these families stretched back in time to the earliest part of the country's history, beginning in the 1700s and before. United through marriage, they came together in the southeastern part of Tennessee in the mid 1800s. Having migrated from the eastern states of Virginia, Pennsylvania, North and South Carolina they became residents of Bradley and McMinn County.

These early families had barely begun establishing their farms, schools and churches when their country was torn apart by the Civil War which began in 1861. In the aftermath of the war many moved on West to escape the destruction and punitive period of reconstruction.

I grew up in the 1940's in a Union household where the conversation was divided between the current war, World War II and the past. I lived with my Aunt and Uncle, Fanny and Dan Trewhitt. Uncle Dan, born in 1867, had grown up in war torn Bradley County. In addition to the adult conversation that swirled about him, he had many memories of his observations of the time. Discussion, reflection and analysis were ongoing -- a compelling topic that would not go away. Uncle Dan's grandfather Levi, had been charged by the Confederacy with taking part in a conspiracy of such magnitude it reached into the White House. He was sentenced to hang by the Confederate Secretary of War, Judah P. Benjamin -- he died in the prison at Mobile while being held by the Confederates. He was an elderly man, in poor health and this act was never forgiven by the family -- a grevious act of cowardice as they saw it. The issue in our household was never one of slavery for the Trewhitt family owned slaves, but one of division of the country. A primary concern was that the predatory countries of Europe who had prowled in North America since its beginning would find a weakened country, divided into factions, easy pickins.

The Confederates had their own point of view, though not expressed in our house. The South had controlled the Federal branches since the country began, but by the mid 1800s the electoral process reflected the changes brought about by the increasing numbers of immigrants flooding into the North. This voting power had given the political edge to the North thus threatening the Southern way of life and their economic system. Based upon agriculture, Southern interests could be overshadowed by the industrial interests of the North. Their solution to "opt out" and attempt to control their future by establishing a separate government would remove the Northern threat.

These families divided between the Union and Confederate cause, represented the dilemma of many in Eastern Tennessee. They would endure the hardship of the War just as they and previous generations had shared in the history of the country, its dark hours and its progress.

The first members lived in humble log homes and traveled by wagon, horseback, and raft. Today's generation enjoys the advances that have come with time. The raft that carried the Hamptons into McMinn County has been replaced by jet aircraft that streak through the skies. The one room school is now a complex system from kindergarten to university. The farmer in his field goes about in air conditioned tractors and uses many other technologically advanced tools.

Descendants of these families have participated in this march of progress -- school teachers, farmers, engineers, acountants, insurance salesmen, Colonels, pri-

CONTENTS

CHAPTER 1

THE SEARCH FOR WILLIAM HAMPTON'S FAMILY IN EARLY VIRGINIA

In the National Archives there is a lengthy pension file pertaining to the military service of William Hampton, a Revolutionary soldier who died in McMinn County Tennessee in 1837. Woven within the statements detailing his military experience in the war, is a great deal of personal information. From clues found in these papers William's life has been traced. The italicized quotes found in the first chapters of this work are from statements made by William when he appeared in various courthouses in an attempt to obtain a pension based upon his years in the war.

"...was born according to the best information he can get on the subject in the year 1761 in the County of Henrico in the State of Virginia..."

The first task was a search for the parents of William. As the early records of Virginia are incomplete this search was not successful. However, some Hampton families who lived at the time and place were found. It is possible that all or some of the Hamptons of this Tidewater region were related and that supportive information may have been lost or destroyed. It is known that records were lost during the Revolutionary War. This is another black mark against Benedict Arnold who sacked Richmond in 1781 and sent up in smoke the records of Henrico County.

One possible antecedent is William Hampton who arrived in the Colony of Virginia in 1620.[1] Thirteen years earlier in 1607 the first settlement had begun when the London Company of England sent out one hundred and forty-three men aboard the ships Discovery, Goodspeed and Susan Constant. This settlement was named James Citty or Jamestown to honor King James I, who was crowned the King of England in 1603. It was here near Jamestown, 141 years after the Hampton's came to America, that William Hampton of McMinn was born.

----

1. The Hampton Families of Virginia, South Carolina and Kentucky. Dr. J. L. Miller, The Times Dispatch, Richmond, Va. 1911.

William born in 1590, was a member of the ancient family of Hampton of Middllesex and Stafford Counties, England. He came to James City, Virginia on the ship Bona Nova. A short time later he was joined by his wife Joan and their three children William, Grace and Elizabeth. Two years after their arrival on March 22, 1622 there was an Indian massacre at Jamestown, all five Hamptons survived. Thomas, the youngest, born in 1623 was the only child born in America. The elder William built his home Hampfield, on land acquired from the King. He held patents for more than 2,000 acres. After William's death his two sons inherited Hampfield. According to an early map, the Hampton family lived on the second ridge within James Citty. (See map on following pages.) In 1677 Thomas, an Episcopal minister, deeded Hampfield to his eldest son John. It is family tradition that Hampfield was a wedding present to John upon his marriage to Mary Mann in 1677. The bride's uncle, John Mann, gave an adjoining tract of land.

John and Mary's son, John II, was born at Hampfield June 3, 1683 and died January 18, 1748.

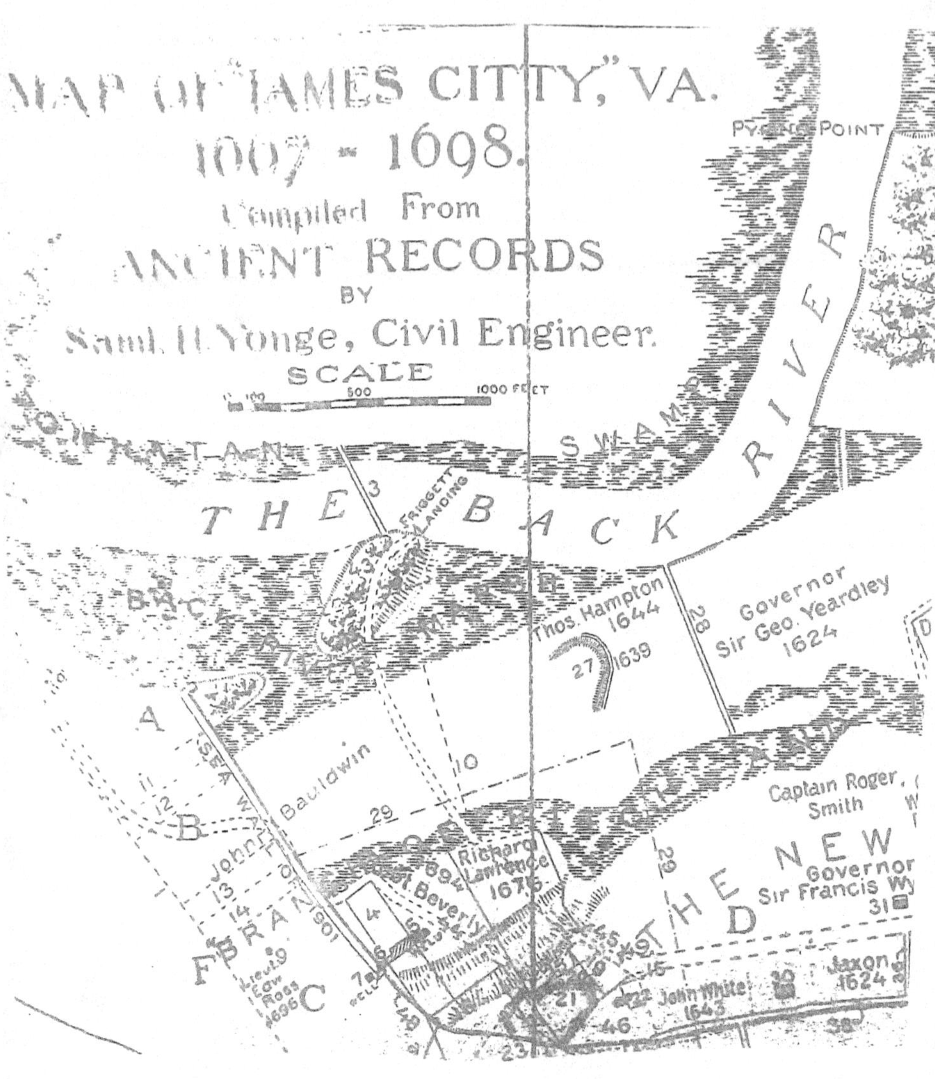

This early map of old "James Towne" reprinted in Virginia Historical Magazine, details the holdings of its'residents. Thomas Hampton's tract is on the second ridge.

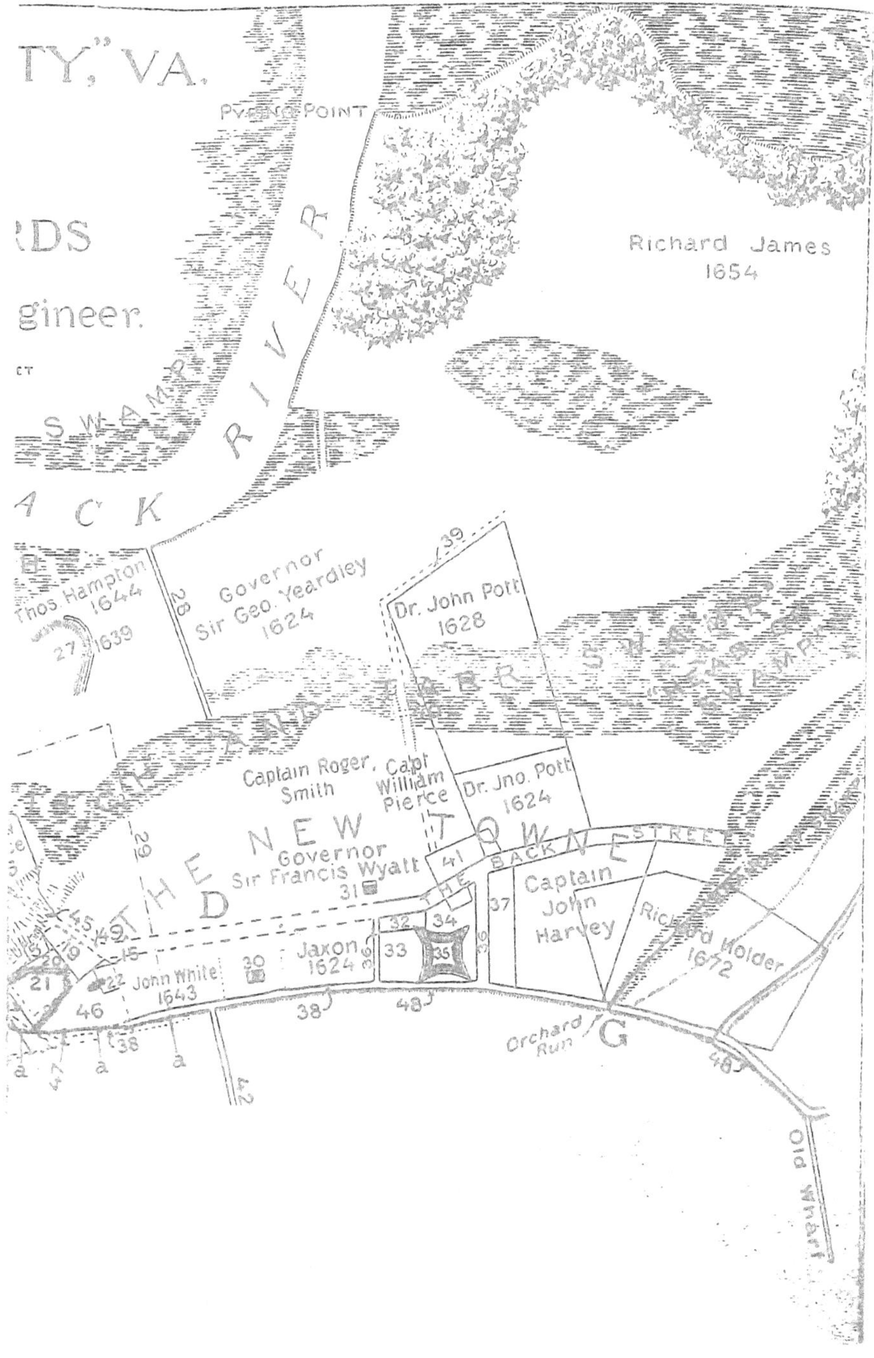

TY," VA.
RDS
gineer.
PYPING POINT
Richard James
1654
SWAMP
BACK RIVER
Governor
Sir Geo. Yeardley
1624
Thos. Hampton
1644
1639
Dr. John Pott
1628
Captain Roger Smith
Capt William Pierce
Dr. Jno. Pott
1624
THE NEW TOWNE
Governor
Sir Francis Wyatt
BACK STREET
Captain
John
Harvey
Richard Holder
1672
John White
1643
Jaxon
1624
Orchard Run
Old Wharf

JAMES CITTY VA. 1607-1698

A - First ridge, "Block House Hill, belonging to John Bauldwin in 1656.
B - Second ridge, containing tracts of James, Bauldwin, Hampton, et. al.
C - Third Ridge, on which stood the third and fourth state houses.
D - Fourth ridge, on which the town was principally situated.

1. Probable western shoreline 1600-1700.
2. Present shore line of mainland.
3. Bridge across Back River on road to Williamsburg.
4. Lot of Philip Ludwell in in 1694, containing ruins of three brick houses.
5. Third and fourth state houses, 1666-1698.
6. "Country House," in 1694.
7. Building reputed to have been a powder magazine.
8. Site of brick fort, 1670-1676.
9. The lone cypress.
10. Northerly line between Richard James and John Bauldwin in 1657.
11. Site of tract of Richard Saunders, 1644.
12. Site of tract Edward Challis, 1643.
13. Site of tract of Radulph Spraggon, 1643.
14. Site of tract of Geo. Gilbert, 1643.
15. Suggested outline of original paled four-acre town.
16. Tract of Edward Chilton, Att. Gen. 1683.
17. Tract of Wm. Edwards, Sr., 1690.
18. Piles of former bridge between island and mainland contructed during first half of nineteenth century.
19. Tract of John Howard, 1694.
20. Tract of Nathaniel Bacon,Sr., 1694. Contains foundation of chimney.
21. Condederate fort contructed in 1861.
22. Ancient tower ruin, inclosed part of old graveyard and foundations of three churches.
23. Probable site of triangular fort constructed 1607.
24. Probable site of bridge (wharf).

John II's third child, Henry was born about 1720 and died in March 1778.

Henry's will, dated May 16, 1778 left to his son Henry Jr., "...to have half of the lands; the Scale tract of land, 225 acres, half of the 1,119 acre Blackburn tract, half of the 900 acres of soldiers' claim lands on the Big Sandy below the mouth of the Kanawha, Sinclair tract of 239 acres in Prince William, 6 negroes and other personal property, besides a fourth of the residuary estate."

Many years later, in the loose papers of Henry Jr., was found a pay voucher belonging to William Hampton of McMinn.

Two additional candidates have been found:

John Hampton was brought to the Colony by Captain William Byrd on March 15, 1675. Far from the aristocratic William a "King's Man," John was an indentured servant. He, along with 121 others, came to work land granted to Captain Byrd in Henrico County, described as being on the north side of the James River beginning at Shoccores Creek mouth, up the river between west and northwest, containing 1,290 acres. Another possible candidate for William's ancestry is the

Hampton family of Manakin Town, a town populated primarily by French Huguenots, religious refugees of the Catholic Inquisition that had been ongoing in Europe for several hundred years. Members of this family were entered on the rolls of the Bristol Parish Church in the mid 1700s as were members of the Trabue family. In his Journal Daniel Trabue[1] described the location of Manakin Town, as "...fifteen miles above the falls of the James River...this falls is where the city of Richmond now is..." Daniel's life closely parallels William's in that they were both born in Virginia in 1761, William in Henrico and Daniel in neighboring Chesterfield County; both served in the Revolutionary War, and by the early 1800s both appear on the tax rolls of Madison County, Kentucky as property owners.

In this Journal, written in the early 1800s, Daniel gives a rare glimpse into the past as he tells the story of his grandfather Anthony Trabue, who fled France in 1687

---

1. Westward into Kentucky, the Narrative of Daniel Trabue, edited by Chester Raymond Young, The University Press of Kentucky, 1981.

and of his great grandfather John James Dupuy.

"There was a bloody persecution against the Dissenters by the Roman Catholicks. The law against the Desenters was very rigid at that time. Who ever was known to be one or evin suspected -- if they would not swear to suite the priest -- their lives and estates was forfited and they put to the most shame-full and cruel tortue and death..." This account describes how "Inquisetors and patrollers" enforced the laws of the church by keeping a watchful eye on the population and hunting down those deemed to be "here-ticks." However, some like the Trabue family did make their escape to places such as England and from there to America. The Trabue family and other French Hugenots settled in Virginia and established a community on the James River. Located about fifteen miles above the falls of the James, the community they established was called Manican Town named after an old Indian town that had been there previously. There were English families mixed in this population and the surname Hampton that appears in the Bristol Parish Church records suggests the Hampton family lived there in the early part of the 1700s. However the records are not conclusive enough to establish a certain link between this Hampton family and William.

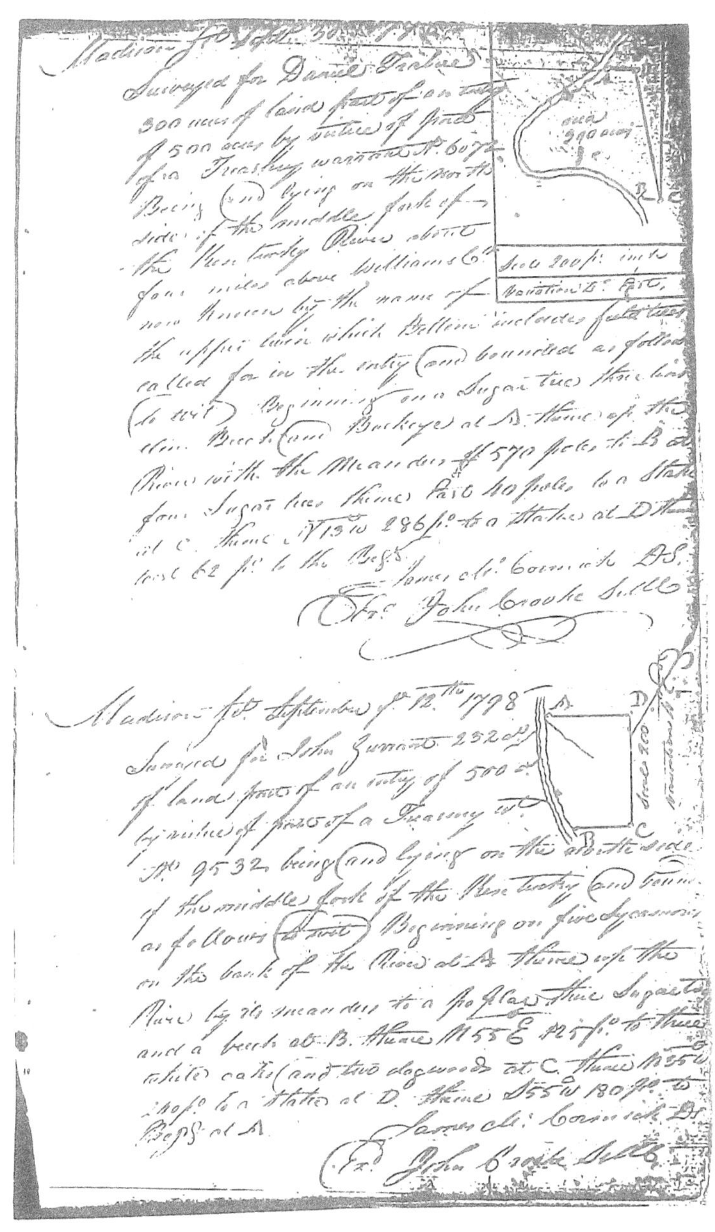

Madison Co Sept. 30 1798

Surveyed for Daniel Trabue 300 acres of land part of an entry of 500 acres by virtue of part of a Treasury warrant No 6072 Being and lying on the North side of the middle fork of the Kentucky River about four miles above Williams Ct now known by the name of the upper [illegible] which Bottom includes part trees called for in the entry and bounded as follows (to wit) Beginning on a Sugar tree three [illegible] elm Beech and Buckeye at A thence up the River with the Meanders of 570 poles to B at four Sugar trees thence East 40 poles to a Stake at C thence N13W 286 po to a Stake at D thence West 62 po to the Beg.

James McCormick D.S.

Exd John Crooke S.K.C.

Madison Ct September 12th 1798

Surveyed for John [illegible] 232 acres of land part of an entry of 500 acres by virtue of part of a Treasury wt No 9532 being and lying on the North side of the middle fork of the Kentucky and bounded as follows (to wit) Beginning on five Sycamores on the bank of the River at A thence up the River by its meanders to a [illegible] Sugar tree and a beech at B thence N55E 125 po to three white oaks and two dogwoods at C thence N35W 240 po to a Stake at D thence S55W 180 po to Beg at A

James McCormick DS

Exd John Crooke S.K.C.

1798 record of Madison County Kentucky describes land purchased by Daniel Trabue.

By late 1700 William Hampton also was a resident of Madison County. This tax record for 1811 indicates that William Hampton (third name from the bottom) living at Muddy Creek, paid tax on property and three horses.

CHAPTER 2

THE PEOPLE AND COLONIAL LIFE

The Colonies were inhabited by people with motives as varied as those that have driven mankind throughout time; religious freedom, political dissent, economic opportunity, greed, escape, adventure, exploitation. The population grew quickly numbering 15,000 by 1650 and 1,370,000 in 1750. There was a strange mixture of religions, nationalities and classes.

Religions:
Church of England - Catholics - Puritans Conformists - Dissenters - Antinomians - Protestants - Dutch Reform - Congregationalists - Quakers - Palatines - Ridge Hermits - Dunkards - Pietists

Nationalities:
English - German - Scotch - Moravian - Irish Swiss Swedish - French Hugenot - Jew - Spanish - Negro

The English were dominant in New England (held by the Puritans), Maryland and Virginia. (Lord Baltimore established Maryland for Catholics.) William Penn, whose father was owed a large sum of money by the King, took payment in land and established Pennsylvania for the Quakers. Early in the 1700s Oglethorpe populated land that would later become Georgia, with a population from the debtors prisons of England. This experiment failed. The French Hugenots were strongest in South Carolina. In addition to the Hugenots there were people from the Bahamas and West Indies. North Carolina's population was primarily German, Scotch-Irish Swiss and French Hugenot.

In the middle states, called New Amsterdam, there were 18 different languages spoken.

Classes:

There were four broad divisions: upper, middle, indentured and slave.[1]

The planter was the aristocrat of the South. He had the appearance of the English

----

1. The Colonies. Reuben Thwaites, Longman, Green and Company, 1890.

country gentleman, the squire. They were the most powerful and few in number. They controlled the government and the courts. Their position was based on wealth rather than family. Their plantations, often thousands of acres, produced chiefly rice and tobacco. A few had degrees from Oxford and Cambridge. They were fashion-conscious, indolent, vain and haughty. They bred horses for racing, gambled and wrestled; valued education, music and the arts.

The middle class, or freeholders, were the majority population. They were small farmers and merchants; undereducated, gamblers, hard drinkers who enjoyed sports.

Early in the 1600s the traffic in human beings began. The destitute, convicts, riff raff, boys and girls snatched from the streets of the cities of Europe. This population of people made up the third group, the indentured white.

More than one hundred years after the Trabue and Dupuy families arrived, John Harrower came to Virginia. Harrower, who had owned a small business in Scotland, had fallen on hard times. England and Scotland, in the early 1770s faced a desperate economic crisis.

Harrower[1] writes "...nothing but money upon interest" could rescue him. Leaving his wife in Lerwick he walked to London, gradually selling off his capital -- a small supply of Shetland stockings as he searched for work. Reduced to the last shilling he was obliged to go to Virginia. He sailed on the Planter to be sold in Virginia. Harrower, who kept a daily log, describes the process in this entry:

"Munday, 16th May 1774...this day severals came on board to purchase servts. Indentures and among them there was two Soul drivers. They are men who make it their business to go on board all ships who have in either Servents or Convicts and buy sometimes the whole and sometimes a parcell of them as they can agree, and then they drive them through the Country like a parcell of Sheep until they can sell them to advantage..."

The fourth group was the Negro slave. Socially he was the least respected but he was expensive. Indentured servants could be

---

1. The Journal of John Harrower. edited by Edward Nile Riley, Colonial Williamsburg, Inc. Williamsburg, Va. 1963.

bought for the price of their passage, usually 6 or 7 pounds. Convicts were cheaper still. These two, the indentured and convict usually did the most servile work.

Royal governors were put in place by the English Kings.[1] In Virginia there was Jefferies, Chickeley, Culpeper, Effingham, Nicholson, Andrus and on and on. All browbeat and robbed the provinces "at their will," publicly hanging those who dared to oppose.

In addition to the hangings, riots punctuated day to day life as did punishments -- stocks, ducking stools, pillories, whipping posts, gibbets, brandings, and mutilations. The second half of the 1600s was a sorry time.

Added to local turmoil were regional problems:

Pirates prowled the Atlantic Coast; Captain Kidd was headquartered in the Carolinas.

Witches were burned at the stake in New England.

Religious tensions culminated in religious battles between various sects.

1.Thwaites, Colonies

Marauding Indians --

The following account comes from Pennsylvania. It is much like accounts from Virginia, New York, and most probably all of the colonies from time to time.

"...the frontiers of this Province have been repeatedly attacked and ravaged by skulking parties of the Indians, who have with the most savage cruelty murdered men, women, and children without distinction, and have reduced near a thousand families to the most extreme distress. It grieves us to the very heart to see such of our frontier inhabitants as have escaped savage fury with the loss of their parents, their children, their wives or relatives, left destitute by the public, and exposed to the most cruel poverty and wretchedness while upwards of a hundred and twenty of these savages, who are with great reason suspected of being guilty of these horrid barbarities under the mask of friendship, have procured themselves to be taken under the protection of the government, with a view to elude the fury of the brave relatives of the murdered, and are now maintained at the public expense. Some of these Indians now in the barracks of Philadelphia ...come as friends to be maintained through the winter that they may be able to scalp and butcher us in the Spring."

Earlier in 1676, the Governor of Virginia, Lord Berkeley, who had an interest in the fur trade, also gave the Indians "protection of the government." Nathaniel Bacon, angered by the murdering of settlers burned Jamestown to the ground to assure "the rogue should harbor there no more." Berkeley was recalled to England.

There was crime -- the following is a petition from South Carolina residents to the court at Charleston.

"...for many years past, the back parts of this province hath been infested with an infernal gang of villains, who have committed such horrid depredations on our properties and estates, such insults on the persons of many settlers, and perpetrated such shocking outrages throughout the back settlements as is past description.

...cattle are either stolen and destroyed, our cow pens are broke up, and all our valuable horses are carried off. Houses have been burned by these rogues, and families stripped and turned naked into the woods. Stores have been broken open and rifled by them. Several traders are ruined.

Private houses have been plundered; and the inhabitants wantonly tortured ...for to be made confess where they secreted their effects from plunder. Married women have been ravished, virgins deflowered, and other unheard of cruelties committed by these barbarous ruffians."

CHAPTER 3

HENRICO, COUNTY OF WILLIAM HAMPTON'S BIRTH

Early in its history Virginia was divided into eight shires -- James City, Henrico, Charles City, Elizabeth City, Warwick River, Warosquoyacke, Charles River and Accomack.[1] Henrico, whose population in 1634 was 419, lay west of Charles City on both sides of the James River and extended indefinitely westward -- presumably to the Pacific Ocean. More than one hundred years later in 1747, Henrico's boundaries were redefined and these boundaries have remained unchanged.

The town of Richmond was laid out for William Byrd II in 1737. Thirteen years later it became Henrico's county seat replacing Williamsburg. Remaining at Williamsburg until 1779 was the Colony's

----

1. History of Henrico County. Louis Manarian, University Press of Virginia, Charlottesville, Va. 1985.

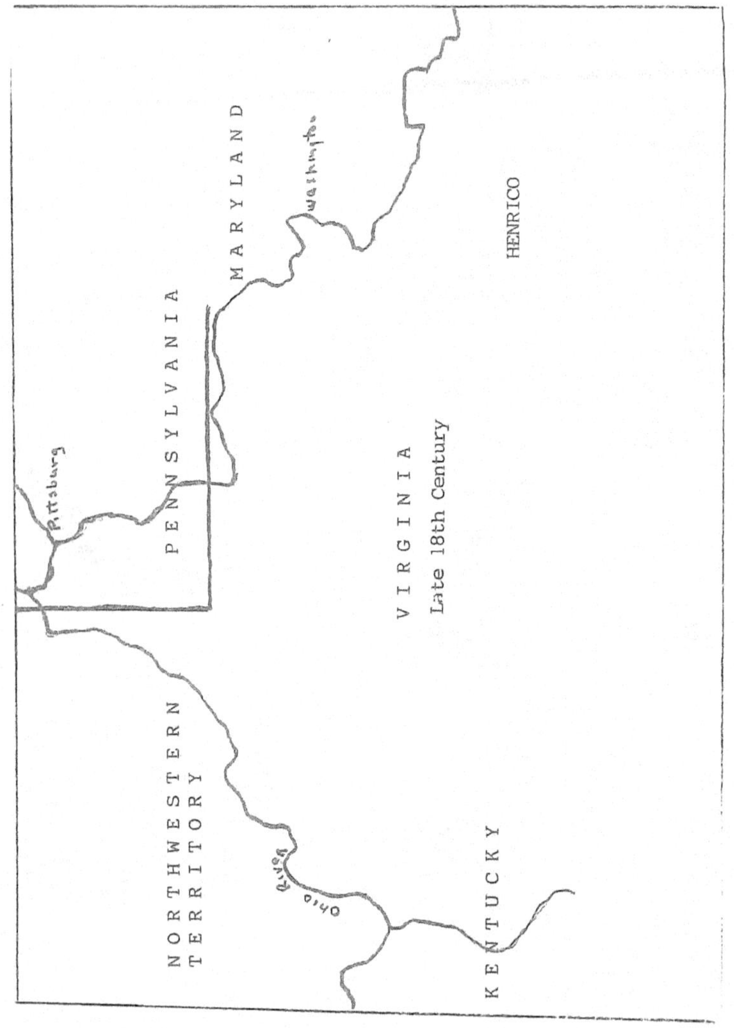

N O R T H W E S T E R N
T E R R I T O R Y
P E N N S Y L V A N I A
M A R Y L A N D
Pittsburg
V I R G I N I A
Late 18th Century
HENRICO
K E N T U C K Y
Ohio River
N O R T H C A R O L I N A

governing body, the House of Burgesses and the Governor.

During the mid 1700s in Virginia, George Washington was an officer in the British Army; Thomas Jefferson born in 1743 and James Madison born in 1751 were growing to manhood.

By the time of William's birth, in 1761, there were 1,470 persons, approximately 400 families living in Henrico. A planter society, based on the English Squire, had emerged in Virginia. Although a handful of towns had been established, it was mostly villages, with an extremely rural population, living in isolation. There were no public schools or social institutions. The College of William and Mary was established in 1693.

Newspapers, begun in New England in the late 1600s, did not appear in Henrico County until the Virginia Gazette began in 1781.

Horse racing was the number one sport and drew much interest.

Currency was the pound sterling, shillings and pence.

There were gristmills, taverns, liquor, clay pits, coal mines, ordinaries, tobacco warehouses, farms, ferries, and a stagecoach from Williamsburg to Alexandria. The trip

NOVEMBER [illegible], 1775.

VIRGINIA GAZETTE.

ALWAYS FOR LIBERTY, AND THE PUBLICK GOOD.

ALEXANDER PURDIE, PRINTER.

AS SALTPETRE is an article much wanted in America, the Committee of Safety earnestly recommend it to the planters of tobacco in this colony to cut down and preserve all their tobacco suckers, and also to preserve the trash, stalks, and sweepings of their tobacco-houses, which are found to be exceedingly useful in the production of that necessary article.

By order of the committee,
JOHN PENDLETON, jun. clerk.

AS the circumstances of the present times make it prudent to guard against the conveyance of intelligence to the enemies of America, by means of certain evil disposed persons, who may travel through the country for that purpose: The Committee of Safety do therefore earnestly recommend it to all magistrates and other officers, civil and military, the members of the several committees, and all others within this colony, to be vigilant in examining all strangers, and suspected persons, whom they may find passing, and to stop such as do not give a proper account of their journey and employment.

By order of the committee.
JOHN PENDLETON, jun. clerk.

WHEREAS lord Dunmore, not contented with having involved the affairs of this colony in extreme confusion, by withdrawing himself unnecessarily from the administration of government, and exciting an insurrection of our slaves, hath lately, in conjunction with the officers of the navy, proceeded to commence hostilities against his majesty's peaceable subjects in the town and neighbourhood of Norfolk; captured man[illegible], [illegible] the property of others, particularly slaves, who are detained from the owners; pol[illegible] all intercourse [illegible] the inhabitants of that borough and the other parts of the colony, except by such as are inimical to the rights of America, by means of whom provisions are supplied to the troops, and intelligence conveyed to his lordship of every material transaction, whilst none of his pernicious designs can transpire in the country until they are matured by the [illegible] The Committee of

TREASURY OFFICE, October 27, 1775.
THE inspectors and other collectors are desired to remember that their accounts are to be settled by the 10th of November, and may be assured that no indulgences will be given.
ROBERT C. NICHOLAS, treasurer.

CONSTITUTIONAL POST-OFFICE,
WILLIAMSBURG, November 3, 1775.
NOTICE is hereby given, that after this week the NORTHERN POST will arrive on thursday evening, and set off every friday afternoon.
A. PURDIE, postmaster.

CHESTERFIELD COUNTY,
October 25, 1775.

AT a meeting of the committee, at the courthouse, the following gentlemen were chosen officers for the militia of this county.
Edward Friend, esq; county lieutenant.
John Bott, esq; colonel.
Robert Haskins, esq; lieutenant-colonel.
Joseph Bass, esq; major.

CAPTAINS.
Thomas Bolling, George Robertson, Robert Goode, Richard Baugh, James Elam, Benjamin Branch, Bernard Markham, Jesse Cogbille, Edward Moseley, James Harris, Creed Haskins, and Joseph Kendal.

LIEUTENANTS.
Richard Booker, Archer Bass, David Pattison, John Osborne, Patrick Wright, Archer Walthall, Stephen Pankey, King Graves, John Hill, Thomas Wooldridge, Samuel Goode, and Benjamin Ward.

ENSIGNS.
John Archer, John Hill, John Fowler, jun. Thomas Osborne, Branch Elam, Thomas C[illegible], Obadiah Smith, jun. George Cogbille, jun. Alexander Baugh, William [illegible], jun. [illegible], and Daniel Wiggins.

Resolved, that publick notice be given to our suffering friends in the county of Norfolk, and places adjacent, who may be compelled to quit their habitations in this time of distress, that the members of this committee will furnish them with every accommodation in their power, and they

the expense of this country; that at the same time they live at free cost at the Congress in Philadelphia they receive large sums to defray those pretended expenses, and wickedly charging the Convention of this colony with the same seditious and similar designs; and that the levies ordered to be made by the committee of this county (by order of the Convention of this colony) for procuring ammunition, and paying other incidental charges, were to be applied to the making gentlemen of themselves; that, under various pretences, they would take every half-bit they had, and then leave them to shift as they could; with other unjust and invidious reflections, of the same nature. And whereas the said Archibald Miller, having been duly summoned to answer the said allegations, did this day appear, the committee, after hearing the depositions of sundry witnesses before taken, and the testimonies of several witnesses now examined, do find the said Alexander Miller has been guilty of the several charges as above alledged.

Resolved therefore, that it be recommended to all the good people of this county and colony to have no further dealings, connexion, or intercourse, with the said Miller; as he appears, from the whole tenour of his behaviour, to be a real enemy to the general struggle of all America, now defending themselves against the tyrannical oppressions of a corrupt British parliament, until he by his future behaviour convince his countrymen of his sincere repentance for his past folly.

Ordered, that the clerk transmit a copy of the above proceedings to Mr. Alexander Purdie, to desire he will publish the same in his publick gazette.
SILAS HART, chairman.

At a committee for the county of Spotsylvania, held at the town-house in Fredericksburg, on thursday the 17th of October 1775. Present 17 members.
CHARLES DICK, gent: in the chair:
Resolved, THAT no provision be allowed to be water-carried from this county, without leave obtained from the committee.

An article in the center of this issue of the Virginia Gazette, October 25, 1775 announces the choice of officers for the Chesterfield County militia. William Hampton had moved from Henrico County to Chesterfield by this time.

took from eight in the morning 'til eleven at night complained one traveler.

Travel was by way of toll road -- Wagon and team .25 cents, plus six cents per wheel, ditto for every riding carriage. Horses mules, horned cattle .03 cents each. The railroad was not to come until the next century.

The courts collected taxes, built roads, levied fines, cared for the poor and orphaned, (the care usually meant for the orphaned to be bonded until the age of 21, and the poor were hustled off to the poor farm or work house) hung the murderers and other miscreants, lopped off ears, lashed backs, fastened into stocks, punished for profanity, cheating and fornication.

Land and personal property were taxed and there were taxes on: rent, sugar, cider, tobacco (sale of), estates, poll, offices, professions, trades, business, wine, rum, slaves, molasses, import duty, painter's colours, paper, glass and yes TEA.

The Colonies desiring development of the country and realizing a larger labor force would be needed decided to increase the population. They turned to the over-crowded cities of Europe. A brisk business developed, one of recruiting and transporting human cargo. They came by the thousands from Dicken's England, Rousseau's France, Ireland and Germany. These people poured out of slums and prisons where life was very cheap as evidenced by the hangings that took place for very small crimes. A poor if not destitute population they arrived in Virginia under the terms of indenture and would serve this period of labor before their "new life" would begin. They became the frontiersmen, fiercely independent, extremely conservative, isolationists, disdainful of authority, violent and undereducated. They lived in log cabins, often ran about naked and had less culture than the Indians according to one observer.

During this period, the mid 1700s, the people of Virginia were at war. British Major George Washington, led the Militia of Virginia. The Militia of Henrico numbered 1,198[1] strong, composed of citizen soldiers who patrolled the county and were subject to call up by the state.

----

1. Manarian, History of Henrico

The French and Indian War begun in 1754, was the final colonial struggle which ended French and British disputes over North American territory. It took place while the Seven Years' War raged between the great powers in Europe. At issue was control of the lands that were drained by the Ohio. At the outset of the war Washington led a small force of colonial troops from the colony of Virginia to force the French troops to withdraw. The French refused and war broke out. Ongoing at the time of William's birth it ended in 1763.

It was an untamed and troubled country that welcomed William. He would have but a few short years of childhood until he too would be caught up in yet another military conflict, the Revolutionary War.

CHAPTER 4

THE WAR

William was 14 when they pushed the tea into the harbor at Boston. It seemed tax after tax had been imposed on the Colonies and they groaned with the weight, and then they growled. Mobs formed in Boston and sought their targets against the Crown. King George II sent General Thomas Gage to put down the rebellion. Gage closed the port of Boston. The government was taken over by the British. Redcoats tramped the streets of Boston. The city was under siege.

John Hancock, whose ship the Liberty had been impounded in the Harbor for the non-payment of taxes, Samuel Adams, Joseph Warren, Paul Revere and Benjamin Church met nightly at the Green-Dragon Tavern[1] for the purpose of keeping an eye on the British and Tories.

The Continentals stored their weapons at Concord. When the British troops began

---

1. The American Revolution. Hugh F. Rankin, G. P. Putnam's Son, New York, 1964.

Major Battles of The Revolutionary War, 1775-1777

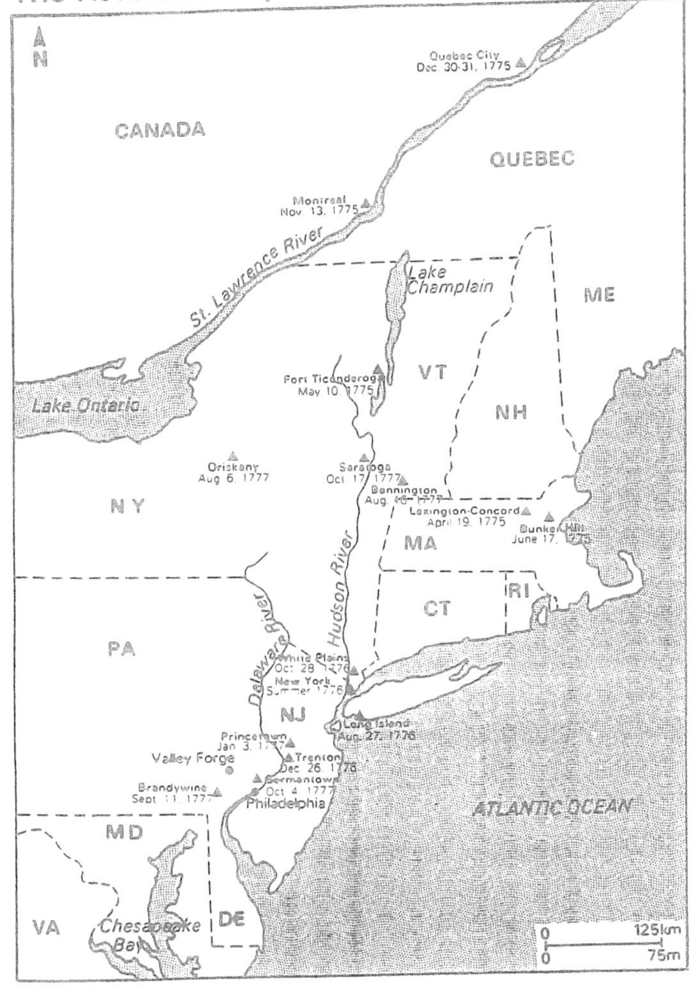

massing at the dock preparing to cross the River Charles, the watch committee knew this arsenal was their destination. Paul Revere made his famous dash in an attempt to rouse the public to save the arsenal.

When word of the British invasion reached the frontiersmen of Virginia they grabbed their squirrel rifles and went.

From this population came William. A planter or a frontiersman??? He could read and write.

At the age of sixteen William became a member of the Second Virginia State Regiment.

"...enlisted in the Army of the United States some time in the Spring of the year 1777..."

The 2nd Regiment of Infantry was authorized by the General Assembly of Virginia in December 1776.[1] Created for local defense, this Regiment was limited to service within the State lines. Late in 1777 the 1st and 2nd Regiments were placed in the Continental Line at Germantown, Pennsylvania to offset

---

1. A Guide to Virginia Military Organizations in the American Revolution, 1774-1787. E. M. Sanchez-Saavedra, Virginia State Library, 1978.

the loss of the 9th Virginia. The 9th was captured to a man and ceased to exist October 1777. In January 1778 the 2nd was formed into a battalion of eight companies, William served in the 5th under Captain Peter Bernard that was raised April 10, 1777.

"... remained at Williamsburg through the Summer when he was 'called to the north' to join General Washington's army at Valley Forge."

The British captured Philadelphia on 26 September 1777. On the night of October 3, Washington attack Howe's army at Germantown. The British sent the Americans reeling. On December 19, 1777 Washington and his men retreated to Valley Forge, marching 12 miles in a snowstorm from a temporary encampment at Gulph Mills. While the British occupied Philadelphia, enjoying the hospitality offered to them by the Loyalists of the city, the Americans shivered at Valley Forge.

Sixteen year old William was among the 10,000 soldiers who began the tragedy at Valley Forge -- 3,000 deserted; 2,000 froze to death or died of starvation and disease.

There were more problems than just the weather at Valley Forge.

Nearby farmers sold to the British for hard cash -- Boston merchants would not move government clothing off their shelves for less than 1,000 percent profit. Profiteering and graft took their toll among the men. The soldier's story that follows gives us a glimpse into that camp.

"...and every night for too many weeks sticklike soldiers stuck their heads out of their smoky huts to cry, no meat! No meat! Firecake and water was their food, bloody footprints in the snow their sign. Their clothes were so ragged and blankets were so scarce that they often sat up all night rather than fall asleep and freeze to death. Many limbs were frozen black." One bitter Continental wrote: "Poor food - hard lodging cold weather - fatigue - nasty cloaths - nasty cookery - vomit half my time - smoak'd out of my senses - the Devil's in it - I can't endure it - Why are we sent here to starve and freeze...?" And from a camp surgeon came the cry "Lord, Lord, Lord, Valley Forge..."

2 | Virginia State Regiment.

Captain Peter Bernard's Co. of the 2d Virginia State Regiment commanded by Col. Gregory Smith.*

Revolutionary War.

Appears on

Company Muster Roll

of the organization named above for the month

of ...., 1778.

Roll dated Valley Forge

May 4 ...., 1778.

Appointed ...., 17

Commissioned ...., 17

Enlisted ...., 17

Term of enlistment ....

Time since last muster or enlistment ....

Alterations since last muster ....

Casualties ....

Remarks: ....

*This company was designated at various times as Captain Peter Bernard's and Capt. John McElheny's Company.

This pay voucher from the files of the National Archives, Washington, D.C. is knowledge certain that William did endure and received six and two-third dollars in May and on June 4, 1778.

"...was put under the command of General Mulenburg on the Schuylkill; followed the British after they had evacuated Philadelphia, and over took them at Monmouth."

The 1st and 2nd Virginia State Regiment joined Mulenburg's brigade. The British General Howe had been replaced by Clinton. The British army and 3,000 Loyalists, left Philadelphia and marched for New York. One observer wrote "...the long red column crawled slowly through the Jerseys, the hot June sun often sent the temperature soaring to a hundred degrees."

Washington started his army marching to intercept Clinton's army. They met at Monmouth Court House on June 28, 1778. The Americans defeated the British at Monmouth Court House. Monmouth was the last major battle of the Northern campaign.

Washington's army had lost its' amateur status at Valley Forge largely due to the drilling and training of Frederick William Augustus Henry Ferdinand, Baron von Steuben. At Valley Forge the previous February, this colorful impostor, rode into camp claiming he had been a lieutenant general on the staff of Frederick the Great in the Prussian army. He had not been more than a Captain. The Americans however, gave him the rank and he turned this mob, mostly made up of teen-age boys, some as young as twelve, into soldiers. Monmouth was the first test. With speed and efficiency the little Rebel army left its winter quarters at Valley Forge and delivered defeat to the British at Monmouth.

"...was taken sick and conveyed to Danbury Auspittle in Connecticut State. Then...took up Winter Quarters at Middle-brook in the Winter of 1778. ...Stony Point was taken by General Wayne. Then marched toward New York and took a place called Fowlers Hook (Paulus Hook)."

This site is today Jersey City, New Jersey. It was the scene of "Light Horse Harry" Lee's triumph on August 19, 1779.

The first and second Virginia State Regiments returned to Virginia late in 1779.

On December 26, 1779 8,000 British troops sailed for Charleston.[1] Clinton commanded.

"...was discharged by his officer sometime in the Spring of 1780, having served out his full three years, which

----

1.Rankin, American Revolution.

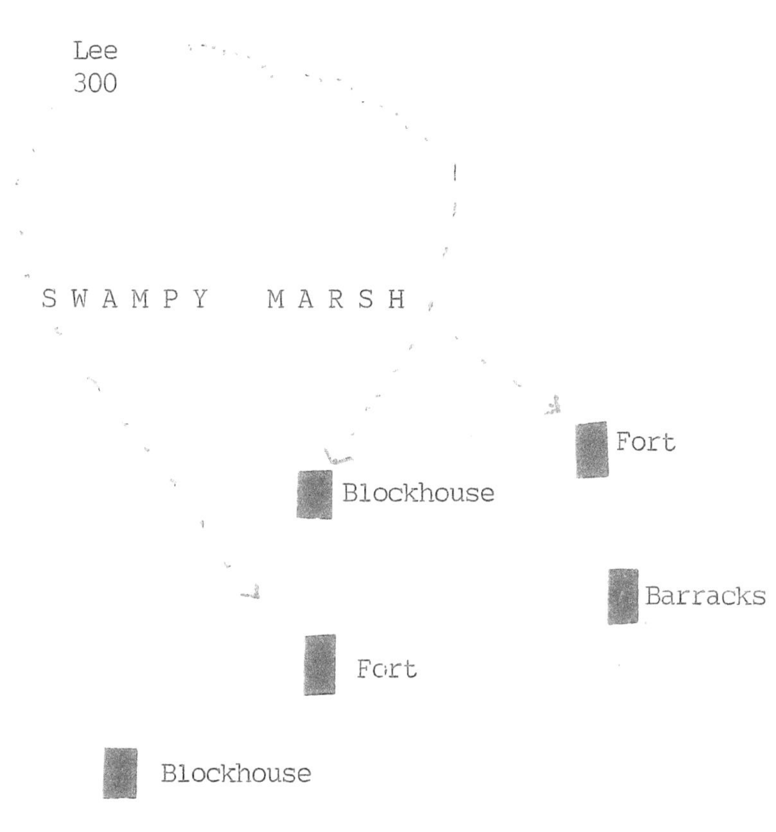

Paulus Hook, a British fortification located in New Jersey (present day Jersey City). This was the site of "Light Horse Harry" Lee's great victory on the 19th of August, 1779.

HUDSON RIVER

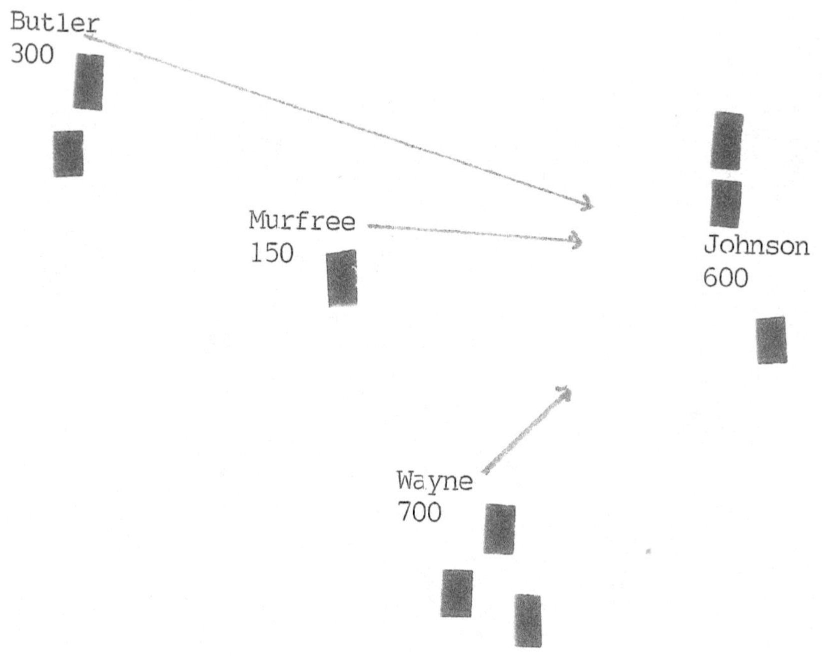

Stony Point, an American fort located twenty-five miles north of New York City on the Hudson River. Captured by British General Clinton on June 1, 1779, the Americans under General Wayne retook the fort in a fifteen minute fight on June 16, 1779.

discharge has been long since lost or mis-layed....was furlowed for three months to go home."

Home was in Henrico County until the close of the War when the Hampton family moved to Chesterfield. Inasmuch as the Counties are adjoining, the description provided by Daniel Trabue[1] in his Journal written in 1827, should reflect events in Henrico. Daniel, returning to Chesterfield from Kentucky in the Spring of 1780, talks about the times.

Daniel's story begins:

"As I went on a long Holston and New River the men was fixing to go aginst the torrys and British. They was very ancious. I did almost conclude to go with them. There were the very men that killed and defeated Forgisson on Kings Mountain. (Trabue is writing from memory and is mis-taken here as this battle did not occur until later that year in October.)

When I went through Bedford at New London, they had about 150 men in custedy. Trying them for Toryism. The fact was the

---

1. Young, Westward into Kentucky.

British had taken Charlestown and our army that was their sent some secret agents to Virginia with Lord Corn Wallace proclaiming in the name of George the 3rd that whoever would throw down their arms of Rebellion and join his Gracious Majisty King George's army he should have free pardon and his great crimes of Rebellion blotted out, and also that when the Rebels shall be subdued shall have a good proportion of these Rebel's estates. These 150 men had joined in with the proclamiton and they ware arrested and in order to get clear the most of them enlisted in the American Army for two years. So the biter got bit. I know some of these men to this day.

When I went but a little further all along the Road the men had but just started to go with General Gates to take Corn Wallace. General Gates seemed to be sure of victory. When I got to Chesterfield near Richmond they -the men - was gone from their also with General Gates."

Lord Cornwallis assumed command of all British forces in the South after the capture of Charleston in May 1780, and marched from Wilmington into Virginia.[1] General Horatio Gates, recent hero of Saratoga, was sent by Washington to liberate the Carolinas. Gates had warned Governor Jefferson "If Cornwallis conquers the southern and eastern parts of North Carolina and extends his posts of communication to Portsmouth, you must expect the weight of the war will penetrate into your bowels and cause such an inflammation there may be consumed the life blood of the State."

The pension paper statements at this point are difficult to reconcile with the history of the War. Perhaps it would be reasonable to believe that 72 year-old William has confused dates.

"...in the Spring of the year 1780 enlisted in the army of the United States at Williamsburg in the State of Virginia for two years..."

William says he no longer remembers the name of his Colonel, but remembers he had a company of Indians and they marched to the Eastern shore of Virginia past Little York and Guinea Island. (Gwynn?)

1.Rankin, American Revolution.

"...marched under the command as in company with a Col Gass (sp)"

"...remained in that section of the country until sometime in the Summer...marched to Little York, from there to Jamestown, from there to a place called Sleepy... then to Petersburg. Stayed there 'til Winter...."

Located on the Appomattox River, Petersburg was the site for the tobacco warehouses[1] and was at this time an important depot of military supplies guarded by 1,000 Virginia Militia. This is what drew the British the following year. In May British General William Phillips advanced on Petersburg with 2,000 troops brought from N.Y. and the 1,000 man force Arnold had brought down a few months earlier. General Von Steuben had been in Virginia a short time with the mission of doing what he could to help mobilize the military resources of the region.

"...was called to the South. Joined General Green's army at the Cheraws..."

General Nathaniel Greene had succeeded Gates. During the period 20 December

---

1.Rankin, American Revolution.

1780 - 28 January 1781 Greene camped on the Pee Dee River[1] in the vicinity of Cheraw (S.C.) with about 1,000 troops.

On January 17, American General, Daniel Morgan was attacked by British Colonel Banastre Tarleton and thus began the battle of Cowpens S.C. Morgan with 1,000 men defeated the British. When news of Cowpens reached Green, his first impulse was to strike the British posts in South Carolina. Instead he went North, his destination Virginia where the turncoat Brigadier General Benedict Arnold was in Richmond. Washington sent 1,200 troops South, under Marquis de Lafayette to the aid of Virginia.

From Trabue's Journal:[2] "In January 1781 the British came to Richmond, 15 miles from where we lived. Brother William and myself got on our horses and went down to Manchester the oppeset side of the River from Richmond. All our county men meet their. We remained their until the neighbouring county also came. And when the British found out so many Militia a gether-

----

1.Rankin, American Revolution.

2.Young, Westward into Kentucky.

ing they burned the ware houses of tobacco and some other houses and went down the River and got in their ships and went off again. Col. Robert Haskins commanded this army. We was soon discharged." Daniel is describing the British capture of Richmond. This force was led by the traitor Benedict Arnold.

On February 23, 1781 General Greene recrossed the Dan into North Carolina and went running South. Jefferson (Governor of Virginia) received intelligence to this effect and promptly ordered the entire militia of five counties to join Greene's forces. For the next two weeks they outdistanced Cornwallis. On March 14, Greene's army lay encamped at Guilford Courthouse.

"...was at the battle of Guilford Courthouse under General Green..."

Trabue[1] talks about Guilford:

"Brother Edward Trabue came home from the Suthern Army. He told us how he was in the battle at Gelford and that he was at Gate' (Greene's) defeat in the battle and

----

1. Young, Westward into Kentucky.

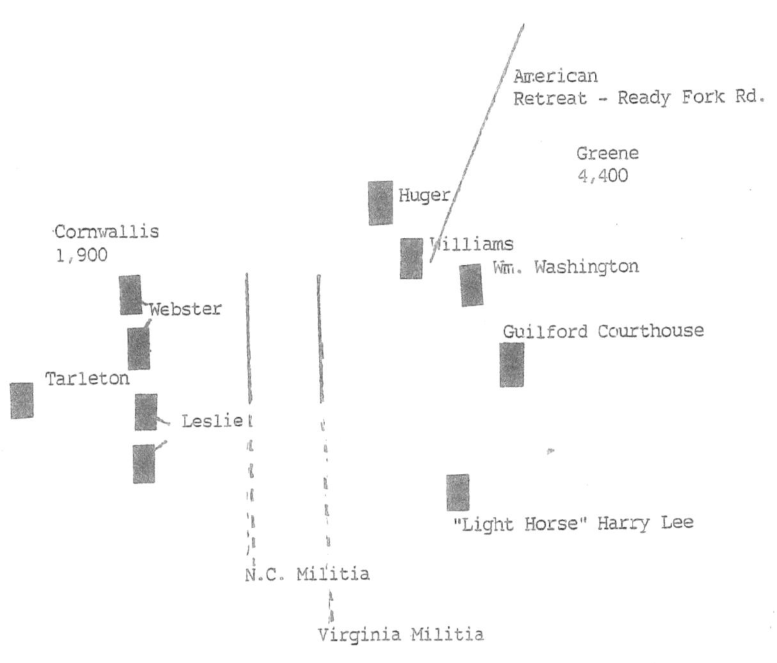

Guilford Courthouse, just north of Greensboro, North Carolina, this battle between the British led by General Cornwallis and the Americans led by General Greene took place on March 15, 1781. The British routed the Americans. It was here at Guilford, that William Hampton ended his soldiering.

as they all broak and run. As he run on some distance a waggoner jumped off his horse and run and left it. Edward took out the saddle horse and mounted him. He looked back and no light horse acoming and the Britesh close by..."

On March 15, 1781 the two armies met at Guilford Courthouse in battle.

Green had 4,500 men defending against 2,000 British and Hessians. The Virginia militiamen were in the second line, about 1,200 strong. The Continental troops from Virginia, including William's regiment were on the third line, about 1,400 strong. On March 18, Cornwallis declared a "compleat victory over the rebels." Many loyalists rode into camp to congratulate Cornwallis. It was however the turning point. Even in victory another piece of the British had been lost as every battle exacts a price from both sides.

William's pension statement, concerning the War, concludes with the battle of Guilford Courthouse.

"...was discharged in Guilford County in the State of North Carolina..."

Did he return home to Chesterfield County from North Carolina?

Trabue[1] talks about Virginia in 1781 --

"We was mustered about the first of March 1781 and started down on the south side of James River. We went near the Dismal swamp and encamped in Babs' Old Field. Our army was about 3,000 all Militia except the Artilera which consisted in about 40 men rank and file. We was commanded by General Mulinburg. We had not been their long before we heard the Drum beat the "general" -- that is to say, "Strike your tents and March." All the soldiers and waiters in the army knows the sound of this beat. If it was at midnight every thing moves:

'Don't you hear the general say,
Strike your tents and march away?

We understood the Britesh was coming on us with a superior force. The British Army moved up the River. We then had to march day and night."

2,500 British embarked at Portsmouth on April 18 and sailed up the James, stopping here and there on missions of destruction.

1.Young, Westward into Kentucky.

Trabue[1] describes Chesterfield County in May:

"The Britesh army was destressing our country very much and had no oppisition. Corn Wallis had his headquarters at Petersburg, and Col Taltern roaving about the country just where he pleased.

The people in Chesterfield was mostly hid in the swomps. These swomps in the winter is wet and ponds of water, but in the summer is dry and very bushy --almost equil to cain breaks. Almost all our young women left their homes and went up the country. When the Britesh would go to a house they would compel the negros and children to go and shew where the meet or brandy or flour was hid out.

My Mother's house was weatherboarded and lathed and plastered inside; and I went on the back side and drawd a plank or two, and put the most of the cloathing and plate and the like, and nailed it up again. No one knew of it but me and my Mother. Some of our meet we hid out, and only some negros know where it was but those we could confide in. My sisters went to an unkil's where it was thought was a very private place. What

---

1. Young, Westward into Kentucky.

arms and ammonition we had we hid out. Brother William and myself when we was at home slept out. Brother Stephen and my Mother stayed at home. Captain Mosley, Brother William, and my self took several tours on the enemie's line in the night. Corn Wallis and Talton left the south side of the river and went on the North side to Richmond."

Through the spring and summer months Richmond continued to be held by the British. Tarleton was racing toward Charlottesville, his objective the capture of Governor Jefferson and members of the Virginia legislature. Jefferson escaped through the woods as Tarleton's men were ascending the hill to Monticello.

Cornwallis was encamped at Williamsburg and Jamestown -- smallpox was everywhere! Anthony Wayne rushed the British Army in a bayonet charge. One observer wrote of the scene "Madness -- Mad Anthony, by God, I never knew such a piece of work heard of -- about eight hundred troops opposed to five or six thousand veterans upon their own ground." Cornwallis crossed the James River and went on to Portsmouth.

By August 1781 the army of Cornwallis was throwing up earthworks as they decided to occupy Yorktown. Some 2,000 slaves (including some from the plantations of Washington and Jefferson) were formed into labor corps. (Negro slaves, promised freedom in return for service, were resold by the British after the war.)

October brought the final battle. Fought at Yorktown, the war's conclusion brought victory to the Americans.

Trabue[1] gives an interesting and unique account of Yorktown. If William Hampton returned to Chesterfield County after the Battle of Guilford it is quite possible he was on hand as many from the countryside were there. The following is from Trabue's Journal:

"...there is now a great difference in seeing people plenty stiring about in the county and at their homes. When Corn Wallis and Talton was roveing about I could hardley see any person. Although the Militia is all called on to go to camp. Now you may often see people -- old men and boys, old woman and girles, and negros --and don't offer to

----

1.Young, Westward into Kentucky.

run and hide and as formerly; but would run to us for the knews, sending letters and other things to their men in camp -- like a little coffey, chockelitt, or cloathig -- and enquereing and saying, 'Do you think Corn Wallace will be taken' 'O yes, and now we are sure to have company along the road that is going to camp." The account continues to describe the arrival of George Washington and of troops from New York.

Both sides made preparation for the battle to come. While the British were hold up in their fortress the Americans brought in supplies and armament. Ditches were dug and batteries to accommodate cannon were placed every few yards. When the battle began bombs fired by the cannon rained down.

Wednesday, October 17, 1781 was the day of surrender. As the British raised their white flag the order to cease fire was given. Two days later, after the terms of surrender had been agreed upon, the British Army marched out and lay down their arms.

CHAPTER 5

ON THE MOVE - "KAINTUCK"

After the War William moved from Chesterfield County to Southwest Virginia. First to Grayson County and then to Washington. From there to Greene County, Tennessee where in 1788 he married Hannah Richardson. Shortly after their marriage William and Hannah moved to Clay County Kentucky and by 1809 to Madison County (Ky.) Where they resided until sometime after 1815.

Southwest Virginia, Tennessee and Kentucky were wilderness, and access was very difficult. From Chesterfield County it was necessary to go North and then West to the Ohio River. For travelers to Southwest Virginia the route was by traveling down the Ohio to the Falls at Kanawha. For William traveling West from Washington County the route was through Moccasin Gap of Clinch Mountain, across the Clinch River through Kanes Gap of Powell Mountain, over Wallen Ridge into Powell Valley, across Powell River, The trail emerged at Cumberland Gap and connected with the Wilderness Road. Alternately they could enter the Kentucky River and travel to the interior. After leaving the River, there were only narrow paths that had been cut by the earlier pioneers, with the exception of the Indian's Warpaths. Only those willing to risk their lives would leave the river and venture onto these.

Early History:

In 1774, at Hillsborough, North Carolina six men came together to form the Transylvania Company.[1] This was a land company formed to purchase 20 million acres from the Cherokee who claimed the land as a hunting ground. This land was enclosed by the Kentucky, Ohio and Cumberland Rivers. The new colony was called Transylvania. Daniel Boone was hired by the company to establish a settlement on the Kentucky River and to cut the Wilderness Road. However, the State of Virginia claimed this wilderness, later to be known as Kentucky, as a part of its territory.

----

1. Glimpses of Historic Madison County, Kentucky. Jonathan and Maud Dorris, Williams Printing Co., Nashville, Tn., 1955.

As a further assertion of its claim, in 1779 Virginia established a Land Office, set up the office of surveyor and began issuing grants or patents. Virginia prevailed. And so this land that was filled with buffaloes and wild turkeys, but very few human inhabitants -- a small band of Chicksaws in the Western part and some fur traders, became the State of Kentucky.

In the early 1800s the northern boundary of Kentucky joined the Northwest Territory. This land today contains the States of Michigan, Indiana, Illinois, Wisconsin, and Minnesota. The Northwest Territory was claimed by various Indian Tribes. Further North lay Canada held by the British, who watched the spread of the upstart colonists. They had not accepted the conclusion of the Revolutionary War as final and were alarmed by the progress of the colonists. Should they gain further land and greater control the job of retaking the colonies would become much more difficult. The Indians and the British had been allies for many years and were joined in the desire to see the colonists contained. Chief Tecumseh led the Indians. In addition to his responsibility as the Chief he was a General in the British Army. And so the stage was set for many years of conflict and finally the War of 1812.

The early settlers endured the raids made by the Indians, and replied with raids of their own. Primarily these were raiding parties of Shawnee or the Wyandot. These raids would sometimes be preceded by an "offer" to come to Detroit and "live under gracious King George III."

The beauty of the wild flowers, forests and streams made a strange backdrop for the daily life of the people whose routines were often interrupted by the arrival of crude litters brought into camp carrying the body of men who had been slain. Raiding parties would be quickly formed to give chase. Conversation was filled with such topics as midnight butcheries, capitivities, horse stealing and the like.

Their forts were designed for protection and their lives were filled with rituals necessitated by the danger. In the morning the first duty was to climb the ladder to the loft and peer through the cracks for any sign of Indians who might be hiding outside the door. The heavy bar placed across the door could not be raised until the strongest was available to lift it for fear a lurking Indian would rush through the door and overwhelm those inside. They were often tied inside the cabin and the cabin set afire. At night rifles, axes and scythes were stored under the bed for ready access. Accounts given during that period talk of nights "when I didn't close my eyes all night." Indians watched the paths that led from the settlements and the settlers watched the paths for Indians. Women dressed as men to make the fort look better protected. Even so, settlers were often captured and then killed or taken to be enslaved.

By the late 1790s the settlers had moved into the interior and the Indians had moved down the Warriors Path. The dust was pretty much settled when William Hampton and his family arrived in Madison County about 1796. Two notable events would soon take place in other Kentucky Counties -- the birth of Jefferson Davis in 1808 and of Abraham Lincoln in 1809. Kit Carson the famous Indian Scout, was born on Christmas Day in 1809 in Madison. Napoleon Bonaparte was on the throne of France and King George III rules England. Thomas Jefferson was

President of the fifteen states that comprised the thirty-three year old United States.

As word spread of the new and wonderful land, the countryside rapidly filled with people arriving by the thousands. They came through the gaps in the mountains, over the Wilderness Road and floated down the Ohio from Pitts Landing (Pittsburgh, Pa.) and road their wagons overland. The "roads" were merely paths formed from buffalo traces.

By 1790 Kentucky's population exceeded 73,000. Land was cheap and taxes in the other colonies high. The people were primarily from Virginia, New Jersey and Maryland -- illiterate, poor country folks. They cleared the land. Shrubs and bushes were grubbed up. Trees were cut down saving the larger ones for cabin building. Limbs and brush were burned and horses pulled the large chained up logs to the building site. There was blue ash, hickory walnut and buckeye. They built rude cabins with port holes, a strong bar across the door, a floor of puncheons and a clap-board roof. Some made do with covered pens and sheds. Paths through the woods connected the early cabins.

One author who lived during this period described a typical scene as a "one-story unhewed log cabin set in a clearing of two-10 acres, surrounded by a brush fence with a number of ragged children playing by the door or under a shade tree."

It was two or three years before the first crop could be brought in. In the meantime they ate a diet of wild turkey and other game without bread. The roots that remained were so thick it was difficult to plow. Often a small boy sat on the horse to guide while father drove the plow. They planted their crops of corn, wheat, hay and vegetables.

By this time the houses were double log, with two square rooms. There was a space left between the rooms called a dog trot. These structures were surrounded by flower and vegetable gardens. There were stepping stones and lilac hedges. Shrubs of calycanthus, mockorange and honeysuckle provided a fragrance and color in the early Spring and Summer. The family burial plot was usually situated behind the flower garden. There was a large fireplace for warmth and cooking. Tester beds, cherry chests and cupboards furnished the rooms.

In addition to the log houses there were the Georgian, Federal, Greek Revival, and Gothic Revival styles of the manor houses belonging to the few wealthy planters who by this time had arrived.

So began the march of progress -- the American Dream. Each generation improving over the last. Lives filled with work, Church and school. These people, most of whom could neither read or write set an early priority on schooling. They spoke in an old English dialect and managed their lives by imitating their parents. They seemed early on to realize the limits this meant and began to establish a school system.

Readin', ritin', and the hickory stick:

The school house constructed of logs usually stood beside a wagon road, one room approximately 16 by 20 feet, with a wooden chimney and puncheon or dirt floor. This structure was built by the community and the schoolmaster was hired by them. These contracts to teach were usually determined by the availability of the schoolmaster and designed around the needs of the parents for their children to help at home. The school year was as short as three months or as long as six depending upon the bargain struck. The people of Madison county paid one pound seven shillings per pupil during the early part of 1800. This amount was nearly always paid in tobacco or bacon, buffalo steak, jerked venison, furs, flax, linsey, potmeal, cattle, corn or whiskey.

Upon arrival the boys removed their hats and made a bow to the master -- the girls courtesied. This courteous behavior extended beyond the school room to all adults they met.

Dr. Daniel Drake,[1] who grew up in Kentucky during this period described his school days in Maysville:

"The students sat on backless benches and recited their lessons out loud, not in unison, but each student endlessly chanting his studies individually. This exercise carried on for hours each day, produced strong lungs and assured the school master that no one was idle. The texts were Dilworth's Speller, The New Testament, Web-

----

1. Pioneer Life in Kentucky, Daniel Drake, Henry Schumann, Inc., 1948.

ster's Speller, Murray's English Reader and Grammar and others. Discipline was emphasized by the switch kept at the ready. The schoolmasters were stern, strict and unsmiling. Mealtime, called dinner, brought the first break in the day. Dinner pails brought from home were spread out on the grass when the weather was mild. Dinner was followed by swinging on grapevines, climbing trees to hunt for birdnests or chasing squirrels. The boys had bows and arrows. There were whistles of paw paw or hickory bark. There was a favorite fame of corner ball, as well as pitching quoits, prison-base and foot races.

At the close of the day the whole school was called up to spell. Following this was dismissal and a scramble for wool hats, sunbonnets and dinner baskets. The dispersion was in a run 'with hopping, jumping and hallowing.'"

In most villages there were variety shops or curiosity shops offering dry goods, hardware, glass and earthernware, groceries, dyestuffs, drugs, ammunition, hats, leather goods, books, stationery, coarse fools caps, wafers, slates and pencils. Among the books were the Bible, hymnals such as Rippon's

Hymns and Watts Hymns, primers, spelling books, arithmetics and almanacs. These goods were all brought from Philadelphia, the only city which imported to small towns and villages of the interior.

Travelers who arrived by horseback, wagon, or stagecoach found lodging and food at the tavern where they slept on the floor or outside in their wagons. This traffic was often made up of men driving wagons filled with merchandise, caravans of migrating people traveling on horseback and gangs of Negroes moving South.

Craftsmen, such as the itinerant tinker who soldered up holes in tin cups and "cast" pewter basins and plates, came to town. They went from dwelling to dwelling looking for work.

Home and hearth - women's work:

Mother cooked, spun, gardened, knitted and a thousand and one things from morning to night. The children's day was filled with chores as well. Their roles as male and female was reflected in the division of labor decreed by custom -- milking was a girl's task and churning a boys.

On wash day water was hauled from the pond in buckets. The washtub was heated from beneath by a fire built of wood. The clothes were hung on the fence to dry. Drinking and cooking water was carried daily from the Spring.

In the Spring the sheep were driven to the pond and washed, then sheared. The wool was "picked" to disentangle the matts and remove the burrs and cockles. It was then carded, spun, dyed, reeled into skeans, wound into balls, knitted and fashioned into a wearable garment. The yellow dye was from the bark of a white walnut tree; red from black walnut and blue from Indigo. These dyes determined the color of the trousers, jackets, coats, caps, mittens and stockings worn. Flax was made into linen for new shirts. Soap and cheese were also made at home.

Crops and hunting - men's work:

Spring was planting time. The earth was so filled with roots often a young boy sat atop the horse and guided while his father drove the plow. Corn was planted in furrows four feet apart. This important crop fed the family as well as the farm animals. In addition to corn there were pumpkins, watermelons, muskmelons, turnips and a variety of vegetables. After the corn was "laid by" in the autumn, wheat was sown. This crop was harvested with a sickle and scythe. As there were no barns or silos, both wheat and hay were stacked out in the field. Corn was taken to the mill to be ground into meal.

In late Fall, when the crops were done, the hunting season began. The tools of the hunters were shotguns, rifles and .32 to .60 caliber flintlocks. By 1810 the deer and wild turkeys, so depended upon by the earlier settlers, had become scarce. Armed not only with their gun but hunting strategies such as ; hunt when the leaves are wet in Fall so animals can't hear you; when there is no wind or he will smell you; not when the snow is falling but when it holds up so you will not leave tracks; wolves must be trapped and turkies will respond to a "gobble" carefully practiced. So armed the men and boys took to the woods.

The day filled with chores for all hands ended much as it began. The animals were brought in and fed. As wolves would carry off and kill sheep they were placed under the cabin at night. Supper was a simple meal of mush and milk. When the meal had been finished and cleared away the Bible was read. Finally the door to the cabin was barred, with the gun under the bed, and the dog placed as sentry outside, the family retired to their beds.

Saturday, going to town day, was devoted to public business, social pleasure, dissipation and for a few, beastly drunkenness. There was horse trading, horse racing, dog fights, cock fights, wrestling or battle between two bullies who may scratch, pull hir, choke, gough each other's eyes, bite off noses -- all encouraged by a shouting crowd of onlookers. There were political meetings followed by epiloges of oaths, yells, loud blows and gnashing of teeth. There were those who got together in the tavern for singing and the ladies who used the time to catch up on the neighborhood gossip.

If it could be said that Saturday was a day for earthly matters and for the revelers of the tavern who had chosen the road to "hell and dammanation," then Sunday belonged to the Church.

Sunday was set aside for those that heard and heeded a higher calling, the pious who sought a path to Heaven through the village Church. While the drunkards and merry makers slept it off they gathered at the meeting house. Most of the people of Madison County were Baptists, as were the Hamptons. The worshipers came dressed in their finest clothes. The ladies in calico dresses, black silk bonnets that covered a cap with flaps tied beneath the chin by a narrow ribbon. The men wore their "Sunday" coat, roram dress hat, their shoes blacked with fat and soot and carrying a walking stick. Children wore their "Sunday go-to-meeting" clothes. The horses were hitched to the fence while the worshipers sat on the backless benches inside listening to a member of the community read from the Good Book or to a circuit preacher who came from time to time. These were the faithful. The Bible and its' laws were the basis for their law and morality, and they believed in the promise that God would punish the rule breakers. It was wicked to treat anything with life cruelly, wicked to waste, wicked to fight or quarrel, to be lazy, disobedient, work on the Sabbath, lie, curse, swear, steal or get drunk. God had told them so in his Word and they did believe with a faith so deep it guided every aspect of their lives.

Viney Fork Baptist Church began in 1797, about the time the Hampton's moved to Kentucky. Located on Dreaming Creek, it would have been some distance from the Hampton home, but possibly the closest established church.

After services, food brought from home was spread upon the ground and picnicking and visiting with friends and neighbors began, sometimes lasting throughout the afternoon until evening service.

Monday morning brought a return to the work week. Up before dawn, make fires for heat in the winter and for cooking. Feed and fodder the horses, hogs and sheep --Johnny cakes for breakfast. The men of the family, accompanied by the dog, often went on an early morning hunt.

Trade:

Commerce begun earlier increased as barges laden with tobacco, lard, flour and meal traveled the 1500 miles from Boonesborough to New Orleans. The trip lasted 40 days and required passports for all who traveled on the waterways as they would pass through the armed forces of three different nations. The Mississippi River was claimed by the British, the land on the Western border of the River was claimed by the French (French Louisiana) and land on the lower Southeastern portion of the River was claimed by the Spanish.

KENTUCKY GAZETTE.

New Series—No. 18. Vol. IV.] LEXINGTON, K. TUESDAY, MAY 4, 1813. [Vol. 27.

KENTUCKY GAZETTE IS PUBLISHED EVERY TUESDAY, BY THOMAS SMITH, PRINTER OF THE LAWS OF THE UNION.

CONDITIONS.

Three Dollars per annum, payable at the expiration of the year, or Two Dollars at the time of subscribing. Persons at a distance [illegible] the paper to be forwarded by mail, must accompany their order with two dollars [illegible] note for three dollars. The postage [illegible] must be paid.

Advertisements are inserted at 50 cents per square the first time, and 25 cents for each continuance.

THE PRINTING OFFICE is kept at [illegible] opposite the Branch Bank [illegible] PRINTING of every description will be executed [illegible] with the whole apparatus used in the [illegible] being entirely new.

LIST OF LETTERS

Remaining in the Post Office at Nicholasville, K. on the 31st of March 1813, if not taken out in three months, will be sent to the General Post Office as dead letters.

John Wa[illegible]	Larkin Garrett
Abraham Head	Thomas Scott
Archer Webber	Joseph Hughes
Robert Clarke	James Baxter
[illegible] Clarke	Thomas Jeffers
[illegible]	Miss Melina Price
[illegible]	John Childers
James Ford	Mrs Catharine Thomas
[illegible] Spears	David Watts
[illegible] Garrett	Joseph M'Cartney
[illegible]	George Chelton
[illegible] Fletcher	Patrick Watson
Johnathan J[illegible]	Robert Grey
George W. Clarke	Miss Mary Thornton
[illegible] Powell	Benj Elliott
[illegible]	Thomas Scott
[illegible] Powell	William Walker
[illegible] Phelps	John Hill
Mrs Jane Williams	Saml Scott
[illegible] Poindexter	Kersey Beale
[illegible] Bell	John Carrell
[illegible] Clarke	Saml Hays
[illegible]	David Ridgley
[illegible] Shelton	Anderson Underwood
Thomas Shelton	William Phillips
[illegible]	Barclay
Edward Kell	Benj Gilbert
[illegible] Corbett	William Heath
Alexander Beasmith	John H. Clarke
George Hightower, [illegible]	Daniel Trenches
David Woods	Leonard Garrett
Jacob Fisher	Moses Wilson

B. NETHERLAND P. M.

FOR SALE.

A BRICK STABLE AND CARRIAGE HOUSE, 33 feet by 22, and a LOT OF GROUND on Upper street, opposite B. Long's carpenter shop, and near Mr Ross's factory—Application to be made to

KENNEDY & BRAND.

April 6, 1813. 14m-tf.

THE subscriber would sell the house and lot [illegible] occupied by W. W. Worsley, esq. in Lexington; the houses and lots on the same street, occupied by Mr Owings and Mr. Lowes; and [illegible] acres of land near Lexington, late the property of Reuben Thurston, Mann Satterwhite, and Daniel Bradford, esq's executors [illegible], and now in the possession of the latter. The terms of the sale would be easy and accommodating to the purchasers.

H. CLAY.

April, 1813 13—tf

State of Kentucky.

Barren Circuit Sct—March Term, 1813.

William Harmon, Compt. against Rebecca Harmon, Defendt. } In Chancery.

THIS day came the complainant by his counsel, and the defendant having failed to enter her appearance herein agreeably to law and the rules of this Court, and it appearing to the satisfaction of the court, that the said defendant is not an inhabitant of this [illegible] it is therefore on the motion of the complainant, ordered that the defendant appear here on the first day of our next June term and answer the complainant's bill, or that otherwise the same be taken for confessed—And it is further ordered that a copy of this order be published eight weeks successively in some authorised newspaper of this commonwealth.

(A copy. Test)

13 RICHARD GARRETT, C. B. C. C.

Fayette County, Sct.

TAKEN [illegible]

Wanted to Purchase.

THREE or four NEGRO BOYS, of ten to sixteen years of age. They must be smart likely boys, or will not do. Enquire of the Printer. 13-tf

Dr. Wm. H. Richardson

HAS removed to Lexington, and tenders his services to the citizens of the town and country, in the practice of

MEDICINE, SURGERY, &c.

In the latter branches of his profession, he will pay particular attention.

He resides in the house lately occupied by Mr. Samuel Trotter, and adjoining the store of S. & G. Trotter.

Lexington, March 27, 1813. 13-tf.

DUANE'S MILITARY BOOKS,

ADOPTED into the service of the United States—for sale at the office of the Kentucky Gazette—and the store of Jeremiah Neave.

HAND BOOK FOR INFANTRY,
HAND BOOK FOR RIFLEMEN,
MILITARY LIBRARY,
MILITARY DICTIONARY,
ALSO,
NIEF ON EDUCATION,
CONDILLAC'S LOGIC,
MONTESQUIEU'S SPIRIT OF LAWS.

All at the Philadelphia prices.

April 12, 1813 11

CASH WILL BE GIVEN FOR

HEMP,

By Samuel & George Trotter.

January 21, 1813. 6-tf

A School,

JESSE PERKINS has opened a school for the tuition of young Masters and Misses, near Sam'l. and Geo. Trotter's new building, on the street leading from Mr. Leavy's store to the steam mill—the house is in a very retired place, in which he will teach SPELLING, READING, WRITING & ARITHMETIC.—Those who may think proper to place their children under his care, may depend upon proper attention being paid to them, as he wishes to keep up a school at that place for a considerable time.

Terms of tuition $2 50 per quarter.

April 19th, 1813 16-3t

I AM authorised to sell that valuable and convenient dwelling house and lot, lately occupied by London Comstock, lying on Mulberry street, Lexington. Any person wishing to purchase would do well to make an early application, as it will be sold at auction unless shortly disposed of at private sale.

I am also authorised to sell another house & lot, lying on Main street, near the upper end—beautifully and pleasantly situated for a family residence. For terms apply at the auction and commission store of

DANIEL BRADFORD.

Lexington, April 20th, 1813 16

Wanted,

THREE or four Tenterer? Fliers, who have been accustomed to work in machinery to whom I will give liberal wages. Also two smart boys of sixteen or seventeen years of age, will be taken as Apprentices to learn the machine making business by the subscriber, living on Water street, adjoining the theatre, Lexington.

JOHN MARAH.

January 25, 1813 6-tf

Jessamine County

TAKEN up by Joseph McKinney, living on Jessamine creek, a BAY HORSE, with a star in his face, all his feet white, a small white spot on his near side, branded on his near shoulder somewhat like a C, about three years old and about 13 1-2 hands high—appraised to $15. December, 4th 1812.

16-3t. JOHN METCALF.

TAKEN up by Daniel Hunt, living in Clarke county on the waters of Indian Creek about two miles from Howard's warehouse, a GREY HORSE, seven or eight years old, fourteen hands and an half high, has been shod all round, but some of the shoes off, his tail has been docked off short, trots and racks very well, no brand perceivable—appraised to $33 before me, this 13th day of Feb 1813.

16-3 M. VIVION.

Mercer Circuit Sct. March Term, 1813

George W. Hoosine? comp't. against Jos. Tibbs? & John Dean?, defendants. } In Chancery

PREVENTION BETTER THAN CURE.

FOR THE PREVENTION AND CURE OF BILIOUS AND MALIGNANT FEVERS, IS RECOMMENDED

Hahn's Anti-Bilious Pills,

Prepared (only) at Lee's old established Patent & Family Medicine Store, No. 56, Maiden Lane, New-York.

THE operation of these pills is perfectly mild, so as to be used with safety by persons in every situation, and of every age.

They are excellently adapted to carry off superfluous bile, and prevent its morbid secretions—to restore and ⟨illegible⟩ the appetite—produce a free perspiration, and thereby prevent colds, which are often of fatal consequences. A dose never fails to remove a cold, if taken on its first appearance.—They are celebrated for removing habitual costiveness, sickness at the stomach and severe head-ache—and ought to be taken by all persons on a change of climate.

They had been found remarkably efficacious in preventing and curing disorders attendant on long voyages, and should be procured and carefully preserved for use, by every seaman.

Hamilton's Worm Destroying Lozenges.

This well known remedy has cured during the last eleven years, an immense number of children and adults of various dangerous complaints arising from worms.

Hamilton's Essence & Extract of Mustard,

A safe and effectual remedy for acute and chronic Rheumatism, Gout, Rheumatic Gout, Palsy, Lumbago, Numbness, White Swellings, Chilblains, Sprains, Bruises, pain in the face and neck, &c.

ITCH CURED,

By once using LEE'S SOVEREIGN OINTMENT.

Hamilton's Grand Restorative

Is recommended as an invaluable medicine for the speedy relief and permanent cure for the various complaints which result from dissipated pleasures; juvenile indiscretions; residence in climates unfavorable to the constitution; the immoderate use of tea; frequent intoxication, or other destructive intemperance; the unskilful or excessive use of mercury; the diseases peculiar to females at a certain period of life; bad lyings in, &c.

Hamilton's Elixir,

Celebrated for the cure of Colds, obstinate Coughs, Asthmas, and approaching Consumptions, and is a certain remedy for the Hooping Cough.

Hahn's True & Genuine German Corn Plaister, Tooth Ache Drops.

A multitude of attested cures performed by the above medicines, may be seen at the place of sale.

The above genuine medicines (with many others of equal celebrity) are prepared from the original receipts of the late Richard Lee, jun. by his widow in New York.

☞ They are for sale in Kentucky (By her particular appointment) at the stores of Waldemard Meeteer, Lexington, and Dudley, Trigg & Dudley, in Frankfort.

Copper for Stills.

THE SUBSCRIBERS are expecting in a few days, a quantity of Copper in Patterns for Stills—which they will sell on reasonable terms. 63-tf.

TILFORD, SCOTT & TROTTER.

Nov 3, 1812.

THE SUBSCRIBER

Respectfully informs the public that he has removed his

COMMISSION STORE,

To the house lately occupied by Mr. Caleward, adjoining Mr W. Leavy's store, where he continues to sell, make and repair Looking Glasses, Picture Frames, gilt and plain; he has lately received an assortment of the most fashionable Looking Glasses, and a most complete assortment of toys for children, more extensive than any before imported, and very cheap.

Likewise—Large Glasses for picture frames
Clock do
Cotton by the Bale
White Lead of the first quality
Box Raisins
Prunes

Silver Platers, Silver Smiths and Brass Founders.

I. & F. WOODRUFF,

RESPECTFULLY inform their friends and the public in general, that they still continue to carry on the above business in all their branches at their former stand, opposite the Branch Bank, on Main-street, Lexington—They return their sincere thanks for past patronage, and hope by their strict attention to business, to merit its continuance.

THEY HAVE, AND INTEND KEEPING ON HAND, A GENERAL ASSORTMENT OF

- Gold & Silver Ware.

Plated Candlesticks, Castors, &c.

OF THE NEWEST PATTERNS.

ALSO,

AN ELEGANT ASSORTMENT OF

Bridle Bits, Stirrup Irons, &c.

OF THE MOST FASHIONABLE PATTERNS

ALL KINDS OF

Carriage and Harness Mounting, Carriage & Gig Springs, Coach Lace, Fringe & Tassels.

ALSO, A GENERAL ASSORTMENT OF

Brass Candlesticks, Andirons, Shovels & Tongs, Door Knockers, &c.

Which they will dispose of very low for Cash.

ALL KINDS OF

Brass Work for Machinery, Clock Work, &c.

CAST ON THE SHORTEST NOTICE.

Still Cocks, Rivets, Gun Mountings, &c

ALWAYS ON HAND.

They have just received an extensive assortment of

SADDLERY, &c.

All of which will be sold on the most reasonable terms for CASH.

☞ One or two APPRENTICES wanted to learn the Silver Plating business.

The highest price in Cash will be given for old COPPER, BRASS & PEWTER.

April 6, 1813. 14—tf.

Barren Circuit Court, State of Kentucky, Sct. March Term, 1813.

William Wilkerson, comp't. vs Sally Wilkerson, defendant. } In Chancery.

THIS day came the complainant by his counsel, and the defendant having failed to enter her appearance herein agreeably to law and the rules of this court, and it appearing to the court by disinterested affidavits that the said defendant is not an inhabitant of this state; It is therefore, on the motion of the complainant ordered, that the defendant appear here on the first day of our next June Term, and answer the complainant's bill exhibited against her in this court, for the purpose of obtaining a divorce in favor of the complainant against the defendant; Or, that on her failure so to do, the complainant's bill be taken for confessed. And it is further ordered, that a copy of this order be published eight weeks successively in some authorised newspaper of this commonwealth.

(A Copy.) Attest,

14 RICHARD GARRETT, C. B. C. C.

State of Kentucky,

Fayette Circuit Court, January Term, 1813

Thomas & Robert Dunn?, complainants, against Thomas Wert?, &c. defendants } In Chancery

THIS day came the complainants, by their counsel, and the defendants John Lepsley, Henry Wilson and Samuel Miller, having failed to enter their appearance herein according to law and the rules of this court, and it appearing that the said defendants are not inhabitants of this commonwealth; It is ordered that unless they appear here on or before the first day of the next June term of this court, and answer the said complainants' bill, the same will be taken for confessed against them. It is further ordered that a copy of this order, be inserted in some authorised paper for eight weeks successively, according to law. And this cause is continued until the next term.

(A Copy.) Attest,

HUBBARD B. SMITH, D. C. F. C. C.

RAGS WANTED

THE Citizens of this place, and county, and [illegible]

OUR GENEROUS AND MAGNANIMOUS ENEMY

We have heard so much of the humanity and tender mercies of the British, we have seen so much in Gov. Strong's Proclamations in favor of the "Bulwark of our religion," and Mr. John Randolph has uttered so many whining praises and shed so many pious tears over the good deeds of our enemy—that the sentiment was stealing into circulation and every British tongue was lisping the praises of their humanity. "Oh! they were the most generous and high-minded nation on earth; the very pink of chivalry; the deliverer of mankind; our shield against that most terrible scourge of the human race, the Emperor of France. They practised every virtue; it was theirs to spare the conquered and pull down the proud;" to pour the balm into the bleeding bosom, to soothe and soften the distress of oppressed and the prisoners; and by the dignity of their principles to frown into silence every grovelling and unfeeling sentiment.

Where were the wrongs of Ireland and Hindostan? They were forgotten. It was forgotten, that the deliverer of Spain and the upholder of the Inquisition was the oppressor of 5 millions of Irish Catholics. It was forgotten that the friend of Prussia was the ravager of India. The conflagration of Copenhagen was forgotten—the pirate of neutral commerce, the kidnapper of American seamen, and the tyrant of the ocean, has friends enough, even in this country, to be hailed as the Bulwark of our religion, and the deliverer of the human race.

What shall we say of her conduct during the present war with the U. S.! It has continued for only 9 months; and yet during that short period of time, what sentiment of generosity or what maxim of civilized war have not her governors and her officers trampled under foot! Let her friends consider the following facts and blush, if they can, for the nation whom they advocate.

FIRST FACT.

Our officers who were taken prisoners at Queenstown, were marched through Canada in ignominious triumph—and finally they were sent to sea on bad and defective rations—robbed of their swords.

The officers of the Nautilus were subjected to the same mean petty-larceny. They were robbed of their clothes & their nautical instruments, without the slightest chance of restitution.

Our countrymen need no pen to eulogise their generosity—yet it is impossible not to compare these tricks with the generous deeds of a Hull, a Decatur or a Bainbridge, who gave up every atom of private property to the owner, & received nothing in return but his thanks. The Governor of Bombay (Governor Hislop, who does not indeed seem backward in his thanks!) is even mean enough to beg Commodore Bainbridge for a service of plate—when during the last war his countrymen went prowling thro' Virginia for plunder, stealing plate and horses, and robbing the very beds of their ticking, to carry off their stolen bacon.

SECOND FACT.

Four hundred of our seamen, taken on board letters of marque under the commissions of the U. S. are at this moment kept as prisoners in the West Indies on half allowance.

THIRD FACT.

Sir John Beresford, "Commodore and commanding the British squadron in the Delaware," has addressed a mean and menacing letter to the people of Lewistown, which would disgrace the merest braggadocio in the world! Mark the circumstances of this noble act! Lewistown is a small village, near the capes of Delaware; the huts of poor fishermen and pilots; the whole of the houses to-

NEW GOODS.

E. WARFIELD is just receiving from Philadelphia and Baltimore, and now opening at his store next door to Tilford, Scott and Trotter's, a large and general assortment of MERCHANDIZE, suitable for the spring season, which he will dispose of on the most reasonable terms for cash, by the piece, or retail; among these goods may be found some choice articles, to wit:

Best Cotton Cards, No. 10,
Waldron's Grass and Corn Scythes,
Elegant fancy patterns of New-England cotton cloth,
Stripes and Plaids,
A variety of fashionable Straw Bonnets,
Boots and Shoes of every kind,
Mantuas, Levantine and Virginia Silks,
Fancy Muslins,
Linen Cambrick,
Assorted Silk Velvets,
Do. Do. Ribbands,
Elegant new patterns of Paper Hangings,
Queens and Glass Ware,
China, Tea and Table Setts,
Ironmongery of every description,
Groceries,
Teas of the best quality,
Best Coffee,
Segars of all kind,
Iron and Nails,
Currying Knives,
Curriers' Fleshers,
Venering Saws, X Cut Saws, Mill Saws, Whip Saws, Hand Saws,
And a great variety of spring fancy Goods.

March 22, 1814. 12-tf

David Todd

Has opened a handsome & general assortment of *MERCHANDIZE*——Consisting of

DRY GOODS,	HARD WARE, &
QUEENS-WARE,	GLASS WARE,

In Anderson's Stone-house, corner near the Market-house, which he will dispose of on low terms.

The business of the firm of David and Sam'l B. Todd, has devolved upon him—The partnership having been dissolved by consent.

Lexington, Nov. 23, 1813 47-tf.

A. [illegible] & Co.

Give four dollars in cash, for good merchantable

HEMP,

At their Rope walk, in the suburbs of the own, on Russell's road.

6-tf February 7, 1814.

Brass Foundery.

I. & E. WOODRUFF, & Co.

CONTINUE the above business at their former stand, and by arrangements lately made, they are enabled to conduct it on a more extensive scale, and to execute every species of casting in Brass or Copper in the best manner and on short notice. A supply of CLOCK WORK, GUN MOUNTING, ANDIRONS, SHOVELS & TONGS, BELLS, &c. always ready. Two or three apprentices, about 16 or 17 years of age, will be taken.

5-tf January 22, 1814

Silver Plating & Brass Foun-

To Merchants.

THE Bank of Chillicothe issues Checks on Philadelphia, Baltimore or Washington City, payable at sight, for a premium of half per cent, and will receive in exchange, in addition to its own notes and specie, the notes of the different Banks in Ohio, Kentucky and Tennessee.

J. WOODBRIDGE, *Cashier.*

March 14, 1814. 11-11t

THE Subscriber has on hand at his Smith Shop, formerly occupied by Wm. Hart, an assortment of the following articles of a superior quality, all of which will be sold on reasonable terms for cash or the usual credits, viz:

Warranted Axes	*Hammers*
Steeled Hoes	*Wedges*
Carey Ploughs	*Drawing Knives*
Common ditto,	*Chains of all kinds*
Grubbing Hoes	*Shovels and Tongs*
Mattocks	*Cranes*
Hinges of all descriptions	*Pothooks*
Carpenters, Hatchets	*Skimmers*
Hand Axes	*Ladles*
Fleshforks.	

The subscriber having five Forges, will be able to execute large jobs on the shortest notice—Horse shoeing will be particularly and carefully attended to.

R. DOWNING.

Lexington, Feb. 26, 1814. 9-tf

Greenville Springs.

THE Subscriber takes this method to inform the public that he has taken the Greenville Springs, near Harrodsburg, and will be ready by the 20th inst. to receive boarders; he pledges himself every thing in his power shall be done to render the situation of those who may call on him comfortable.—The large and numerous buildings on the premises will enable him to accommodate a large company. He will be supplied with liquors of every kind—his stables are large and shall be well filled with hay and grain of every kind—he hopes that by an unremitted attention to his duty, he will be enabled to give general satisfaction.

H. PALMER.

April 1[illegible] 1814. 15-tf

WANTED TO HIRE,

A NEGRO BOY about 14 or 15 years of age. Apply to R. MARSH.

May 2, 1814. 18-tf

WANTED,

TWO or three Apprentices to the House Carpenter and Joiner's business.—Also, two Negro men on hire, for whom a liberal price will be given.—Apply to

17-3t THE PRINTER.

TAKE NOTICE.

ALL persons are hereby forewarned from fishing or fowling on the premises of the undersigned, as we have been considerably injured by such practices.

JAMES GREGG, Adm'r. of Samuel Gregg, dec
HENSON WILLIAMS,
FULTON THOMPSON.

April 25, 1814. 17-5p

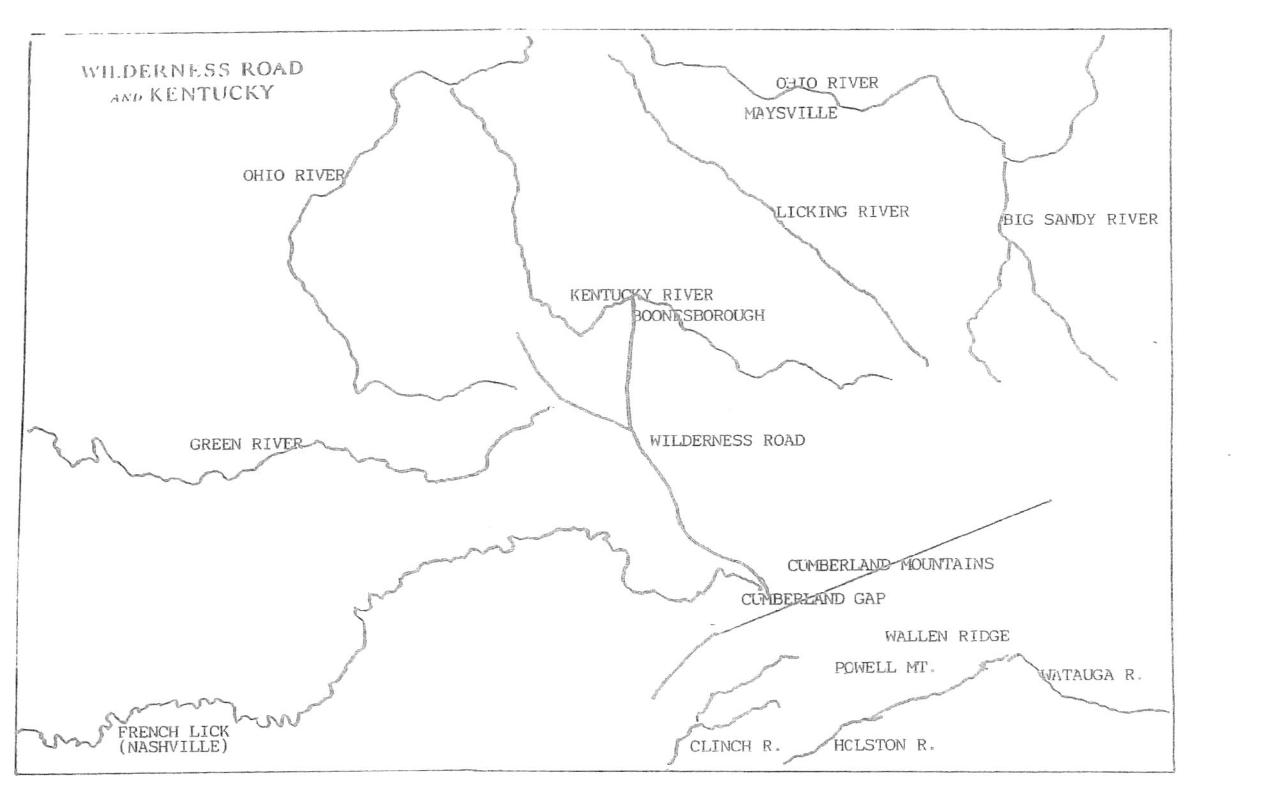
WILDERNESS ROAD
AND KENTUCKY
OHIO RIVER
MAYSVILLE
LICKING RIVER
BIG SANDY RIVER
OHIO RIVER
KENTUCKY RIVER
BOONESBOROUGH
GREEN RIVER
WILDERNESS ROAD
CUMBERLAND MOUNTAINS
CUMBERLAND GAP
WALLEN RIDGE
POWELL MT.
WATAUGA R.
FRENCH LICK
(NASHVILLE)
CLINCH R.
HOLSTON R.

Late 1700s

CHAPTER 6

1812 -- WAR RENEWED

The War of 1812 really began with the War between France and England in 1793. Napoleon Bonaparte Emperor of France and master of all continental Europe and George III King of England were the ruling heads of the warring factions, at least until George went insane in 1811 and was replaced by the Duke of Wales. The War was a trade war with the purpose of destroying the trade of each nation, by blockading each other's ports and interfering with ships on the high seas. They boarded each other's ships taking off sailors to be impressed into service by the opposing force, and confiscated cargo. Caught in the crossfire were the developing colonies who were dependent upon England and Europe for trade -- their raw materials for finished goods. The American vessels were boarded and fired upon as well. Native born American sailors were declared to be British and taken "by mistake" to serve on the British ships.

President Madison, on June 1, 1812 asked Congress to declare War on Great Britain on the basis of interference of the United States trading ships and the British support of the Indians in the Northwest Territory. The battlefield for these two combatants however would not be the high seas. The United States Navy had no battleships, and only seventeen frigates and sloops of war vs the British who dominated the high seas with nearly 1000. So the Americans planned a three way attack on Canada, from Detroit, Niagara River and Lake Champlain. It was this land attack that involved the men of Kentucky.

In 1812 the population of Kentucky was 400,000. Out of this number came forty regiments of militia and a number of battalions and companies, more than 25,000 men. About sixty-four percent of all soldiers killed were Kentuckians, 1,200 men.[1]

The Americans were under the direction of Major General William Henry Harrison - Major General of the Kentucky Militia who

----

1. Kentucky Soldiers of the War of 1812. compiled by Minnie S. Wilder and G .Glenn Clift, Genealogical Publishing Company, 1969.

would later become President of the United States. Harrison was known for his heroism during the Indian war, Battle of Tippecanoe when he defeated Tecumseh's half brother, the Shawnee Prophet.

On September 3, 1812 Kentucky's troops arrived at Piqua, from here a detachment was sent to rescue Fort Wayne. The remaining troops advanced on Frenchtown a small Canadian outpost on the Raisin River twenty-six miles south of Detroit[1] and captured it January 18, 1813. On the 22nd of February British troops under the leadership of General Henry Proctor attack the Americans. After killing more than 100 Kentucky riflemen and capturing about 500, the Americans surrendered. Following the surrender two hundred blackened Indian warriors, placed as guards of the wounded prisoners by Proctor, mad with victory, invaded the stockade and tomahawked, scalped, and butchered the wounded men. This brutal massacre inflamed the American army and led to the

----

1. American Military History, Army Historical Series, Maurice Matloff, U.S. Army, Washington D.C. 1973

battle cry of "Remember the Raisin" that would sweep throughout the country.

Soldiers surnamed Hampton served in the 10th Regiment of the militia. This regiment was under the command of Colonel Boswell, their Captain was Peter Dudley whose company was known as the Light Infantry Blues. Whether any of these Hamptons were William's sons cannot be ascertained as the names of all of his sons are not known. Additionally, records of this War are incomplete and information available is meager. The men who served were James, James Jr., Thomas and Wade. William's son James would have been twenty-two years old at this time.

James, James Jr., Wade and Thomas enlisted in the Light Infantry Blues on the same day, the 29th of March 1812. This singular account of the men under Captain Peter Dudley happened sometime after the River Raisin massacre, in the Spring of 1813 near Fort Meigs which was located in northern Ohio near the western end of Lake Erie.

The Americans had suffered a tremendous loss on the left bank of the Maumee River at the hands of the Indians. On the bank opposite this scene, General Clay attempted to land the six boats under his command.

Five of the boats were swept away by the swiftness of the current that had been swollen by the heavy rains. The remaining boat "...containing General Clay, with Captain Peter Dudley and fifty men, kept the stream, separated from the rest, and finally landed on the eastern bank of the river opposite to Hollister's Island. There they were assailed by musketry from a cloud of Indians on the left flank of the fort, and by round shot from the batteries opposite. Notwithstanding the great peril, Clay and his party returned the Indians' attack with spirit, and reached the fort without the loss of a man.

Colonel Boswell's command in the other boats, consisting of a part of the battalions of Kentucky Militia under Major William Johnson, and two other companies of Kentucky levies, landed near Turkey Point. He was immediately ordered by Captain Hamilton, General Harrison's representative, to fight his way into the fort. The same Indians who assailed Clay disputed his passage. Boswell arranged his men in open order, marched boldly over the low plain, engaged the savages on the slopes and brow of the high plateau most gallantly, and reached the fort without suffering very serious loss. There he was greeted by thanks and shouts of applause, and met by a sallying-party coming out to join him in an immediate attack upon that portion of the enemy with whom he had just been engaged, pursuant to Harrison's original plan of assailing the foe on both sides of the river at the same time. There was but a moment's delay. Boswell on the right, Major Alexander and his volunteers on the left, and Major Johnson in the centre, was the order in which the party advanced against their dusky foe. They fell upon the savages furiously, drove them half a mile into the woods at the point of the bayonet, and utterly routed them. In their zeal the victors were pursuing with a recklessness that if continued, would have resulted in disaster like that which overwhelmed (William) Dudley. Fortunately, General Harrison, always on the alert, had taken a stand, with a spyglass, on one of his batteries, from which he could survey the whole field of operations. He discovered a body of British and Indians gliding swiftly along the borders of the woods to cut off the retreat of the pursuers, when he dispatched a volunteer aid (John T. Johnson, Esq.) to recall his troops. It was a perilous undertaking. The gallant aid-de-camp had a horse shot under him, but he succeeded in communicating the general's orders in time to allow the imperiled detachment to return without much loss.

General Harrison now ordered a sortie from the fort against the enemy's works on the right, near the deep ravine...."

If James Hampton of the 10 Regiment was William's son he survived the war and on the 14 of September 1815 he married his neighbor's daughter Gemima Wells.

Prior to 1818 the Hamptons moved to Montgomery County and from there to Delaware County, Indiana. In July of 1825 they arrived in McMinn County Tennessee.

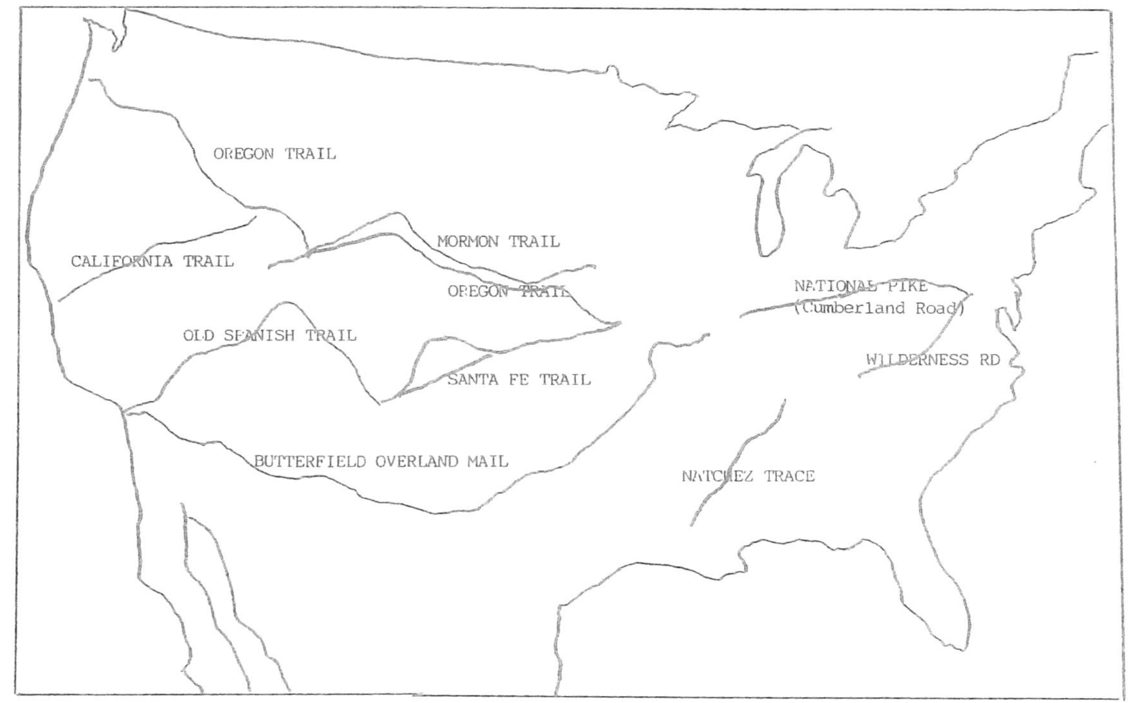

Major Roads and Trails, 1780-1860

CHAPTER 7

TENNESSEE - THE HAMPTON'S AT CALHOUN

"...then to McMinn County in the State of Tennessee where he now resides and has resided for seven years."

The 480 square miles that make up McMinn County are located in the foothills of the Great Smoky Mountains. Before the advent of the white man it was a dense forest, a beautiful woodland of stately oaks, pines and other native timber. This wooded land with its streams of clear water fed from nearby springs and from rivulets that came from the sloping hillsides was populated with great herds of wild animals coming down to the fertile valleys to graze. This was the home of the Cherokee Indians and one of their favorite hunting grounds. In 1819 this land known as the "Hiwassee Purchase" was bought by the Federal Government from the Cherokee nation. Talks between the Indians and the white men had begun two years prior to the signing of the Treaty. The Cherokee were divided on this issue and many opposed the Treaty. The two factions within the tribe were hostile. By the time the Treaty was signed 5,000 to 6,000 Cherokee had moved beyond the Mississippi. For those Indians leaving the white men offered transportation by raft, a rifle, ammunition, a blanket and a brass kettle or a beaver trap and finally land was promised on the Arkansas and White Rivers as a reward for moving. As required by the Treaty each Cherokee was given 640 acres and citizenship. The citizenship was largely rejected and the land accepted. However, the land was soon lost to speculators.

With the arrival of the white man timber was cut and the land cultivated. Little settlements sprung up here and there and the sound of the woodsman's ax and of domestic life replaced the "war whoop" and the chanting sound of the Indians.

Major John Walker, who was part Cherokee, established the first town in the County on his 640 acre reservation -- Calhoun. The name Calhoun was decided upon in honor of a famous South Carolinian, John C. Calhoun, the Secretary of War.

The first circuit court was organized at Calhoun in the Spring of 1820 and was presided by Judge Charles Keith until 1844. A native of Jefferson County, he moved to McMinn when chosen as Judge. He was succeeded by J. C. Gaut. Benjamin Hambright, whose name appears on many of William Hampton's papers was the Register from 1820 until 1836. Early records of the court have been lost. In 1823 this court was moved to the town of Athens.

Athens would become the second town. It began as a settlement known as Pumpkin Hill.[1] Elijah Hurst, a early settler and one of the Commissioners appointed to lay out the town, gazing at the beautiful landscape said to his fellow workers "I suggest that we give this little town the name of Athens because of its beauty of location."

By 1828 a brick building, forty by sixty-six feet and standing two stories high was erected on Athens' public square. This was the new courthouse. Prior to this time a log jail had been completed. In 1835, Planter's Bank opened its doors and by 1838 it was joined by State Bank. There were half

----

1. Leaves from the Family Tree... McMinn County Penelope Johnson Allen, Chatttanooga Times, 1933-1937.

a dozen doctors and several attorneys. Mud holes filled the courthouse lawn. A jockey lot was located in a section set apart for the convenience of horse swappers and farmers who came to town in horse drawn vehicles. Oil lamps illuminated Athens. They were usually out by 9 O'clock which was considered bedtime. The lamplighter carrying his ladder, would make his rounds as twilight began to fall.

The first church was a log house built by the Baptists, the Methodists followed soon after. A Presbyterian Church was erected in 1823. The Hiwassee Baptist Church was established the 3rd Saturday in December 1824 in the house of Sterling Camp. At its beginning, this church met in the homes of its membership.

It was here to the Hiwassee Baptist Church William, Hannah and their children came on June 6, 1829. From this date the family and its many members are noted in the Record. The last entry is for February 2, 1872.

The minutes of the Hiwassee Baptist Church have been preserved and are an interesting source of information pertaining to the life of the community and its members.

Book One of the Minutes of this Church covers the period January 1825 to January 1842. The preface begins: "The members whose names are here enrolled are constituted a Church of the order of the United Baptist by presbytiers elders Jesse Dodson, Samuel Short and John Courtney on the third Saturday in December 1824 and to be known by the name of the Highwassee Baptist Church -- Sterling Camp, Anna Camp, William Varnell, John Roberts, Rebecca Roberts, Simeon Oswalt, John Varnell, Elizabeth Varnell, Sally Brookshire." There are thirty-four names on the first list. There are several black members as evidenced by the following entries made in the minutes:

"Saturday March 18, 1826 -- received Sister Funna a woman of color under watch care.

July 1831 -- Received Polly a woman of color belonging to the widow Woolf.

October 1832 -- ...received Joseph Camp a man of color...

January 1833 -- ...black woman by name of Rossy.

June 1834 -- ...received by letter David a man of color owned by John Simmons...

March 1840 -- ...received by letter...Sarah a slave of Robert Hanks..."

The minutes of the church reflect its concern with such routine topics as members coming in and going out, collecting money, baptisms, funerals and poor attendance.
November 1828 -- "...Brother Edmonson to go to Brother Oswalt to invite him to come to church and let us know his reasons for staying away, also Brother Roberts to do same for William Varnell, also John Varnell invite Brother Rease."

Additionally the Church was the arbitrator of morality. Many entries pertain to the breaking of the rules by its members.
Saturday, April 1827 -- "Postponed case of Brother Rease of misusing a bound boy and requested help of Eastanalle, Zion Hill and Friendship Churches."
Friday October 10, 1828 -- "...took up the case of Brother Shearwood Rease and James Hickey -- accusation Brother Rease layed against Brother Hickey a false statement. Second hurt is Hickeys declaring a none fellowship with him. Third hurt is that Brother Hickey acquested Brother Rease of that which is falst. Fourth, Brother Hickey answered to the first charge Not guilty the second charge guilty -- Church says that Brother Rease has not established the

charge. Saturday: The Church takes up the matter from the beginning again and after labouring with them again we still say that Brother Hickey has not falsified his word." This case concludes in November as the two resolve their differences in a meeting held at the Eastanalle Church.

March 1841 -- Rebecca Fowler is charged with dancing...

April 1841 -- Charles Amos having refused to come to the church...is excluded because of the charge of drunkeness...

May 1841 -- Rebecca Fowler, not having heeded the church, was excluded...

The second book of minutes continues to bring up charges of drunkeness, falsehoods, swearing, dancing and in one instance a member "...absented herself for some days with a married man in a scandalous manner and was excluded. Another was charged with disorderly conduct in Charleston.

November 1849 -- William Melton, James Hampton's son-in-law, husband of Rebecca, is asked to "...notify Charles Catelow to come to next meeting and make satisfaction to a charge of immoral conduct..." By February Castelow is excluded for this charge, along with Polley Tommas for fornication.

In addition to its other duties the Church takes up the business of probate at least in this one instance.

January 1841 -- "Received a letter from Sherwood Rees complaining of Sterling Camp's estate and John Courtney deceased because they refused to pay to the order of Rees with ten years interest 74.38 in the month of Feb 1831."

February 1841 Church rejected the charge of Sherwood Rees against Sterling Camp and the estate of John Courtney. "...1st because those means of reconciliation laid down in Matthew 18:15-17 were not attended to be the said Rees. 2nd it appeared that the defendants denied the demands of the plaintiff."

February 12, 1831 -- "...3rd the Church is requested by the plaintiff to exercise a power in the distribution of their deceased brother's estate that belongs to the civil authority alone..."

On November 15, 1851 land was deeded to the Church to be used for a public grave yard. The land was conveyed by Thomas Camp and others to Oswell M. Lyner, James M. Waling, Trustees of the Church. "For the respect that we have for the United Baptist Church of Christ known as the Hiwassee

Church, and for the purpose of a public grave yard, we do hereby give transfer and convey to Oswell M. Lyner and James M. Waling, Trustees of the said church and their successors in office a certain tract of land in the State of Tennessee McMinn County, Hiwassee District, Second range West of the Meridian fourth fractional township, twenty eight section and part of the North east quarter of said section, beginning at a stake, thence south thirteen poles so as to leave the grave of Sterling Camp dec'd two poles East of said line, and in the center of said tract north and South thence East thirteen poles, thence North thirteen poles, then West thirteen poles to the beginning, containing by estimation one acre, to have and to hold the same to the said O.M. Lyner and J.M. Waling and their successors in officer forever, we do covenant with the said O. M. Lyner and J. M. Waling and their successors in office that we are lawfully seized of said land have a good right to convey the same and that it is unencumbered this 15th November 1851. Signed Thos. Camp; Wm. C. Porter, Sarah McNight; Mary Bates; John Hambright; Wm. Camp -- Attest Wm. McKnight and Eli Hellums.

The black arm of the church began when Brother Joe Camp requested, through O.M. Liner the privilege of holding meetings across the river and receive members of his own color which was granted at the December 1855 meeting. However, blacks continued to be received as members and are baptized into the original church.

The Forest Hill Academy, the first school was near the Cumberland Presbyterians camp-ground.

Forest Hill, established in 1826, was located near a large spring about a mile northeast of Athens on the old Post Road. In 1922 Charles Grandison Samuel, son of the school's president, gave the following information in answer to a Civil War veteran's questionnaire.[1] Mr. Samuel had been a Captain in the Confederate Army.

"I was born at old Forest Hill Academy one mile east of Athens, February 18th, 1833. My father was President of Forest Hill from 1830 to 1850. I went to school at old Forest Hill Academy from the time I was

---

1. _Tennessee Civil War Veterans Questionnaires,_ Tennessee State Library and Archives, Nashville, Tn.

five years old until 13 then I worked on the farm for two and one-half years. I helped clear ten acres new ground, grubbed, ploughed same ground with bull tongue plow. I helped chop our sprouts and cleared corn hills with the hoe; worked side by side with my father's old negro man. This work was part of my education. It built me up physically and made me understand labor was honerable and right. My father and mother both taught in the school room from early morn to dewey eve. During vacation my father took his boys William, Robert, Benjamin, Pat and myself and went a mile to the farm and cleared. It was considered highly honorable for the President of a college and all his sons to work on a farm. We all wore Indian mocassins, shoes made by Indians. We were told by the old men if we would learn to work we would make good men. Everybody in those days engaged in all kinds of work, the idler was avoided. In my young days a boy or man that idled away his time was looked upon as no good, no account.

Forest Hill Academy was launched by the Athens people in 1828 and my father took charge of it in 1830. This was the only school any ways near. There were a few public district schools meagerly attended. Forest Hill school became famous. Students came from as far as Knoxville to complete their Latin and Greek. The school was maintained by private subscription. My father's salary was $1300 per year. It opened each year and continued until the middle of the following July. Ended with a great public examination. Every boy and girl in Athens and around Athens, as well as some from Georgia, Alabama and Mississippi attended the school. My father and mother and Prof. Alderhoff and Prof. Knabe of Belgium were the teachers. I was the school mascot. By the age of eleven I had read Leber R... History, Sa... Ovid Caesar, Horace Cicero.

On the grounds of the Academy there was a great spring and an old stamping ground for public gathering and barbecues and camp meetings. The Cumberland Presbyterians built a large shed...would seat thousands... father was a strong Clay Whig but liberal in his...toward all other parties...the great statesmen of Tennessee made speeches during their campaigns under this shed... I was a little bare footed boy running round with my breeches rolled up to my knees... my older brothers had written Clay with polkberry juice on their straw hats and I had written Polk on mine... about 1840 when I was about seven years old....Jones and Polk was setting in my father's porch talking about the removal of the Indians. We boys came up and Polk called me to come up...asked who wrote Polk on my hat... told him I did... I said soon as I saw you ride up on that big black horse...you was the man that should be at the head...they all laughed...I howled out Hurrah for Polk...on the same porch I have seen John Bell, Trousdale Gentry, Landon C. Haynes, Crozier, W. G. Brownlow, Gustave Henry, Aaron V. Brown, Peter Turney, Return J. Meigs, Judge C.F. Keith, Nixon T. Van Dyke, John Ross, Cherokee Chief, Jack Walker, Indian Chief ... Polk, statesman... last time I was in Nashville during the lifetime of his widow I called to see her and related the little episode of my boyhood...she laughed..seemed to enjoy it. Many noted men graduated at old Forest Hill Academy."

First stores were opened by James and Isaac Fyffe and Mathew and William Smith. 1

1.Allen, Leaves...McMinn County.

James Gettys and Squire Johnson were tanners, Joel Brown had a tailor shop, Peter Kinder was a hatter, Dempsey Casey a saddler, George Sehorn, a silversmith, and Julius Blackwell a coppersmith.

The Valley Freeman, begun in 1824 was the first newspaper. This paper continued until about 1834. By 1827 the Hiwassean, & Athens Gazette was printed in a log cabin three miles northeast of Athens.

The Tennessee Journal and the Hiwassee Patriot, a Whig sheet was published for a short time beginning in 1837. A bitter Democratic paper, The Athens Courier began about the same time and continued until 1853.

Reading through old copies of these newspapers published during the late 1820s through the 1840s, provides a glimpse into the issues of the time.

Saturday, February 24, 1827 the Hiwassean & Athens Gazette carried a story of national interest headed TEXAS. The topic is a Treaty between the republic of Nacogdoches and sundry tribes of Indians. "Whereas the government of the Mexican States have by frequent insults, treachery and oppression, reduced the White and Red emigrants from the

Hiwassean, & Athens Gazette.

Athens, Tennessee, Saturday, February 24. 1827.

PUBLISHED Every Saturday morning [illegible] THREE DOLLARS within six months, or [illegible]

Valuable property FOR SALE. THERE will be offered for sale, in the town of Athens, on Tuesday, the 6th day of March next, THE FOLLOWING TOWN LOTS belonging to the late firm of M'Ewen & M'Kamy. HALF OF Lot No. 7, [illegible] LOTS [illegible] BRICK Dwelling-House, Kitchen, Smoke-house and Lumber-house. ALSO, SIX LOTS [illegible] Two acres each. ALSO, 160 Acres [illegible] Fifteen Acres [illegible] 12 Months, [illegible] Athens, Feb 6, 1827.

Look Here!! THE subscriber respectfully informs the citizens of Hiwassee district, and the public generally, that he has commenced, and will carry on the Wagon-making Business in Athens, [illegible] ONE OR TWO BOYS, [illegible] A FIRST RATE WORKMAN, [illegible] CHARLES W. MARTIN. Athens, Feb 6, 1827.

Apple Trees. [illegible] ALSO, Seedlings, [illegible] RICH'D. C. WATERHOUSE. [illegible]

Take Notice. ALL persons are hereby warned from trading for A Note of Hand, [illegible] JAMES SWAN. [illegible]

Sale postponed. sheriff's sale. BY virtue of a writ of [illegible] And to me directed, [illegible] I will expose to public sale, [illegible] LAND, lying in M'Minn county, [illegible]

TEXAS.

From the Natchitoches Courier.

Treaty between the republic of Nacogdoches and sundry tribes of Indians.

Whereas the government of the Mexican United States, have by frequent insults, treachery and oppression, reduced the White and Red emigrants from the United States of North America, now living in the province of Texas, within the territory of the said government, into which they have been deluded by promises solemnly made, and most basely broken, to the dreadful alternative of either submitting their free born necks to the yoke of an imbecile faithless and despotic government miscalled a republic; or of taking arms in defence of their unalienable rights, and asserting their independence They—viz: The white inhabitants now assembled in the town of Nacogdoches, around the independent standard, on the one part, and the red emigrants who have espoused the same holy cause on the other, to prosecute more speedily and effectually the war of independence, they have mutually undertaken, to a successful issue, and to bind themselves by the ligaments of reciprocal interests, and obligations, have resolved to form a treaty of union, league and confederation.

For this illustrious object, Benjamin W. Edwards, and Harmon H. Mayo, agents of the committee of independence, and Richard Fields and John D. Hunter, the agents of the red people, being respectively furnished with due powers have agreed to the following Articles.

1 The named contracting parties bind themselves to a solemn Union, League and Confederation in peace and war, to establish and defend their mutual independence of [illegible] of Joseph [illegible] from thence West by the compass, without regard to the variation to the Rio Grande, thence to the head of the Rio Grande, [illegible] with the mountains [illegible] head of Big [illegible] thence north to the boundary of the United States of North America thence with the same line to the mouth of Sulphur Fork, thence in a right line to the beginning

The territory apportioned to the white people shall comprehend all the residue of the province of Texas and of such other portion of the Mexican United States, as the contracting parties by their mutual efforts and resources may render independent, provided the same shall not extend further west than the Rio Grande.

3. The contracting parties mutually guarantee the rights of Empresarios to their premium lands only, and the rights of all other individuals, acquired under the Mexican government, and relating or appertaining to the above described territories, provided the said Empresarios and individuals do not forfeit the same by an opposition to the independence of the said territories, or by withdrawing their aid and support to its accomplishment

4 It is distinctly understood by the contracting parties that the territory apportioned to the red people, is intended as well for the benefit of the tribes now settled within the territory apportioned to the white people, as for those living in the former territory, and that it is incumbent upon the contracting parties of the red people, to offer the said tribes a participation in the same.

5. It is mutually agreed by the contracting parties that every individual red and white who has made improvement within either of the respective allied territories and lives upon the same, shall have a fee simple of a section of [illegible] tion mutually stipulate that they will direct all their resources to the prosecution of the heaven inspired cause which has given birth to this solemn Union League & Confederation, firmly relying upon their united efforts, and the strong arm of heaven for success.

[illegible] By gentlemen just arrived from col. Austin's settlement, Texas, we are informed that gov. Saucedo has arrived there from St. Antonio, with one hundred and fifty Mexican [illegible]

AN EARLY NEWSPAPER --published at Athens, Tennessee.

THE ATHENS UNION POST.

LIEUT. N. SMITH BOYNTON, EDITOR.

ATHENS, TENNESSEE,

THURSDAY, SEPTEMBER 17TH, 1863.

OUR MISSION.

We issue the first number of the ATHENS UNION POST, with the belief that it will do much toward opening the eyes of the people of East Tennessee in regard to the policy now being pursued, and to be pursued by our Government. We hope that the people, whether heretofore loyal or disloyal, will not misconstrue our motives. We want them to fully understand our intentions and govern their opinions accordingly.

We do not come among you as a victorious foe to oppress, or to crush out your liberties. We do not wish to seal your lips by iron rule, or military power; but with the sword in one hand to drive out and put down the enemies of our country, whether they have taken up arms through malicious or mischievous motives, or having been influenced so to do by the counsel of wicked ambitious leaders—while with the other hand we extend to you the olive branch of peace, asking you kindly to return to your allegiance to that government under which you have heretofore lived so happy and prosperous; under which you have enjoyed those blessed rights and privileges that you could not enjoy under any other form of government that exists upon the face of the earth, to-day.

We are not your enemies, but your friends. You have been led to believe that we come among you, to destroy your property, to devastate your fields, to ravish your unprotected women, to jeopardize your lives and their lives. These false statements have been made to you by unprincipled men in order to draw your love and affection away from the government you have in former times respected and worshiped.

Who three years ago did not feel proud to be called an American citizen? Who three years hence will not feel ashamed and mortified to be called a Confederate? Many of you who have joined your fortunes with the South, in the mistaken idea of fighting for your rights, may still think it an honor to be connected with the fast falling Southern Confederacy. Unprincipled men have often for a time exhibited an outward pride in boasting of their bad deeds—but sooner or later they realize their disgrace and ignominy.

Many of you have already witnessed the truth of the statement. Can any deny but that those, who, through fear of being punished for their traitorous conduct towards their Government, fled from this place on the approach of our army, felt their cheeks tingle with shame, and their consciences—if they had any—did not smite them?

The sooner the people of the South throw aside the idea that the Southern Confederacy is right, and the Union wrong, the more honor will it be to them in the future.

We come among the people of East Tennessee not as Yankees, Ohioans, Illinoisans, or Michiganders, but as American Citizens; determined to restore the Union again to its original position among the nations of the world; and as soon as you who are disloyal become loyal, peaceable, AMERICAN CITIZENS, and set about to restore law and order, our mission will be accomplished, and we will return to our homes again, feeling that we have done a noble work.

rights and privileges have you enjoyed since you embraced the false doctrine of secession, that you did not enjoy before? The bug bear of secession was the negro question. Have you the same protection now over that institution that you had when we lived happily together?

Have the fugitive negroes been any less since the war than they were before? Has not the South lost more of that peculiar property in the two last years than ever before? Most certainly she has; and who is to blame?

The South has cursed President Lincoln for issuing his Proclamation of Emancipation, and claim that he had no right to adopt such a policy, that it infringed upon their rights. What presumption! that a nation has no right to weaken her enemies who are seeking to destroy her. For a moment let every southern man take a common sense view of this hated policy, and not allow themselves to be carried away by prejudice and passion.

Our enemies of the South own between three and four millions slaves. These slaves are employed in the field raising cotton, corn, sugar, rice, produce of all kinds, with which the enemies of our government subsist their armies. They employ them on their fortifications, in their entrenchments; at every place that they can be made available.

Now is it not to the interest of the Government of the United States to take away this formidable force? Would not any nation resort to the same measures for self preservation?

But it is said by some that the proclamation will not, and does not, reach the slaves in the extreme Southern States, and as it still protects the institution in the loyal slave states, it is weak and powerless. If this is so, why raise such a hue and cry about it?

And how simply ridiculous it is to ask of the government they have sought to destroy, protection to that property which is used so effectually against it. It would be as consistent to ask the government to protect their arms and munitions of war; and to raise objections to the policy of capturing those found in arms against us, and making them prisoners of war.

"All we want is to be let alone," say our secession friends south. Did they expect to be let alone when they attempted to destroy the best government that the sun ever shone upon? Did they expect to be let alone when they sought by force of arms to establish the dangerous and destructive doctrine of State Rights, which if established would sever our once powerful country into numerous petty governments, so weak and insignificant that the nations of the old world would look upon us with contempt?

"Let us alone," is the motto of the highwayman, while he cuts your throat, and robs you of all you possess. "Let us alone," while we undermine the foundation of our noble institutions and bring ruin and desolation upon our country. "Let us alone," while we are endeavoring to establish out of the ruins of a free republic, an aristocratic monarchial form of government.

It is time that the people of the South opened their eyes to the true state of things, and learn, before it is too late, that evil may grow and flourish for a time, but sooner or later it will have to give way to the onward tread of Truth and Justice. They never can succeed in their mad attempt to separate this Union, cemented by the blood of our revolutionary forefathers, both North and South. If a portion of the people of the South have so lost sight of the fact, that those noble men who laid the foundation of this government, upwards of eighty years ago, knew no North, no South, no East, no West, but labored for their common country, it is time that they should remove the scales from their eyes, look into the past and imitate the ways of our fathers.

That this wicked rebellion will be crushed, and the offenders—the leaders—be brought to justice, is only a question of time. Just as sure as the sun rises in the east, and sets in the west, just

This newspaper was published by the Union Army during its' military occupation of Athens beginning June 10, 1862. This occupation continued until sometime in the Fall when they retreated in front of the Confederate forces. East Tennessee changed hands several times during the War. Nashville, gained by the Union early in 1862 remained in Union control. Andrew Johnson was appointed military governor and served until the War's end.

ATHENS UNION POST.

VOL. I. "THE UNION MUST AND SHALL BE PRESERVED." NO. 1.

ATHENS UNION POST.

LIEUT. N. SMITH BOYNTON, EDITOR.

ATHENS, TENNESSEE.

THURSDAY, SEPTEMBER 17TH, 1863.

OUR TERMS.

RECRUITS WANTED!

Attention East Tennessee ans!

PROTECT YOUR HOMES AND FIRESIDES!!

ATHENS, Tenn., Sept., 10th, 1863.

TWELVE MONTHS!

HEAD QUARTERS,

This September 1863 issue of the Union Post contains a "Recruits Wanted" bulletin -- John B. McCracken enlisted the previous June.

United States of North America now living in the province of Texas, within the territory of the said government, into which they have been deluded by promises solemnly made and most hourly broken, to the dreadful alternative of either submitting their free born necks to the yoke of an imbecile faithless and despotic government miscalled a republic; or of taking arms in defense of their unalienable rights, and asserting their independence.... The White inhabitants now assembled in the town of Nacogdoches, around the independent standard on the one part, and the Red emigrants who have espoused the same holy cause on the other, to prosecute more speedily and effectually the war of independence, they have mutually undertaken, to a successful issue, and to bind themselves by the ligaments of reciprocal interests, and obligation have resolved to form a treaty of union, league and confederation.."

Another story from the same issue and dated the previous January 10: "By gentleman just arrived from Col. Austin's Settlement, Texas we are informed..." This goes on to describe hostilities between Commanches and the Mexicans. The Commanches are estimated at between five and six thousand with some estimates as high as fifteen thousand warriors. "...the Indians have been at war with the Spaniards ever since they have been in the country, but their war fare has been of late, carried on by small parties, whose principal object is to plunder. There are ten or twenty other tribes but their numbers are small."

Beside the Texas story is this advertisement. "Look Here!! says the first line "The subscriber respectfully informs the citizens of Hiwassee district, and the public generally that he has commenced and will carry on the WAGON MAKING BUSINESS in Athens, where all kinds of work in his line of business can be had on the best of terms... one or two boys from fifteen to eighteen years of age, of sober and industrious habits, will be taken as apprentices to the above business...

Charles W. Martin Athens, February 6, 1827

Beneath Martin's ad is one for Apple trees. "I have a great number of proper size for setting out... particularly the New York or Green pippin...with other Winter, Fall and Summer grafts. Also seedlings which I will sell on 12 months credit.

Rich'd. G. Waterhouse February 13, 1827

Continuing from the Hiwassean -- Town lots are offered for sale "On Tuesday, the 6th day of March next, the following town lots..." Also described is a brick dwelling house, kitchen, smoke and lumber house.

A copy of the Tennessee Journal, dateline Athens, morning February 4, 1834 at the upper left states "Published weekly by J.M.Gibbs at $3 per annum...no subscription received for less than 12 months; nor discontinued unless at the option of the Publishers... country produce will be received in payment for subscriptions at the market value if delivered at the offices within the year. Advertisements will be inserted on the usual terms."

Each edition of the paper carried a list of letters to be picked up at the post office. On the first of January 1834 one of the names in the list is Jemina Hampton, the wife of James.

The February 4, 1834 issue of the Tennessee Journal has a lengthy article entitled Boston Manners. In this article Mr. Grant Thornburn describes a steamer trip up the Hudson -- a trip he took with the purpose of observing the behavior of his fellow passengers. His interest is caught by two

...ffs' Sale.

...venditioni exponas, issued ...Court of McMinn County ...d,

...will sell

...e door in Athens, on Sat... ...y of March next, all the ...interest and demand that ...ch has to a certain Town ...of Athens, Known in the ...in the out Lots as Num... ...y a judgment and cost that ...William Lowry obtained ...lch before Fulsp[illegible] Lane

...BEAVERS, Sheriff. ...1834.

No. 24. $...

...riff Sale

...venditioni Exponas issued ...Court of McMinn County ...d,

...will sell

...se in Athens, on Saturday ...March next all the right, ti... ...est and demand that Jub ...ertain House and Lot in the ...known as

No. 37,

...ment and cost, that James ...against said Hall before ...a Justice of the Peace for

...BEAVERS Sheriff. ...1834.

No. 24. $...

...iff's sale.

...a Fieri Facias issued from ...t of McMinn County and

...will sell,

...se in Athens, on Saturday ...March next, all the right, ...interest and demand that ...est has of, in and to, ...h East quarter, and his ...half of the South west ...on 19th, Township fourth ...t ode.

...same that said Bryles ...the same more or less—to ...ent and cost that James, ...I against said Bryles, in ...rt of McMinn County.

S. BEAVERS, Sheriff. 1834.

No. 24. $5.

...of John Hamilton and William H. K. Shelton

No. 1039

levied on as the property of said M'callister, to satisfy a Judgment in favour of York and Riggs. sale in legal hours unless previously satisfied

WM. JONES. Sheriff. of Marion County.

January 7, 1834.

No. 24. $9.

A List of Letters remaining in the Office at Calhoun Tennessee on the 1st January 1834, if not taken out before the first April next will be sent to the General Post Office as dead letters Viz.

Carroll Elijah	Lowry Sarah
Clark David	Lowry Alex
Callen Geo A	Mitchell Wm 1,
Dunmeraut Demarquis	M'Callon Geo—9
Fan Matilda Mrs 2	Morgan Silas
Fitzgerald Aaron	M'Camish John
Freeman Lewis	Okelly Benj
Gardiner W G capt	Phillips Henry
Hampton Jemima	Parsons Thomas
Harp Thomas	Rornagay Geo D
Hang Wm	Repter James
Harris James G	Troup James
Hellams John	Turbet Sally Mrs
Iamon Benj	Williams William
Jack Jeremiah	Webb Julius
Jimerson Benj	Wardlaw Michael
Lankford Robt	
Lattemore Dan Reed	

NOTICE.

ALL persons are hereby forwarned from trading, with, or crediting or harbouring, my wife Mary Harris, on my account, as I will not pay any debts of her contracting

JOHN HARRIS.

August 17, 183...

WAGONS WANTED.

Sixteen first rate Road Wagons with bodies of the largest kind, each to be drawn by a first rate six horse teams complete in Gear and Harness, will find employment during the removal of the present Emigration of Cherokees from their homes to their respective points of Embarcation upon the rivers; by the owners of such enrolling their names immediately at the agency.

The said Wagons to be called upon at any time between the 1st & 20th day of February next—to go to ...

Sheriffs Sale.

By virtue of a venditioni exponas issued from the court of pleas and quarter sessions of M'Minn County, and to me directed,

I will sell

at the Court House door in Athens, on Saturday the 22d of February next, all the right, title, claim, interest, & demand, that James King, administrator of William King. Has of, in and to, the one half of the south west quarter of section 23d, Township fourth, range first, east of the Meredian.—To satisfy a judgment and cost that Sampson Dedrick & co. obtained against said King, before Robert M. Swan Esqr. and will be sold unless debt and cost are previously satisfied.

S. BEAVERS, Sheriff.

January, 7th 1834. no 23. $3.

Sherifs Sale.

BY virtue of two venditioni exponas, issued from the county court of M'Minn, and to me directed,

I will offer

for sale at the Court House door in Athens, on the first day of March next, all the right, title, claim, interest and demand, that Gilbert Cruse. Has to the sixth part, of an undivided Estate of Benjamin Riddle Deceased the land on which said Cruse now, lives, to satisfy four executions, one in favour of Charles Royester, for Murrell and Humphreys, one in favour of Murrell and Humphreys, and two in favour of Humphreys. Each obtained against said Cruse—and will be sold unless debt and cost are previously paid.

S. BEAVERS, Sheriff.

January 7th 183 4. $3.

Sheriff's Sale.

By virtue of a venditioni exponas issued from the County Court of McMinn County, and to me directed,

I will Sell

at the Court House door in Athens, on the ...

Gemima Hampton's name appears in the article above listing "...letters remaining in the office at Calhoun..." Printed in an early McMinn County newspaper, the article is dated January 1834.

young lovers "...on board you may easily distinguish them from those who have been buckled together in a holy alliance ...for provided you are a keen observer of nature, you will see the fair new... cling fast to the arm of her natural support upstairs and downstairs to the table, or to the promenade, always linked together as close as the bands of matrimony can tie them. Even in a crowd, where they can't go abreast, you may see her pressing sideways along still grasping the arm as if she was afraid he might drop into oblivion. After supper, and when most of the passengers have retired, you may see them pacing the deck, or sitting in a lonely corner, like the turtle dove on a solitary tree, repeating their ...of love. There they sit 'til midnight.... They now walk to the door of the ladies' cabin but hitherto they may go, but no farther... they shake hands, part as if it were forever, she to sleep if she can and he to the bar to drown his sorrow in a glass of champagne..."

In stark contrast and on the same page: "Committed to the jail of McMinn County, Tennessee on the 1st inst. a Negro man by the name of Tim, who was brought to Athens two or three days previous by a white man calling himself Prescot, who claimed said negro was his property and offered him for sale but whilst negotiations to that effect it was thought that this conduct looked suspicious and he and said negro was questioned separately as to their real names, occupations etc... their statements were contradictory... The negro is 5 feet 8 or 9 inches high, stout built, about 30 years of age, and quite intelligent, wore a brown home spun coat, and had other clothing all home made, the owner of said negro is requested to come forward prove his property, pay charges and take him away or he will be dealt with as the law directs.

John Austain, Jailor January 4, 1834

The following notice was placed in the same issue: "I forwarn any person from trading or taking an assignment for a note of hand executed by me to James Keyton on the fourteenth day of October 1830 for the sum of sixteen dollars and twenty-five cents which was to be discharged in wheat, rye and corn; payable about the 15th of November next as I am determined not to pay said note except compelled by law as it was defraudently obtained from me.

Samuel T. Biddle January 24, 1834

The publishers of Novelist's Magazine of Philadelphia offer a premium of $750 to the author of the best novel on a national subject. The manuscript to be delivered on or before the first of April 1834.

There are notices of Sheriff's sales -- public auctions to be held at the Court House door. The most usual cause for the sale of these properties is to satisfy debts or to settle estates.

Dry goods are offered by the local tradesmen -- fancy staple merchandise declares one heading: Just received from Baltimore and Philadelphia silks, merinos, wool shawls, calicoes, cambricks, blue, black, brown, olive, grey, mixed, mulberry and drab cloths... various colors and qualities...china...handkerchief, coffee, sugar, allspice, ginger, Epson Salts, shoes, hats, caps, whips...lace edging, shovels, spades, hoes and forks, paints, oil, Patent medicines and a splendid assortment of books and stationary all of which will be sold for cash and will receive in exchange for beeswax, beef hides, cotton, flax and tow linen.

January 1st 1834

The entire first page of a June, 1834 issue of the Tennessee Journal, published at

Athens is taken up by an abstract from a journal pertaining to a Congressional convention held in May of that year.

The following were placed in the ad section of an 1838 edition: Wool carding machines for sale... pocket book found... Notice: further emigration of the Cherokee Indians is suspended until the first of September next. Persons wishing to enter their...in the United States service at the time specified, can send their names in for enrollment and when they are wanted due notice will be given. John Page, Captain and Principal Disbursing Agent, Calhoun, Tennessee

June 20, 1838

Peter Hampton the oldest son of James and Gemina answered this call.

The ads from The Journal continue: $30 Reward for runway "...mulatto boy named Cy, belonging to Thomas Crutchfield of Athens, Tennessee... there is reason to believe he will seek shelter in the Cherokee Nation and aim to make his escape in that way."

May 24, 1838

There are sixteen letters of testament to the wonders of Dr. J. H. Bacon's cures for a variety of diseases and disorders.

H | Lindsay's Reg't Mtd. Vols. | Tenn.

Peter Hampton

Pvt { Capt. Morrow's Co., Lindsay's Reg't Tennessee Mtd. Vols.

(CHEROKEE WAR.)

Appears on

Company Muster Roll

for July 11 to Aug 21, 1837.

Joined for duty and enrolled:

When July 11, 1837.*

Where Fort Cass *

Period 3 years.*

Present or absent Present

H | Lindsay's Reg't Mtd. Vols. | Tenn.

Peter Hampton

Pvt { Capt. Morrow's Co., Lindsay's Reg't Tennessee Mtd. Vols.

(CHEROKEE WAR.)

Appears on

Company Muster Roll

for Sept & Oct, 1837

Joined for duty and enrolled:

When July 11, 1837.*

Where Fort Cass, *

Period 12 ~~years~~.* mos.

H | Lindsay's Reg't Mtd. Vols. | Tenn.

Peter Hampton,

Pvt { Capt. Morrow's Co., Lindsay's Reg't, Tenn. Mtd. Vols.

(Cherokee War.)

Age ...... years.

Appears on

Company Muster-in Roll

of the organization named above. Roll dated

Cherokee Agency July 11, 1837.

Muster-in to date July 11, 1837.

Joined for duty and enrolled:

When July 11, 1837.*

Where Calhoun *

Period One years.*

H | Lindsay's Reg't Mtd. Vols. | Tenn.

Peter Hampton

Pvt { Capt. Morrow's Co., Lindsay's Reg't Tennessee Mtd. Vols.

(Cherokee War.)

Appears on

Company Muster Roll

for Nov & Dec, 1837.

Joined for duty and enrolled:

When July 11, 1837.*

Where Fort Cass *

Period 12 ~~years~~.* mos.

Present or absent Present

Military records of Peter Hampton, Cherokee Removal.

84	Lindsay's Reg't Mtd. Vols.	Tenn.

Peter Hampton

Pvt { Capt. Morrow's Co., Lindsay's Reg't Tennessee Mtd. Vols.

(CHEROKEE WAR.)

Appears on

Company Muster Roll

for Jan & Feb, 1838.

Joined for duty and enrolled:

When July 11, 1837.*

Where Fort Cass*

Period 12 mo years.*

86	Lindsay's Reg't Mtd. Vols.	Tenn.

Petter Hampton

Pvt { Capt. Morrow's Co., Lindsay's Reg't Tennessee Mtd. Vols.

(CHEROKEE WAR.)

Appears on

Company Muster Roll

for Mch & Apl, 1838.

Joined for duty and enrolled:

When ...., 183 .*

Where ....*

Period 12 ~~years~~* Mos.

Present or absent Present

Stoppage, $......100 for ....

Due Gov't, $......100 for ....

Valuation of horse, ... $100

H	Lindsay's Reg't Mtd. Vols.	Tenn.

Peter Hampton

Pvt { Capt. Morrow's Co., Lindsay's Reg't Tenn. Mtd. Vols.

(Cherokee War.)

Age .... years.

Appears on Co. Muster-out Roll, dated

Fort Cass Tenn, July 12, 1838.

Muster-out to date July 10, 1838.

Last paid to Apr. 30, 1838.

Clothing account:

Last settled ...., 183 ; drawn since $......100

Due soldier $......100; due U. S. $......100

Am't for cloth'g in kind or money adv'd $......100

Due U. S. for arms, equipments, &c., $......100

Bounty paid $......100; due $......100

Remarks: ....

Book mark: ....

N Bradshaw

(361) Copyist.

Restoring all to good health and often for "very small sums of five or ten dollars."

Wanted to Purchase... An intelligent likely black or mulatto boy as a waiter, from 12 to 20 years of age. A liberal price in specie, will be given for one that will suit. Enquire at Mr. Mounte (sp) Store at the Agency. July 25, 1838

Notice the subscriber wishes to procure specie currency for which he will give drafts on New York, in sums to accommodate those who wish to make the exchange. Application to be made to him, at Fort Cass, Cherokee Agency, after the 3rd of August. Rich'd. Bennett, Paymaster, U.S.A.

August 1, 1838

There are several ads beginning: Estray, placed by people looking for horses and people who have found horses looking for their owners. Sorrels, bay mares, bald faces white feet, cropped ears, brands, marks, blazes, measured in hands and years.

And there is the following bounty offer: $100 Reward "For the apprehension and delivery of Benjamin Shipley, in Hamilton County so that he may be ...for an attempt to murder Archibald McCallie of said county by shooting him through the arm and hip on

Saturday the 23 of June 1838. Said Shipley is about six feet high, stoutly built, rather rawboned --is considered a stout man, his skin is tolerably fair, and somewhat freckled but generally sun-burnt, fair hair, and pale blue or grey eyes ...given to intoxication...boisterious and uncontrollable when drinking ...and is sort of a blacksmith. Thos. McCallie July 11, 1838

J. S. Bridges lives on the farm next to James Hampton. He places the following ad: "Wanted immediately, five thousand pounds of soap of which I will give six pence per pound delivered in this place. Also, for sale five hundred bushels of corn, three miles from Athens.

J. S. Bridges, Athens, 11 July 1838

The September 17, 1841 copy of the Athens Courier carried the following accounts:

On the front page is the tragic account of Aaron Burr and his daughter. Burr who had scaled the heights to the vice-presidency and as a result of his duel with Hamilton became a fugitive from justice. Finally, the story describes how his daughter "his all on earth" in a privately chartered vessel set sail to visit him in his old age and was lost when the vessel foundered and she never arrived..."the last link was broken."

But not all stories were so serious. A light-hearted social event held at the Washington Hotel is described in the following account. "The Ball" ...held on the evening of the 9th inst. at the Washington Hotel was passed most agreeably... the dancing goddess thronged the Hall at early evening and from the first peeping-out of the stars until the very witching hour when ghosts do stalk abroad joy, innocent joy held the ascendant. Lovely forms moved lightly through the mazes of the merry dance while bright eyes beamed joyously amid the guileless pastime. The girls were beautiful, the boys were happy -- the supper was magnifique -- the wine was delicious -- the music excellent -- and in a word the whole affair was first rate... it will gratify our young friends to learn that on Wednesday evening next, our host will give another entertainment of the same agreeable nature."

A notice regarding the militia: "Major General Brazelton will attend and review the several regiments in the Fifth and Sixth Brigades...on October next." Soldiers from

McMinn made up the 31st, 32nd and 33rd Regiments of the Sixth Brigade.

T. B. Emerson & Co. near Athens, manufacturers of paper advertised for "Rags! Rags! Rags! offering for all clean linen and cotton rags 1 cent per pound...

G. J. Worsham of Chestua Mills thanked the people for the patronage accorded him during the last ten or twelve years of his services as a millwright and announced that he has permanently located in Polk County near Armstrong's old ferry.

The schedule and prize money for horse races held at the local track, was carried in this article: The Athens races over the Boston Race course will come off Wednesday the 17th of November. 1st day -- Purse $100 mile heats; 2nd day -- Purse $150 2 mile heats; 3rd day -- Purse $250 3 mile heats. On Tuesday previous to the regular meeting, a sweepstake for 3 year colts will come off, mile heats $50 entrance...on Saturday a sweepstake for 2 year colts, one mile out $30 entrance half forfeit.

The Athens Courier of Friday, September 3, 1842 gives a glimpse into Athens: J. M. Gibbs, proprietor of the Washington Hotel, in an advertisement for the hotel states "has provided good stables and provinder and a careful and attentive caler."

There is a notice that the law firm of Cannon and Stephenson is open for business.

A. O. Keyes, is identified as a school commissioner and Edward A. Atlee is an expert saddler, harness maker, coach and wagon maker who "will construct even wheel-barrows." Mrs. Brown notified the public that she would take a few young girls at her home to teach them "oil and water colors and the pianoforte." The Athens Female Academy was quite active.

The big news of the day was the armed occupation of Florida.

Another article gives the information that there are "over twelve hundred thousand persons in England and Wales living on alms."

In addition to the daily newspaper was the delivery of the mail. The Post Office Department records indicate that the Athens Post Office was established January 31, 1823. By 1830 there were five post offices and postmasters in McMinn County. The Athens post office was located at the court house, James Fyffe, postmaster. James S. Bridges was the postmaster at Calhoun. The remaining offices were Cobbs, David A. Cobbs, postmaster; Columbus, Samuel McConnell; Holt's Store, James H. Reagan.

The earliest record of the Athens office shows in 1824 there were two routes:

1. From Knoxville, by Marysville, Morgantown, ...Ferry, Colwells? Athens, Calhoun, Rossville

2. From Murfreesboro, by Winchester, Jasper, Rossville, Springplace, Talons? Chestnut Hill, to Athens.

The mail was delivered by stagecoach drawn by six horses, sulkies and on horseback. Relays were about fifteen miles apart. The horses went in a full gallop. In this area of McMinn County the horses were changed at the Hiwassee... and at Sweetwater.... "Nette Wattee??" as it was known in the early days.

The Bridges Hotel was built early in the history of McMinn. David Crockett stayed there on his way to Texas. Henry Clay drank at the hotel bar when he was a candidate for President in 1844. General Sherman stayed there the night he left Chattanooga and went to the relief of General Burnside at Knoxville. Before the railroads came to Tennessee the Bridges stop was a relay for the stage.

The Rogers Tavern was erected about the year 1829 by Tim Rogers, prominent citizen of Calhoun. The building is frame with columns on the long porch so popular with the old colonial style houses. During the stagecoach days it was one of the relays between Chattanooga and Knoxville. John Howard Payne, author of Home Sweet Home was a guest at this tavern while on a visit to John Ross Chief of the Cherokee. Payne and Ross often dined at the hotel and drank from the bar.

Between 1861-65 many notables whose names are familiar to students of history stopped at the Rogers Tavern. It was for several days the headquarters of a Division from Ohio while enroute to Chattanooga. The soldiers camped on the banks of the river southwest of the old ferry while the commanding officer and his principal aide, put up at the Tavern. General Sherman when he marched to Knoxville to relieve federal forces being besieged by Longstreet was a guest at the Tavern overnight. General Bragg, who had his headquarters in Chattanooga and who was an intimate friend of

Major McConnell, Captain Lafferty and Captain Dill all residents of Calhoun was at several different times a guest.

The first manufacturing plant in McMinn County was established in 1829, at the little village of Mount Verd within three miles of Athens.

Charles W. Metcalf and his sons began the Mount Verd spinning mill. There were only a few dwellings and no business houses in the little village of Mount Verd. Metcalf first erected a small frame structure and later enlarged the plant by adding a substantial brick structure. He employed approximately 100 boys and girls. This plant was famous throughout a wide territory surrounding it for its cotton yarn. This yarn was used as a warp for the making of cloth in the home looms and for knitting hosiery. The greater part of the employees in the Metcalf thread factory were girls as in those days it was considered unwise to educate girls, but instead, they were taught it was their duty to earn their living by work. The boys attended school if so situated near enough to an institution of learning. Later, if the parents were financially able, the boys would be sent to the Old

Forest Hill Academy near Athens located near the Ingleside Spring.

The plant seldom shut down. It was operated by water power, its machinery being uncomplicated and hence shutdowns were rare. The mill ran right on, never stopping for want of orders and seldom failed to fill orders on schedule. Operators were never idle.

In addition to the thread factory, Metcalf manufactured castor oil, made from the castor bean. Several hundred acres of fertile land near the Mount Verd village were used for the cultivation of this crop. Wagon loads of the beans were hauled to the plant by growers in the surrounding territory. Metcalf disposed of the finished product by hauling in wagons to the different sections of the country and exchanging the oil for groceries. Thus a "barter and trade" center sprang up. Sugar, coffee, tobacco, etc. brought back from the market was sold at retail in the company's store. Augusta, Georgia was the principal trading point for the product and it required several weeks for wagons to get the product to market and return. The finished castor oil was put into containers, holding from one-half to one gallon of oil each. The manufacture and sale of the oil enabled Metcalf to secure the necessary articles for his retail trade. It afforded the growers of the bean to exchange their crop for groceries.

The railroad, that would replace the wagons of Metcalf's mill had its beginnings in France many years earlier. The following newspaper account tells of its awkward start.

"Speeding diabolically at the rate of three miles an hour inventor Frenchman Sugnot's 1769 model steam locomotive noisily overturned. French public authorities demanded this three wheel monster be immediately locked up. This parent of the steam engine was considered to be a menace and danger to public safety. No longer was it to be allowed to run freely along the common road, accompanied by shouting happy French children, barking dogs and blinking onlookers and to stop every 15 minutes to build up its white steam pressure."

The first Tennessee railroad dirt was broken in 1837 at Steed's Crossing two miles west of Athens by the Hiwassee Railroad Company. The line was to run from Athens, Tennessee to Dalton, Georgia. Methodist

Minister David Sullins wielded the pick that broke the first railroad earth. T. Nixon Van Dyke hauled away the first cart load of dirt. "Railroads may mean a great deal in Tennessee someday, said Mr. Van Dyke at the big celebration barbecue... why the time may even come when a man can eat his breakfast in Knoxville, have dinner in Athens and actually eat his supper in far away Cleveland." The distance between Cleveland and Athens is approximately 26 miles!

Bill Peak, who lived four miles from Calhoun on the farm upon which he was born and spent all his life, remembered when the first train came across the bridge..."a large crowd gathered to see the train into Calhoun, men, women and children...this was about the year 1850."

A description of day to day life in McMinn during this period is reflected in the passages that follow. Extractions from questionnaires filled out in 1922 by Civil War veterans[1] who were children in the 1830's and 40's, provide a look at school, home, church and other features of daily living.

----

1. Civil War Questionnaires, Tennessee State Library.

John Hart - Born in McMinn, our property was worth about $4,000.00. We lived in a log house with two rooms and a porch. Owned 833 acres. Father did general farm labor, plowing, chipping, ditching and many other kinds of work. Mother cooked carded and spun and wove cloth and done common house work. Belonged to the Baptist Church.

David Jennae - Born in McMinn and lived in a three room log house. Father ran the farm, mother the house, cooking, spinning, weaving and knitting. I attended school for ten years.

J. B. King - I was born in McMinn. We had a farm of 500 acres worth about $10,000.00. House one story frame building, had seven rooms.

James Benjamin Liner - Born in McMinn. My father was James Smith Liner, my mother Lucy V. Aul. We owned 200 acres Red Hill, poor land worth $1,500.00. Our house was log and frame. All white men in this section worked and worked together. I was a member of the Hiwassee Baptist Church for 64 years.

William Henry Patterson - Born February 2, 1842 in McMinn. My father was a renter. We lived in log houses. I chopped, grubbed, split railes, made hand plowing from the time I was nine years of age every year until the war as a hired hand on other men farms. I done all kinds of farm work. My father done all kinds of work done on the farm. At that time he plowed, hoed, soed harvested puld foder raised sheap, flax and cotton and all crops raised on the farm. Raised hogs, cattel and horses. My mother cooked spun cotten, flax, wool and tuc and wove the same into cloth for family use. We had no negroes or any kind of servants. All such work as mentioned above was ingaged in by all the community except two or three of the baser specemon of the community who was not reliable nor honest. Some of them owned Negroes and most of them worked their children with their negroes and hired help on the farms. Back in those days the people were more social than now. At corn shuckings, log rolings, house raiseings and so on the slave owner was just one of us. Often the intelectual advantage fell to non-slave holders. There was a political difference of opinion as to the rite to own Negro property but boath sides owned Negroes so the difference was not on the ground of holding or not. All young men were ingaged in working at some thing. Some of them exercised econemy while others was extravagent. But all had an oppertunety alike except those who were of the low class.

William Harrad - I was born 8 September 1844. Pa left in '46 war of Mexico and never returned. Mother died when I was only three months old, then I was left in the hands of a slave holder and as oft happens sure did see one hard time. I did farm work, plowd, hoe, don all kinds of farm labor done on a farm.

George Washington Brown - I was born May 27, 1822. Father and I boarded at the Mayo Hotel in Athens. Mother died when I was six months old and he never married again. I spent my boyhood days helping on the farm (father kept a family on a farm to take care of me when I was a small boy). ...hunting, fishing and trapping. I did not have to work, and I was just like all other boys who have everything they wish, not so fond of it. When I was about four years old I was out playing and an old Indian kidnapped me. His name was Falling. He was very kind to me and I learned to love him very much. Father offered a reward of $900 and Uncle Abraham found me after about

12 or 14 months. I was so fond of the old Indian and begged so hard for him that father put him on one of his farms so that I could be near him. I learned the Indian language and we had wonderful times together hunting and fishing.

My father designed and directed the making of all kinds of furniture, cabinets and coffins. On account of religious belief father kept no slaves. Mother kept a personal servant, but no more because she honored father's religion.

Honest toil was considered as very respectable; it was the man who had nothing and "loafed" who was looked down upon. The poor white boys worked and a few of the wealthier boys. The men who idled were arrested under the Vagabond Act and made to work. I knew one man, John Henderson, who was bid off at six and one-half cents and put to work by the buyer. Afterward he bought his freedom, later bought a farm for $15,000.00. He would often laugh about being sold for six and one-half cents. I was about eighteen at that time. Men were not looked down upon for not owning slaves, but they were looked down upon for laziness and for not trying to accumulate anything.

My father was a land owner and he was industrious, consequently he was highly respected. It was the lazy fellow whose habits were not above those of the negro who was not respected.

My grandfather, Aaron Brown, lived to be over eighty. He served in the Revolutionary War but I do not know in what capacity. He fell and totally disabled himself about ten years before his death and his wife, Naoma Brown, supported the family by baking and selling ginger cakes and cider. In addition to keeping the family out of the proceeds from her ginger cakes and cider, Grandmother Brown bought a farm for which she paid $800. The same farm in that section of the country today (1922) would be worth about $100,000. When grandmother's children were grown she adopted another little girl to raise. This little girl found her dead in bed one morning. As grandmother weighed 300 pounds it was decided she had smothered to death. I was very small at that time. I suppose seven or eight, but I remember that all of the country attended her funeral. I have been told that on account of her industry she was held in very high esteem in her community. She was a member of the Presbyterian Church. She was over ninety at the time of her death. To the union of Aaron and Naoma Brown there were born the following children; Brooks, Abraham, Joseph, Jess, Sarah and Naoma. Brooks Brown, my father, was a furniture and coffin manufacturer; uncle Abraham Brown was a wagoner, hauling produce of all kinds from Tennessee to Georgia; Uncle Joseph was a printer; Uncle Jess assisted my grandmother Brown in selling her cakes and cider; Aunt Sarah was a painter. An English publisher came to the country and persuaded Uncle Joe and Aunt Sarah to return to England with him. Aunt Sarah's salary was $1,500 besides extra money she received for her paintings. I remember that my great-grandfather and great-grandmother Babb (Grandmother Brown's parents) lived in a small log house. They owned a small farm of about fifty acres. They both lived over one hundred years. I have heard it said that great-grandmother Babb lived 116 years. She was a very small woman. Grandmother Brown often carried her in her arms and called her baby. I remember that as a child I was not very fond of my great-grandfather Babb because he once tapped me over the head with an axe handle. I had slipped his axe out and gapped it. The name of Mother's father was John Crawford of Athens, Tenn. He owned more land than any other man in Athens at that time; he also owned the largest dry goods store in Athens at that time; he owned five houses and lots and nine slaves. Usually a good strong negro man was worth $800; a good negro woman, $600. However, Grandfather Crawford paid $1500 for his blacksmith negro.

Daniel L. Buckner- We lived in a log house with framed addition with four rooms and basement. My father was a millwright and then took up dentistry. I spent most of my time with my father in the dental office. I went to school in a little log house at Mouse Creek known as the Wassom Schoolhouse and one near Riceville known as the Riceville Academy. There was considerable interest in school at that time. The old blue black was the favorite and you could have heard us about six hundred yards getting our spelling lessons and even farther than that when the teacher said "put up your books and take your dinners."

Uriah Payne - Born in McMinn 89 years ago. My parents owned 220 acres and two slaves; total value $800.00. My father farmed and my mother did cooking on the fireplace, weaving on homemade looms, spinning and making cloths. I attended Queener School and Carlock School.

Henry Morrison McKenzie - My parents owned several tracts of land. 160 acres cost $1,800 to $2,000. I lived in a frame house, five rooms in Riceville. We had seven slaves. Father was a merchant, mother ran the hotel. Mother did all kinds of work in the house and hotel, cooking and spinning, weaving -- made all every day wear of clothes for... and slaves. We had seven slaves, three grown women rest children. Oldest boy same age as I. I went to school at the Academy in Riceville.

Jacob Elias Sliger - Born in McMinn in 1822. Father Adam Sliger. Owned 160 acres worth $300.00. Lived in a log house with four rooms. Plowed the ox and used the hoe, cut grass with blade and grain with the reaphook and cradle. Mother did cooking, spinning, weaving for the family until children was large enough to help. Also work of the kind for other people to help support the family. He went to the Little Tick School. (Note: Jacob Sliger served in the 36th Infantry, Confederate Army. James Hampton was also in the 36th.)

Rev. David Sullins - Born in McMinn. Father was a farmer and stock raiser. Owned 1,000 acres in McMinn County worth about $15,000. We lived in a log cabin for five years then a two story log house, that was added with a brick chimney. There were nine rooms, including the kitchen. I did all sorts of work on the farm, plowing, hoeing, reaping and sowing. Father managed the farm and his stock, doing part of the work himself taking the load of the hands. Mother did cooking, spinning, weaving and making clothes for the family. Usually hired a colored man and his wife from other slave holders. I attended Forest Hill Academy then Emory and Henry College in Virginia. The Academy was three miles away at Athens.

Benjamin Swafford -- Born in McMinn 82 years ago. Owned 300 acres worth $2,500. Lived in a log house with three rooms. On the farm, plowed mostly but hoed if necessary, pulled fodder, gathereth $2,500. Lived in a log house with three rooms. On the farm, plowed mostly but hoed if necessary, pulled fodder, gathered corn and pease, cut some wood but mostly hauled, did not split rails or do much heavy work for want of strength. My father did all kinds of work needed on the farm and mother did all the work needed about the house and worked by pine blaze 'til late bedtime every winter night to make clothes for the family and now if I wanted to wright a book I could expand without truble. If a man had any disrespect for honest labor, common sense policy would have kept his mouth closed on that subject. I attended Mossy Creek College known now as Femon & Naman College. My father was Thomas Major Swafford. His farm was four miles from Calhoun. My mother was Nancy Almira Liner daughter of James and Elizabeth Liner who lived near Calhoun.

CHAPTER 8

BRADLEY COUNTY BEGINS IN 1830s

Bradley was cut out of land purchased from the Cherokee Indians in a Treaty known as the Ocoee Purchase. Two factions among the Cherokees emerged as before in the McMinn, or Hiwassee Treaty. John Ross, a Cherokee, led the group opposed to ceding the land to the white people. John Walker and several other half-breeds were for cessation. Walker lived on the McMinn County side of the Hiwassee River and had for many years sold goods from a log house erected at Charleston.

A council was held in Red Clay Georgia in August 1834 and without the sanction of Ross, Walker and his group made a treaty ceding the land to the United States. This was considered a treasonous act by the others and John Walker Jr. was put to death by two fellow Cherokees, James Foreman and Addison Springston who ambushed and shot him. He died nineteen days later. Final ratification of the treaty did not take place until John Ross agreed to sign May 23, 1836. As soon as this was accomplished troops were sent into the nation to gather up the Indians preparatory to their removal. Generals Scott and Wool were in command, with headquarters in Charleston. Barracks and other buildings were erected there covering an area of nearly ten acres around which was a stockade. The removal was begun in 1837 but not completed until the following year.

The survey of land was begun in the Spring of 1837. The baseline of the survey began at a large mass of limestone on the Hiwassee River opposite Charleston and ran to the Georgia line. In March 1838 an entry taker's office was opened at Cleveland and the land was placed for sale. For the first four months the price was $7.50 per acre; the next four -- $5.00 after which it was reduced to $2.00 and then $1.00, finally the last was sold in 1841 for one cent per acre. By 1840 the population of Bradley was more than 4,000.

Although the treaty with the Indians was not signed until 1836, white people had begun to drift into the area from McMinn and other surrounding counties by the early thirties. An early resident who lived in the County during this period described his community of Laurel Hill[1] located in the southeastern section of the county:

"...cabins must be built, large logs hewn into shape and fitted into each other by means of notches at the end, for walls. The cracks between the logs were filled with short pieces of wood, around which was daubed a plaster made of clay. The doors were made of heavy pieces and the floor of logs hewn flat, called puncheon floor. The chimney was made of sticks and clay, the roof of clapboard or long oak shingles fastened by heavy logs. There were no nails in them of course, The windows if any, had greased paper for glass with a heavy shutter to close in rough weather. Next came the clearing of the land, plowing and cultivation of the soil. The settlers farming tools were as primitive as his cabin. He used the faithful ox believing the horse was too speedy for a beast of burden. The horse did pull the plow. The neighbors gathered

---

1. <u>Brief Sketch of a County Neighborhood, Laurel Hill,</u> T.E. Thatch, 1894.

together for house raising, log rolling and corn husking.

...the first school...puncheon floor, with a log cut out for a window and almost one whole end of the house for a fireplace. The teachers wages ranged from twelve to eighteen dollars and when wages reached twenty dollars everybody wanted to follow. School began at sunrise and kept until sunset, with but little recess. The text books consisted of Webster's blue backed speller and the Testament. The exercises of the day were rather monotonous, all spelling aloud, until Friday afternoon, then a spelling contest ensued in which all engaged that could spell by heart.

There were no churches in the settlement and but few ministers. So the people would hold services at a neighbors house and then began to use the school house for a church. The boys would have great fun sometimes at these meetings. If a bat came in the house while the preacher was preaching, the boys would gather the broom and their hats and kill it while the preacher would take a rest and then go on with his discourse. In time a separate building was erected for the church and a circuit rider sent.

The people were English, Dutch, Irish, lived in little log huts, worshiped in the same way, poor men, but men of character. These were the days of hogs and hominy.... The delicacy for the table was dried pumpkin. Their means of travel were walking or riding horseback."

The county government was organized in May of 1836.[1] A site was chosen for the county seat and named Cleveland. Cut out of land that was largely wooded and swampy the village began with a few log buildings. By the late 1830s the population had grown to 500 and the village became a new frontier town. There were schools, including the Oak Grove Academy, a school for males, churches, blacksmith shop, tavern, grocery, dry goods store, a saloon, hotels. There were harness-makers, saddlers, tailors, tanners, blacksmiths, lawyers, physicians, and teachers. The log court house stood on the southwest corner of the public square until

---

1. Bradley County and the Town of Cleveland Tennessee East Tennessee, Historical and Biographical, R. M. Edwards, A.D.Smith and Co., 1893.

one night late in the year 1839, when a crowd gathered and declared the structure a "disgrace to the rising greatness of the town," and in between swigs of the whiskey bottle they dismantled the structure. It was replaced with a brick one. There was a jail located near the courthouse. Previous to this time, criminals were sent to McMinn County.

The streets were unsealed, wide pathways that had been cleared of trees. Deeply rutted and filled with stumps they were a hazard to the traffic of the day, horsedrawn vehicles, as well as those on horseback and foot. Muddy during times of rain and winter's snow the dust flew in the summer's heat and dryness.

The traffic of the streets reflected the activity of the daily lives of the people. Wagons laden with manufactured goods came into the town from the northern city of Baltimore to be sold by the local merchants. Produce from the local farms left in wagons going South headed for Georgia's markets. The stagecoach came through bringing passengers and mail. There were also the activities of the local hotel and the saloon. The streets bustled on Saturday. It was "trading day" for the farmers, and the day court convened. Many came to spectate the "doins of the court."

Early records of this court reflect the activity of its erring public. The first indictment was found against Jerry and Elias Towers for malicious mischief. The charge: throwing down a fence belonging to Robert Watkins -- the case was dismissed. The first person convicted was Green W. Whitt, a grocery keeper who engaged in a fight. The first delegate to the penitentiary was William Bailey who was given a three year sentence for horse stealing. The first capital offense was brought against Abraham Scott charged with the murder of Farry Barnes. Scott died before the case concluded.

Tuesday, December 24, 1838 Spencer Beaver, Sheriff and Jailor of McMinn County appears to petition the court for payment for "keeping Wafsaha, a Cherokee Indian in the Jail of McMinn County..."having held the Indian for one hundred and fourteen days at thirty seven and one half cents per day" he requests payment of $42.75. Additionally, he requests "...for conveying said Wafsaha from the jail of McMinn County to the Court

House in Cleveland fifty two miles going to and returning from, at ten cents per mile making $5.10."

Thursday, December 27, 1838 Hamilton B. Gather pleads guilty as charged to gaming.

Friday, December 28, 1838 John Cockram is charged with larceny.

Saturday, December 28, 1838 William Peoples is charged with incest.

Saturday, December 28, 1839 William Williams is charged with forcible entry.

Monday, May 1, 1840 John McHaffee is found by the jury to be guilty "of felonious taking and carrying away of a certain midling of bacon of the goods and chattels of Ruth Price in manner and for as charged in said Bill of Indictment and the jurors aforesaid having on their oath aforesaid further ascertained and said that the said John McHaffee for the offence aforesaid shall undergo confinement in the jail and penitentiary house of this State for the term of one year..."

Wednesday, December 30, 1840 Calvin Wrinkle and Lewis Holdman, laborers, "not having the fear of God before their eyes but being...seduced by the instigation of the Devil on the twenty second day of August in the year of our Lord, one thousand eight hundred and forty with force and arms in the County of Bradley aforesaid and within the jurisdiction of the Honorable Court in and upon the body of one Andrew J. Hodges then and there being in the face of God and the State of Tennessee feloniously willfully deliberately maliciously premediatedly and with malice aforethought did make an assualt and that the said Calvin Wrinkle... a certain pistol of the value of five dollars then and there...wounding the said Andrew J. Hodge did then and there instantly die...did commit murder in the first degree...."

January 1, 1841 Henry Driskel "...did feloniously and fraudulently make prepare and complete one piece of adulterated coin in imitation of one silver dollar, called a Spanish mill dollar." Guilty of counterfeiting.

Saturday, September 6, 1845 Henry Marvel returns a bill of Indictment for Bigamy. It seems he married Amanda while his marriage to Polly was still intact.

Reps Mabry appears in the court records several times beginning with this account in the months of April 1843: John Carden vs Reps Mabry "Came the defendant by his attorney and on his motion a rule is granted him to show cause why the plaintiffs petition should not be dismissed."

September 1, 1843 Reps Mabry vs William Gray: "This day came the defendant by his atty and on his motion a rule is granted him compelling the plaintiff to give security in this cause..."

December 28, 1843 Repts Mabry vs Alva Prewitt: "Trespass-- This day came the plaintiff by his attorney Levi Trewhitt Esqr. and entered a nolle prose qui as to Alva Prewitt, one of the defendants in this cause."

December 28, 1843 Repts Mabry vs Morton Gray: "This day came the defendant by his attorney and the plaintiff..." This is difficult to read but seems to deal with a default.

December 30, 1843 Repts Mabry vs Thomas Ma?: "Came the defendant by his attorney and on his motion a rule is granted..." Seems to be requiring security be given by the plaintiff.

May 8, 1844 Repts Mabry vs. Thomas Ma?: " The rule heretofore entered in this cause not being complied with..."

May 10, 1844 Reps Mabry vs Thomas Ma?: "This day came the plaintiff by his attorney John C. Mullay Esqr. and on his affidavit..."

May 10, 1844 Reps Mabry vs Morton Gray: "This day came the parties by their attorneys and this cause is continued next term of this court..."

May 11, 1844 Reps Mabry vs. Thomas Ma?: "Ordered by this court...."illegible.

September 2, 1844 Reps Mabry vs Morton Gray: "On motion of the defendant's attorney it is ordered by the court that the plaintiff give security for the prosecution of his said suit, on or before the second day of the next term of this court or the cause will be dismissed."

January 8, 1845 Reps Maberry vs Mathew Gray: Appeal - "This day came the parties by their attorneys and..."

January 11, 1845 John Carden vs Reps Mabry: "This day came John C. Gaut, Esqr. attorney..."

May 10, 1845 John Carden vs. Reps Mabry: Controversy - "This day came the parties by their attorneys and ...to wit

Samuel Blevins, Rufus Clement, H...Fitzgerald, Robert S. S..."

These disputes, though difficult to read and in some instances illegible, seem to involve property. Reps purchased land in partnership with Morton Gray and others.

Newspapers:

The Cleveland Dispatch and the Cleveland Banner began publication in the early 1850s. The Dispatch was politically a Whig paper while the Banner presented the other side -- Democrat. The following material, taken from the pages of these two papers, give a hint of what the people of Bradley were reading and insight into the interests and issues of the time.

The September 13, 1851 edition of the Cleveland Dispatch carried a lengthy story entitled "What is Cholera" that discusses at great length the symptoms and treatment of this disease; travelers returning from Russia mention that all exotic necessities of life, such as colonial produce have reached enormous prices, sugar costs 15 cents per lb. and coffee in proportion. The beet root sugar works of Russia seems to be no longer able to meet demand; and there is

The Cleveland Dispatch, Volume 1, Number 19, printed during September 1854.

FAIR WARNING!

[illegible]

THOMPSON & DYSON.

In Chancery at Benton.

Thomas H. Callaway, vs. Joseph H. Bradley, Samuel Pate, and Night

[illegible]

THE ÆTNA Insurance Company, Of Hartford, Connecticut.

Cash Capital $300,000.

[illegible]

C. L. HARDWICK, Agent.

Just Received.

[illegible]

TIBBS & HARDWICK.

Sheet Iron and Tin Plate.—[illegible]

C. H. MILLS & CO.

ATTACHMENT.

[illegible]

SELLING OFF AT COST!!

C. H. Mills & Co.,

[illegible]

C. H. MILLS & CO.

Come ye Afflicted and Buy

Dr. Christie's Galvanic Belts, [illegible]

THOMPSON & DYSON.

Wool Carding.

[illegible]

Ovens, Lids and Potters, just received and for sale by D. C. KENNER.

CHEMICALS.

Just recieved direct from the Manufacturer:

[illegible]

THOMPSON & DYSON.

Valuable Land for Sale

[illegible]

NASHVILLE, TENN.

BREAKFAST HOUSE,

E. TENN. and Ga. R. R.

J. S. Bridges

[illegible]

Thompson & Dyson,

(Successors to Brown, Wells & Johnson)

Wholesale and Retail Druggists,

CLEVELAND, TENN.

[illegible]

A Bargain to be Had.

[illegible]

To Rail Road Agents.

[illegible]

NEW GOODS!!!

FOR SALE AT LOW DOWN

CASH PRICES!!!

J. M. JOHNSTON & CO., [illegible]

Cheap Goods;

[illegible]

Family Groceries!,

[illegible]

J. M. JOHNSTON & CO.

Glass! Glass!! Glass!!!

[illegible]

THOMPSON & DYSON.

NO CREDIT.—E. Tenn. & Ga. R. R.

[illegible]

FOR DUCKTOWN.

TRI-WEEKLY LINE OF HACK.

[illegible]

DEFRIESE & ANDERSON.

For Sale.

[illegible]

The Farmers' Tobacco.

[illegible]

Crocks, Jars, and Jugs.

[illegible]

C. H. MILLS & CO.

1000 FINE CIGARS, [illegible] D. C. KENNER.

Just Received.

[illegible] HUDSON, WELLS & JOHNSON.

Ploughs, Straw Cutters, and Corn Shellers for sale by D. C. KENNER.

Flax Seed Wanted.

[illegible] C. H. MILLS & Co.

10 [illegible] D. C. KENNER

27000 FINE CIGARS [illegible] D. C. KENNER.

PHILADELPHIA

Type and Stereotype Foundry.

NEW BOOK OF

SPECIMENS OF PRINTING TYPE,

PLAIN AND ORNAMENTAL,

RULES, BORDERS, WOOD CUTS, &c. &c.

[illegible]

L. JOHNSON & Co.

Just Received!!

[illegible]

C. H. MILLS & CO.

Seamless Bed-Spreads.

[illegible] C. H. MILLS & CO.

NEW ARRIVALS.

[illegible]

THE DRUG STORE.

SAVANNAH, GA.

[illegible]

GREENVILLE & CO.

O YES! O YES!!

Just received, and for sale at wholesale [illegible]

[illegible]

Salt Petre.—[illegible] THOMPSON & DYSON.

5,000 Fine Cigars.

[illegible] THE DRUG STORE.

125 Sacks Salt— Just received and for sale by W. R. PICKENS & CO.

Shoot Luke or give up the Gun.

[illegible]

NOTICE! NOTICE!!

[illegible]

W. R. PICKENS.

NOTICE.

[illegible]

HUDSON, WELLS & JOHNSON.

$10 REWARD.

[illegible]

Cooking Stoves, just received and for sale by D. C. KENNER.

Box Stoves and Parlor Stoves, just received and for sale by D. C. KENNER.

FALL AND WINTER

GOODS,

[illegible]

READY-MADE

[illegible]

C. H. MILLS & CO.

VALUABLE TOWN PROPERTY

FOR SALE IN THE THRIVING TOWN OF

CLEVELAND, TENN.

[illegible]

SAM'L R. FAIN.

WM. TAYLOR & CO.,

Warehouse & Commission Merchants,

Receiving, Forwarding and General Agents,

MONTGOMERY, ALA.

[illegible]

GILMER, TAYLOR & CO.,

Commission Merchants

For the sale of

WESTERN PRODUCE & GROCERIES,

MONTGOMERY, ALA.

Warehouse on Commerce & Tennessee Streets.

[illegible]

Cleveland Dispatch classified ads, 1854.

Cleveland Dispatch classified ads, 1854.

this "Excitement and rashness seem to go together as naturally as sin and profanity. Get a man's dander up and he is sure to do the rash, as a woman is to get into all sort of notions when she has plenty of dollars and little sense. You must keep cool if you desire to have no acquaintance with the Rash family."

Half of one column is devoted to a poem entitled "A Love Story." There is business news also, discussing the role of the Blue Ridge Railroad and the importance of railroads to commerce and development. "The Blue Ridge Railroad is the work by which the city of Charleston and the State of South Carolina propose to secure to themselves a portion of the trade of the Mississippi Basin. In building this road they are only acting in obedience to an idea which has lead every city of any considerable importance and anyone that proposed commercial greatness as its future, to construct or undertake works of a similar character for similar objects. The Valley of the Mississippi is looked upon as the seat where is to be the greatest development of wealth, population and trade on this continent.... Charleston is the only Atlantic City with the exception of Richmond, that does not possess its appropriate and peculiar railway extending to the Mississippi basin..."

Another story from Wisconsin -- "There is a fast boy out in Madison the capital of Wisconsin, who if he gets no backsets will scarcely fail to reach Congress or the penitentiary one of these days. His school teacher, a young lady, was prosecuted by his parents for pretty severely welting the young rascal's back for his badness. The case went to the court and the verdict of the jury was 'served him right.' We give one of the items of the boy's testimony, the wit of which atoned for its rudeness. He asked her to do a sum for him which was to subtract 9 from 28. One of the counsel asked him if he could not do it without her assistance. Boy, 'I might but the arithmetic book said I couldn't subtract 9 from 8 without borrowing 10 and I didn't know where the hell to borrow it.'"

The Cleveland Dispatch, February 8, 1855 -- India is the title of this front page story. It is an extraction of a letter read before the Mercantile Association of Cincinnati."...he began his lecture by observing that all western nations, however widely they may wander or however changed may be their circumstances, still look up with reverence to Asia as their common mother... All modern forms of civilization seem to have an earlier form of civilization as their basis...England to Italy, then to Greece...to Egypt...its civilization had been brought from some southwestern Asiatic source."

Reference is made to an article carried in the Banner to the Governor's election. "...for several weeks past, observed manifestations, through the Whig newspaper of an earnest desire that Col. Gentry should be our next candidate for Governor." The article concludes "...we shall rejoice to see Col.Gentry Governor of the State of Tennessee, as we believe he certainly will be, should he undertake the canvas." This endorsement must have been unusual, a Democrat paper supporting a Whig candidate!

A prize winning essay on the Sabbath, written by a journeyman printer from Scotland is printed in full. "...young fellow think how the abstraction of the Sabbath would helplessly enslave the working classes with which we are identified. Think of labor that is going on...continual and eternal cycle, limbs forever on the rack, ...the eyeballs forever straining, the brow forever sweating, the feet forever plodding, the brain forever throbbing, the shoulders forever drooping, the loins forever aching, and the restless mind forever...."

There is a poem for Snuff Dippers and a lengthy obituary for William Capers, a Methodist Minister.

The Cleveland Dispatch, February 8, 1855,"...an editor speaking at a woman's rights convention says: 'persevere ladies petticoats will rise by and by.'"

"...the late storm was severe in Lancaster, Pennsylvania..."

"...a matron of Virginia appeals through the Richmond papers to the ladies of that state asking them to petition the legislature to contract for the purchase of Mount Vernon, reserving to itself the title but allowing the women of America to pay for it."

"...advice to ladies -- a Vermont editor gives this advice to ladies 'When you have got a man to the sticking point -- that is when he proposes, don't turn away or effect a blush or ask for more time, all those tricks are understood now; but just look him right in the face and tell him to go and order the furniture.'"

Even though the Civil War at this point was just five years distant, the local newspaper seems to pay little attention. This letter occupying a position on the front page with its oblique reference to slavery is the only article in the paper mentioning the issues surrounding the War. This would suggest that such matters were not a daily topic. The writer juxtaposes the issues of slavery and the suffering of women in England. Resentful of the British criticism of American treatment of slaves, the writer responds with an account depicting the harsh, severe, institutionalized treatment of women in Britain.

The Cleveland Banner, December 12, 1856 "Suffering in England and America -- our good friends, the British have always a good many tears to shed over the sufferings of the slaves in America but they are very callous and hardened against all unfortunate cases at home. For instance recently an unfortunate woman who had formerly been a governess to a high family was picked up in the streets of London in a state of exhaustion. She had eaten nothing for two days and had no home. The police took her to a hospital but the hospital authorities after consideration decided that she had no right there and without offering the poor creature any nourishment, they sent her to the workhouse where she died. Again, in the Marlebone Workhouse a woman was most dreadfully beaten by the master for some infraction of the rules of the establishment. This case was laid before the authorities and the master resigned...the Poor Law Commissioners refused to receive his resignation thus sanctioning his doings. ...these are notes taken from London papers representing judicial proceedings of half a week! And yet the same papers are loaded with grief at the state of crime in the United States growing out of slavery."

In 1861, as the Civil War began, Bradley County's population had risen to 11,701 whites and 58 free blacks; in the community of Charleston there were 400. In addition there were 1200 slaves owned by 170 masters. General Hurlburt,[1] writing in his book Histo-

---

1.<u>History of the Rebellion in Bradley County East Tennessee</u> J.S. Hurlburt, Downey and Brouse, 1866.

ry of the Rebellion, states "the slave trade existed in Bradley to a limited extent. The notorious William L. Brown...rebel Congressman Tibbs, John Osment, John Craigmiles, Jacob Tibbs, and William B. Graddy were perhaps the only persons in the county who made the traffic a regular business. Most of these would bring into the county from Richmond, Virginia or from some other slave mart, ten or fifteen negroes in a gang, and sometimes more and dispose of them in the vicinity to the highest bidders. William H. Tibbs, serving in the rebel Congress at Richmond, would avail himself of this opportunity and universally bring home a company of slaves as a matter of speculation."

CHAPTER 9

WAR WITHIN A WAR
THE EAST TENNESSEANS REVOLT

At the outbreak of the War division existed from the world community to the local community i.e., England and France sympathized with the South, Russia with the North. Young men of the North went South and young men of the South went North to join the army of their choice. Arguments, debates, points of view, came from the pages of newspapers, the political stump and from the pulpit. In East Tennessee this division was so intense it became a war within a war.

The first State to secede was South Carolina, doing so December 20, 1860. Within six weeks Mississippi, Florida, Alabama, Louisiana, Georgia and Texas joined South Carolina. In January Tennessee's Governor Isham Harris put the question of secession to the vote. On February 15, the Cleveland Banner (a Southern Cause newspaper) gave an account of the outcome "...the returns leave no reasonable doubt that the Convention has been voted down by an immense majority." Tennessee for now, would not join the Confederacy. In April speaking before the State legislature Governor Harris, disappointed by the election results countered the outcome "...I respectfully recommend the perfecting of an ordinance by the General Assembly, formally declaring the Independence of the State of Tennessee of the Federal Union, renouncing its authority and reassuming each and every function belonging to a separate sovereignty."

On June 8, amid cries of foul from Unionists, another election was held and by a 61,000 majority separation was approved. Tennessee, the last State to join, became a member of the Confederacy. Tennessee raised 100,000 troops for the Confederate Army and 30,000 for the Union.

Support for the Unionist movement came primarily from residents of several Eastern Counties, Bradley and McMinn among them. Following this second election which they believed to be illegal, and charging that the election had been held in a fraudulent manner with unqualified voters "stuffing the box," they formed their own government led by Congressman Thomas A.R. Nelson, William G. Brownlow (Brownlow would be elected Governor of Tennessee after the war), Connolly F. Trigg, Horace Maynard, Senator Andrew Johnson and others. Senator Johnson was elected Vice-President of the country in 1865 and would succeed Lincoln in that office after Lincoln's assassination.

Meeting at Greeneville, the county seat of Greene County, on the 17th of June they petitioned the Governor for the "privilege of East Tennessee to withdraw as a part of the State..."

By July it was reported that the Unionists were 10,000 strong "...under drill and armed with rifles and shotguns." Another communique dated August 6, 1861 sent by General Zollicoffer to Adjutant General Cooper advises the Lincoln government has sent "a very large amount of arms and ammunition" to Kentucky.

Insight into the "Insurrection" as it was often called, is provided by correspondence preserved by the National Archives,[1] exchanged between Jefferson Davis, President

---

1. War of the Rebellion, Official Records of Union and Confederate Armies, Washington, D.C., 1880-1901.

of the Confederate States of America, his Secretary of War Judah P. Benjamin, their generals and colonels, as well as other subordinate officers. Also included is correspondence from officials of the railroads with lines through East Tennessee. The following excerpted material taken from those letters describes the developing events as the Unionists formed their resistance:

October 1861, General Zollicoffer to Colonel Wood: "Watch the movements of the Lincoln men in East Tennessee. Restrain our ultra friends from acts of indiscretion. Promptly meet and put down any attempted open hostility. But I have observed heretofore that a few of our friends about Knoxville are unnecessarily nervous; give their expressions of apprehension only their due weight."

Jefferson Davis ordered all citizens of East Tennessee to take an oath of allegiance to the Confederate government or leave the country by October 1861. Some left and some observed the oath by day and packed bullets by night.

We, ——— ——— and ——— ———, acknowledge ourselves indebted to the Confederate States of America jointly and severally in the sum of $10,000, but to be void if ——— ——— shall faithfully and honestly support the Constitution and laws of the Confederate States of America and if he shall faithfully and honestly render true allegiance to said Confederate States in all things; and if he shall not directly or indirectly by writing, talking or otherwise seditiously or rebelliously attempt to excite prejudice in the mind of any person or persons against the existence, perpetuity or prosperity of said Confederate States; and if he shall not in any manner directly or indirectly aid, assist, encourage or advise the United States or any officer, agent or adherent thereof in the present war against the Confederate States.

Witness our hands and seals this —— November, 1861.

——— ———

——— ———

I do solemnly swear that I will faithfully and honestly support the Constitution and laws of the Confederate States of America and I will faithfully and honestly render true allegiance to said Confederate States in all things and in every particular; and I further swear that I will not directly or indirectly by talking, writing or otherwise seditiously or rebelliously attempt to excite prejudice in the mind of any person or persons against the existence, perpetuity or prosperity of said Confederate States; nor will I in any manner directly or indirectly aid, assist, encourage or advise the United States or any officer, agent or adherent thereof in the present war against the Confederate States.

——— ———

———

This oath was taken by many of the residents of East Tennessee.

November 4, 1861, Reuben Davis to Jefferson Davis: "By request of Mr. Samuel Tate I write to you this morning. He is just from East Tennessee and says he considers the command of General Zollicoffer in great danger; more from the rear than the front. Feelings of decided hostility are again being exhibited by the citizens, and in his opinion there is danger of aid being given to Lincoln by the people of East Tennessee at an unexpected moment and seizure of the railroad. He requests me to suggest to you the necessity of rendezvousing several regiments immediately. I give you this information at his pressing instance. Election Wednesday. Result doubtful."

The young men Lincolnites, who wanted to join the Union Army crossed the northern border into Kentucky.

November 4, 1861, J. P. Benjamin, Secretary of War from Colonel W. B. Wood: "I have today written to General Cooper in reference to the state of affairs in East Tennessee and the necessity of re-enforcements being sent immediately; but as there is a misapprehension in reference to the feeling of the late Union party existing abroad I have requested Mr. Archer, of Richmond, now on a visit here to call on you and give you fuller information than I can write. In addition to what I have written to General Cooper, I will say that there can be no doubt of the fact that large parties numbering from 20 to 100 are every day passing through the narrow and unfrequented gaps of the mountain into Kentucky to join the enemy. My courier just in from Jamestown informs me that a few nights ago 170 men passed from Road County over into Kentucky. I do not believe that the Unionists are in the least reconciled to the Government, but on the contrary are as hostile to it as the people of Ohio and will be ready to take up arms as soon as they believe the Lincoln forces are near enough to sustain them. I do not believe that the Southern men here are alarmed or nervous. They are as brave and fearless as any I ever saw but they do live in constant apprehension that a general uprising and rebellion may take place at any day. I submit the matter to the determination of the Department assuring you that I will do all that I can with 200 infantry and one company of cavalry to prevent any disturbance."

The reports of men moving into Kentucky are followed by reports of bridges being burned. The following four letters were written on the same day November 9, 1861.

General A. S. Johnston to Governor Isham Harris: "...destruction of the railways and telegraphs near Chattanooga, Cleveland and Dalton (Ga.) cannot be the work of the enemy's troops buts of the disaffected in North Alabama and East Tennessee."

S. Cooper from General Zollicoffer: "Colonel Wood of Knoxville writes that last night Hiwassee bridge and two other railroad bridges near Chattanooga were burned. Attempt on Strawberry Plains bridge failed. No cars from East. Feared that the Union bridge is destroyed..." He orders more troops.

Honorable John Letcher from William Moore, Justice of the Peace, Washington County, Virginia: "...the bridge across the Holston was burned last night by about fifty Union men...a Union force is now assembling near Watauga bridge reported to number about 500 for the purpose of attacking Col. McClellan's troops now stationed at the bridge and burning the bridge...all communication between here and Nashville is cut off...appeal to President Davis to call out the militia..."

The next four letters are dated November 11, 1861.

J. W. Lewis, Superintendent of East Tennessee and Virginia Railroad, writing from Cleveland (Tenn.) to Jefferson Davis: "Several bridges burned on East Tennessee road. The country is in great excitement and terror."

R. L. Owen, President Virginia and Tennessee Railroad to Benjamin: "...the camp of the enemy is at N.G. Taylor's five miles distant, with about 400 men. Another camp at Elizabethtown two miles further is said to contain 500 men...there is no doubt but that re-enforcements are every moment reaching them from Watauga County, N.C. and Johnson, Carter and Washington counties, Tennessee. These counties can furnish about 2000 Lincolnites and each fresh occasion emboldens them. They threaten to burn Watauga bridge tonight. Should they be successful it will bring forward hundreds now quiet..."

Adjutant General Cooper from Colonel W. B. Wood: "Three bridges burned between Bristol and Chattanooga, two on Georgia road. Five hundred Union men now threatening Strawberry Plains, fifteen hundred assembling in Hamilton County; and a general uprising in all the counties..."

The same day, another letter from Cooper to Wood: "...the whole country is now in a state of rebellion. A thousand men are within six miles of Strawberry Plains bridge and an attack is contemplated tomorrow...I learned that another camp is being formed about ten miles from here in Sevier County... they are being re-enforced from Blount, Roane, Johnson, Greene, Carter and other counties. I need not say that great alarm is felt by the few Southern men. They are finding places of safety for their families and would gladly enlist if we had arms to furnish them. I have had all the arms in this city seized (Knoxville) and authorized Major Campbell to impress all he can find in the hands of Union men who ought now to be regarded as avowed enemies for the use of the new companies. I felt it to be my duty to place this city under martial law as there was a large majority of the people sympathizing with the enemy and communicating with them by the unfrequented mountain paths..."

East Tennessee was surrounded on three sides by the Confederacy. Confederate troops were sent in to "keep the order." The order placing Knoxville under martial law would continue until 1863 when the Union Army gained control and they became the occupying force.

November 12, 1861, Jonesborough, Tn. A. G. Graham to Jefferson Davis: "Civil war has broken out at length in East Tennessee. In the late election scarcely a so-called Union man voted. Neither Mr. Nelson nor any of the released men who had been sworn to be faithful to the Southern Confederacy voted upon the occasion and there appeared a simultaneous assault upon our line of rail-roads from Virginia to the Georgia line. In this county (Washington) the secession strength is about equal to the Union force but our force is much weakened by five volunteer companies now in the service. In Carter and Johnson Counties, northeast of this, the Union strength is not only as formidable but it is as violent as that of any of the Northwestern Virginia counties. Had they the power not a secessionist would live in this region. The hostile element in those counties and also in Greene is so strong that I give it as my firm conviction that it will neither abate nor be conciliated. They look confidently for the re-establishment of the Federal authority in the South with as much confidence as the Jews look for the coming of the Messiah and I feel quite sure when I assert it that no event or circumstance can change or modify their hopes. In this state of affairs this part and indeed all of East Tennessee will be subjected during the war to apprehensions of internal revolt more or less remote as the tide of war turns in this direction. The recent bridge burning in this section was occasioned by the hope that the Federal troops would be here in a few days from Kentucky to second their efforts. We will crush out the rebellion here in a week or ten days but to prevent its recurrence should be a matter of anxious consideration. Upon this subject I have the honor of making the following suggestion to your excellency: The expatriation requiring alien enemies to dispose of their effects and leave their families should be enforced. Should they not do so voluntarily on proof being submitted that they were in arms or hostile to the Government they should be forced to leave on due notice with their families. A man with his family with him in the North wil do us no great harm. He will not enlist for he will have to support his family..."

November 12, 1861, Governor Harris to Jefferson Davis: "...Union men are organizing...this rebellion must be crushed out instantly, the leaders arrested and summarily punished. I shall send immediately about 10,000 men to that section..."

November 19, 1861, Colonel Leadbetter from J. P. Benjamin: "Send all the prisoners known to be criminals or to have borne arms against the Government to Nashville to be tried for high treason..."

Andrew Johnson's family received mention in the exchange between Lieutenant Colonel Mackall and Brigadier General Zollicoffer.

November 20, 1861, Colonel Mackall from F. K. Zollicoffer: "I sent a few men up to Greenville to arrest Andrew Johnson's sons and son-in-law."

November 20, 1861, Benjamin from Colonel Wood: "The rebellion in East Tennessee has been put down...their camps have been broken up and a large number of them made prisoners..."

The correspondence now turns to the problem of how to punish and control the insurgents.

November 20, 1861, Madison T. Peoples (Okolona, Tennessee) to Benjamin: "...if they are all prosecuted every citizen of East Tennessee must be arraigned before the court or brought up as witnesses...martial law ought to be enforced in every county in East Tennessee to hold these bad men in proper restraint..."

November 25, 1861, Benjamin to Colonel Wood: "...I proceed to give you the desired instructions in relation to the prisoners taken by you amongst the traitors in East Tennessee...all such as can be identified as having been engaged in bridge burning are to be tried summarily by drum head court-martial and if found guilty executed on the spot by hanging. It would be well to leave their bodies hanging in the vicinity of the burned bridge...ringleaders must be sent at once to Tuscaloosa to jail as prisoners of war..."

One such ringleader was 65-year-old attorney, Levi Trewhitt. Levi's grandson Daniel, would join the McCracken family in the 1920s when he married Fannie, daughter of Jackson and Nancy McCracken.

January 20, 1861, Jefferson Davis from Colonel Gillespie, Colonel of the 43rd Regiment of Tennessee Volunteers: "...on the 19th day of November last I arrested and brought to this place Levi Trewhitt, esq., of Cleveland, Tennessee. This arrest was made under an order from Col W.B. Wood, commanding the Sixteenth Alabama Regiment, who at that time was the commander of this post. The arrest was ordered because Mr. Trewhitt was suspected of knowledge of the burning of the railroad bridges and the plans by which it was done. He was retained here from some weeks and then sent to Tuscaloosa by order of General W. H. Carroll, who succeeded Colonel Wood in command. There was no trial or investigation of the charges so far as I know or have understood."

Mr. Trewhitt died in the prison at Mobile.

As the Confederacy continued their hold on the Eastern counties the following orders went out in late April to remove the families of the Unionists leaders that remained:

April 24, 1862, M. T. Haynes to W. M. Churchwell: "Mrs. Maynard applies for passports for two servants understood to be slaves. I am directed to ask you decision as to whether they are her property or not."

April 25, 1862, Provost Marshall Churchwell, Knoxville issues a passport: "The following named persons are allowed in charge of Lieutenant Joseph of Norfolk, Va., Mrs. Horace Maynard and three children."

April 26, 1862, Mrs. Andrew Johnson from Churchwell: "Your note to Maj. Gen E. Kirby Smith has been referred to this office and I am directed respectfully to reply in order to give you more time to make your arrangements for leaving. The time is extended thirty-six hours from the delivery of this second note when the major-general hopes you will be ready to comply with his request. You can go by way of Norfolk, Virginia north, or by Kingston to Nashville. Passports and an escort will be furnished for your protection."

April 28, 1862, Churchwell to Campbell: "My mission to Mrs. Johnson was unsatisfactory. She said she would not go North but Judge Patterson and her son Charles have assured me that she would go. You will please state what goods and chattels she will be allowed to take with her; also how much money and if you are willing that her son Charles shall accompany her. He is a young unmarried gentleman and I think should go with his mamma. Mrs. Carter will go unhesitatingly but has a sick child just now but can go in a few days. She says she has not the funds. She is in bad health and must take a nurse with her, a slave. You will answer by 12 O'clock."

By April 30 Mrs. Johnson moved on by way of Norfolk. Other families of those identified as "leaders" were removed in just the same way.

Late in April a general order was given by the Adjutant General's office to enter the prisons where Union men are being held and conscript them into the Confederate army. With these lasts tasks completed the "Insurrection" had been put down. The Confederate grip would last until 1863.

An elderly East Tennessean, many years later when asked by his grandson who won the war "Son, he replied, it don't really make much difference who won the whole war -- in East Tennesse, everybody lost!

CHATTANOOGA, *June 28, 1861.*

HON. ROBERT TOOMBS,
Richmond:

I came through East Tennessee yesterday. Saw some of our friends, but many more of our enemies. There is truly great disaffection with those people. It is currently reported and believed that Johnson has made an arrangement at Cincinnati to send 10,000 guns into East Tennessee, and that they have actually been shipped through Kentucky to Nicholasville, and are to be hauled from there to near the Kentucky line and placed in the hands of Union men in Kentucky on the line to be conveyed to Union men in Tennessee. They openly proclaim that if the Legislature refuses to let them secede they will resist to the death and call upon Lincoln for aid. Nelson, Brownlow, and Maynard are the leaders. If they were out of the way we would be rid of all trouble. That they will give us trouble I doubt not unless they are promptly dealt with. They rely on aid from Southeastern Kentucky and Lincoln. You must see Davis and get him to order Floyd down to about Cumberland Gap to intercept these arms if they attempt to cross into Virginia. Governor Harris has ordered one regiment to the various passes on our northern border, but the people here say they are not sufficient. A number of Union companies are forming and drilling daily in the disaffected districts for the avowed purpose of resistance. Let the Government look closely to this movement. Unless nipped in the bud it may become very troublesome.

In haste, yours, truly,

[4.] SAM. TATE.

NASHVILLE, *June 29, 1861.*

JEFFERSON DAVIS,
President:

The developments in East Tennessee and Kentucky are such that the Governor deems it inadvisable to move any regiments to Virginia at present.

S. R. ANDERSON,
Major-General.

[4.]

Official Records - CSA Correspondence.
Senator (R. Tn.) Andrew Johnson, supplied guns to Unionists in East Tennessee.

CLEVELAND, TENN., January 6, 1862.

Col. CHARLES M. MCGHEE.

DEAR SIR: I have received your request to write you the facts about the arrest of James S. Bradford by Capt. W. L. Brown's command, and he was a few days after sent to Tuscaloosa. The nature of the charge against him I am ignorant of. I feel confident that his arrest and transportation from here must have been done under a misconception of his position as regards the rebellious feeling that has disturbed East Tennessee, and had an investigation been allowed that he would have been discharged without spot or blemish. It is true he was originally a Union man and at the beginning of the secession amongst us had considerable influence with the party but before the period at which our State linked her future with the Southern Confederacy he became a loyal Southern man and from that day exerted all his influence and power for peace and submission. I know that it told to such a degree that their numbers were greatly lessened amongst us.

When we learned an armed body of men had assembled at Clift's for the purpose of resistance—the people in the county being much alarmed—some of his original Southern personal friends desired he should go over there and use his influence to get them to disperse. He consented to do so and informed me of his intention but I opposed his going fearing it might bring him into trouble from the Union people. He replied that his neighbors were anxious for him to go and as he was reflected on to some extent for former Union sentiments he felt it his duty to do all in his power to arrest the evil. He remained only a few hours at Clift's, stayed over night at Col. C. D. Luttrell's and returned there the day he was at Clift's. Colonel Luttrell who is an out-and-out original Southern man approved of and encouraged his mission to Clift's. He was there several days before the forces moved on Clift's camp and at home as they passed his house. So soon as he returned from the camp he informed me he could do nothing with them and [illegible] came into town and so informed my Southern friends. He even said it was dangerous to speak of peace to the motley crew.

I do not desire as you know to have any man released who in any way encouraged rebellion; but Bradford I know is an innocent man and is a good Southern man and so shown himself from date named and I would therefore be glad to see him released.

FRANCK W. LEA.

Confederates now in control, have arrested 2,000 or so "ringleaders." Clift driven from Hamilton County, near Chattanooga, continued his military activities for the Union in the northeastern part of the State.

HEADQUARTERS,
Knoxville, January 11, 1862.

HON. J. P. BENJAMIN, *Secretary of War, Richmond, Va.*

SIR: On the 9th instant I telegraphed* the Department that a writ of habeas corpus had been issued by the circuit court of the State of Tennessee and served on me in the case of Daniel Smith, charged as an accessory to the crime of bridge-burning.

To the writ I made answer that the prisoner had been seized in obedience to instructions of the War Department at Richmond and held as a prisoner of war; that he had been duly transferred as such to my custody and is now held by me commanding Confederate forces in East Tennessee. But the court claims that the validity of the answer must be tried and decided by the court. Judge [George] Brown who issued the writ is a Southern man and desires only to do his official duty. Some other judges of the State exercising the same authority may be less worthy of confidence and this question of jurisdiction between the military and civil authorities assumes much gravity whether it be decided by loyal or disloyal judges.

In the condition of the country immediately subsequent to the bridge-burning I should have paid no respect to a writ of habeas corpus. The military law of self-preservation prevailed at that time. But the circumstances are now less urgent and I infer that the Government does not wish to suspend the writ. Martial law might be proclaimed locally and the lawyers here think that the writ would thus be suspended. I do not see how so long as Congress has not suspended the writ.

The judges generally and perhaps without exception would decide that a man taken literally in arms against the Government is a prisoner of war. But there must occur many cases of serious guilt wherein the prisoner will be turned over to the civil courts to be bailed out and tried by his peers. If the military have any function or mission to perform in this disturbed country their efforts in that behalf will be frustrated by the interference of the civil courts for the military will be brought into contempt.

To-day I am served with another writ by Judge Brown including the cases of six or eight prisoners to be brought before Judge Humphreys' C. S. court, on the 16th.

I hope to receive from the Department full instructions for my guidance in all such cases.

Very respectfully, sir, your obedient servant,

D. LEADBETTER,
Colonel, Provisional Army, C. S.

OFFICE OF DEPUTY PROVOST-MARSHAL,
Athens, Tenn., January 27, 1862.

Col. JOHN E. TOOLE, *Provost-Marshal, Knoxville, Tenn.*

DEAR SIR: I am gratified to hear that the thirty-nine caught in the mountains are dying. It is better for the country and better for posterity that they should die young—that is, as young as they are. The Captain Pierce who was conducting them hence is again in these parts. He was recently in Meigs and McMinn operating for more recruits. He told an old lady whose son he got into that unfortunate gang all about his affairs and made many apologies for letting her son get caught. She betrays him and if I had six or eight good cavalry I think I could get him. He has a partner by the name of Matthews in the same neighborhood whom I will try to get.

I suggest that as the conscripts have not been run out of Monroe County yet you try to get Captain Clark's cavalry company belonging to Colonel Ashby's regiment detailed for Captain Hicks and let me borrow a few men from him occasionally. If not this some other company. My vineyard is getting a little foul again. Last Friday I hired a horse and rode out to Dixon's factory and arrested two conscripts (one of them old Dixon's son) whom he had got detailed to guard his factory, and they were doing so by sleeping in the building. I overhauled that concern pretty thoroughly, searched the house and Dixon's residence for arms which were reported to me as being concealed there. I have no doubt that old Dixon and all he has connected with him are doing all they can for Lincoln.

I arrested his boss for saying that the next morning after the Holston and Watauga bridges were burnt a man said to him: "Well, there is good news." "What is it?" said he. "All the railroad bridges are burnt from the Georgia line to the Virginia line except the one at Loudon." He denied that he told that such a thing had been said by him and when I proved to his face that he had told this story he said he could not recollect who the man was. I took him before a magistrate and made him swear that he could not recollect who the man was. I let him go because the factory was spinning gun-cotton for the Government so they said and it could not run if he was taken away. He is there yet and thinks he is safe. What ought to be done with such a devil and with the whole set?

I will see about the cattle driving from Charleston. Cannot you send me copies of factory bonds? There are wagons slipping off from this county to Kentucky. I hear of it after they are gone. Buch inquires about his account.

Your obedient servant,

JNO. M. CARMACK,
Captain and Deputy Provost-Marshal.

CONGRESS HALL, *January 28, 1862.*

Hon. ROBERT OULD, *Assistant Secretary of War:*

The friends of the State prisoners from East Tennessee confined at Tuscaloosa or Mobile are very desirous of having their cases acted upon promptly by the Department. May I ask your early attention to the subject.

Yours,

THOMAS M. JONES.

WAR DEPARTMENT, C. S. A.,
Richmond, February 4, 1862.

Hon. L. C. HAYNES, *Knoxville, Tenn.*

SIR: On the 28th of January last Brigadier-General Withers was directed to release Samuel Hunt with other political prisoners upon their taking the oath of allegiance to the Confederate States.

Your obedient servant,

J. P. BENJAMIN,
Secretary of War.

KNOXVILLE, TENN., *January 27, 1862.*

His Excellency JEFFERSON DAVIS,
President Confederate States of America.

SIR: The Army of the Cumberland is utterly routed and demoralized. The result is regarded with the profoundest solicitude. * * * There is now no impediment whatever but bad roads and natural obstacles to prevent the enemy from entering East Tennessee and destroying the railroads and putting East Tennessee in a flame of revolution.

Nothing but the appointment to the command of a brave, skillful and able general who has the popular confidence will restore tone and discipline to the army and confidence to the people. * * * Cannot you, Mr. President, right the wrong by the immediate presence of a new and able man?

Yours, truly,

LANDON C. HAYNES.

TO THE PUBLIC:

The militia draft under the State laws having been suspended by the proclamation of Maj. Gen. E. Kirby Smith he also suspends the operation of the conscript bill in this department. It is expected all good citizens will return from Kentucky. They will not be molested if they come to remain and cultivate their farms and take care of their families.

W. M. CHURCHWELL,
Colonel and Provost-Marshal.

HEADQUARTERS DEPARTMENT OF EAST TENNESSEE,
Knoxville, April 28, 1862.

General S. COOPER,
Adjutant and Inspector General, Richmond, Va.

GENERAL: I have the honor to report that a portion of the Fourth Regiment Tennessee Volunteers (Colonel Morgan) will leave to-day for Milledgeville, Ga., in charge of Union prisoners. The officer of the detachment is directed to report afterward with his command to the military authorities at Savannah, Ga. In more than one communication Brigadier-General Stevenson has reported many desertions from this regiment to the enemy and urged its removal from Cumberland Gap. Because of this and the general character of the regiment for disloyalty I have thought it best to send it beyond the limits of this department. Being thus removed beyond the influence of friends in the ranks of the enemy it is thought these men may make loyal and good soldiers. I trust my action in this matter will meet the approval of the Department.

Very respectfully, your obedient servant,

E. KIRBY SMITH,
Major-General, Commanding.

HEADQUARTERS DEPARTMENT OF EAST TENNESSEE,
Knoxville, April 28, 1862.

Brig. Gen. D. LEADBETTER,
Commanding, &c., Chattanooga, Tenn.:

A citizen cannot be tried by a military court for an offense committed in a district before the declaration of martial law. The offender will be held for trial by some court in Georgia having jurisdiction of the case. This decision of the Attorney-General does not apply in cases where soldiers who are not citizens are upon trial.

H. L. CLAY,
Assistant Adjutant-General.

STATE OF TENNESSEE,
Bradley County:

Personally appeared before me, the undersigned, an acting justice of the peace and duly authorized to administer oaths within and for the county and State aforesaid, G. R. Hambright and Benjamin Hambright, men of undoubted truth and veracity and entitled to credit when on oath, and made oath in due form of law that at and about the time the rebellion was taking place in East Tennessee there was some disquietude in the settlement in which they resided in said county, and that there was some talk among the neighbors as to what they should do relative thereto and as to going and joining Clift who they understood was encamped for the purpose of going to Kentucky and consequently a meeting of divers of the citizens for the purpose of taking steps in the premises, and affiants learning that fact went to the residence of Levi Trewhitt whom they understand now to be confined at Tuscaloosa or Mobile as a prisoner of war and procured him to go and be where these said persons were to assemble, who did go to said place and there opposed every thing or movement that had any tendency to a rebellion in East Tennessee and through his influence and exertions the people in said settlement were quieted and all tendency to rebel in said settlement was put down by his advising them against rebellion and to go on with their ordinary business and let Clift and his rebellion alone and keep themselves out of rebellion, and thereby the citizens went on with their ordinary business and none went into the rebellion to the knowledge of affiants.

BENJAMIN HAMBRIGHT.
G. R. HAMBRIGHT.

Sworn to and subscribed before me the 16th day of January, 1862, and I certify that the said G. R. Hambright and Benjamin Hambright are both men of undoubted truth and veracity.

J. B. HUMPHREYS,
Justice of the Peace for Bradley County, Tenn.

The following letters pertain to Levi Trewhitt, grandfather of Daniel Trewhitt who married Fanny J. McCracken.

STATE OF TENNESSEE,
Bradley County:

Personally appeared before me, the undersigned, an acting justice of the peace and duly authorized to administer oaths within and for the said county of Bradley and State of Tennessee, Edmund Ramsey, a man of undoubted truth and veracity and entitled to credit when on oath, and made oath in due form of law that, in the summer of 1861, there was a company of men organized in the settlement where he resided who called themselves as home guards, furnishing their own arms, &c., and after General Zollicoffer issued a proclamation requesting said companies to stop drilling, Levi Trewhitt, whom he now understands to be confined in Tuscaloosa or Mobile as a prisoner of war, used his exertions and influence to get said company to cease drilling and by the aid of his exertions and influence said company was procured to cease drilling and obey said proclamation; and further states that at or about the time it was understood that Clift was encamped with a regiment of men in Hamilton County about forty miles distant on the north side of Tennessee River there was some disquietude among the citizens in the settlement where he resided and a meeting of some of the citizens for the purpose of taking steps, and a different meeting from the one in the settlement of G. R. and Benjamin Hambright as to going and joining the said Clift, and at said meeting said Levi Trewhitt opposed everything that had any tendency toward a rebellion, and advised the persons there assembled to keep out of said rebellion and not to join or go to Clift but to go on with their ordinary business, and by the aid of said Trewhitt's exertions and influence said disquietude was suppressed and said persons procured to go on with their business, and no person to affiant's knowledge went to said Clift or into the rebellion in any manner.

E. RAMSEY.

Sworn to and subscribed before me the 16th day of January, 1862, and I certify that the said Edmund Ramsey is a man of undoubted truth and veracity.

J. B. HUMPHREYS,
Justice of the Peace for Bradley County, Tenn.

STATE OF TENNESSEE,
Bradley County:

Personally appeared before me, Joseph H. Davis, an acting justice of the peace for the county of Bradley and duly authorized to administer oaths within and for the county and State aforesaid, Alexander A. Clingan and made oath in due form of law that at or about the time of the rebellion in East Tennessee and at the time he understood that Clift was encamped in Hamilton County on the north side of Tennessee River about twenty-four miles from the residence of affiant Levi Trewhitt, whom affiant now understands to be confined at Tuscaloosa or Mobile as a prisoner of war, came by where affiant was and procured affiant to go with him to where some persons were to assemble for the purpose of taking steps as to what they should do and to assist him in suppressing anything that might occur tending to a rebellion and affiant did go. At said meeting the said Trewhitt made a speech or talk to the persons there assembled and advised them to keep out of all rebellion and especially to keep out of the Clift rebellion and to go on with their ordinary business and by the aid and assistance of the said Trewhitt said persons all agreed and promised to keep out of all rebellion and go on with their ordinary business.

A. A. CLINGAN.

Sworn to and subscribed before me the 17th day of January, 1862, and I certify that the said Alexander A. Clingan is a man of undoubted truth and veracity.

JOSEPH H. DAVIS,
Justice of the Peace for Bradley County, Tenn.

The cases of James S. Bradford, Levi Trewhitt and others.

RICHMOND, VA., *January 20, 1862.*

His Excellency the PRESIDENT OF THE CONFEDERATE STATES.

SIR: In passing through East Tennessee I have been informed by a gentleman of integrity and whose loyalty to the Confederacy has never been questioned that some forty-five or fifty of the citizens of that section of country have been arrested by persons having or assuming to have military authority under this Government; that after arrest the most of them have been told they must volunteer or be sent to the Government prison at Tuscaloosa, Ala., and that those who refused to volunteer under such compulsion have been sent to and imprisoned at Tuscaloosa where they now remain.

The names of the persons thus dealt with as far as my information extends are as follows: Dr. John G. Brown, Charles B. Champion, James S. Bradford, Allen Marlow, Sidney Wise, John F. Kinchelow, Samuel Bunn, ——— Potts, W. R. Davis, ——— Gamble, Thomas I. Cate, John Beene, sr., and John Boon. These men were arrested by a captain of Tennessee cavalry and as I learn without ever having been before any tribunal, civil or military, without any specification of charges and without the examination of a single witness they were hurried off to imprisonment. Levi Trewhitt, William Hunt, Stephen Beard, John McPherson, George Munsey, ——— Thompson were taken to Knoxville but had no investigation before any tribunal. The first two were sent from thence to Tuscaloosa. The remaining four were released either on parole or unconditionally but after returning to their homes they were arrested by the captain of cavalry before alluded to and also sent to Tuscaloosa. As I am informed none of the persons whose names I have given were taken in arms or suspicioned of having been in arms against the Government.

I was requested to bring these facts to the attention of the Tennessee Congressional delegation. I learn that many if not all of them have received corroborative information. By their request I have been induced to bring the subject to your attention that justice might be done in the premises and the character of the Government vindicated. It is insisted and I presume correctly that the terror engendered by these arrests was an efficient cause in changing public sentiment in East Tennessee.

Respectfully,

JNO. [illegible]

[Indorsement.]

Secretary of War, for attention.

Those who acted for the Government can inform you whether political arrests were made and prisoners sent to Tuscaloosa as herein affirmed.

J. D[AVIS].

KNOXVILLE, TENN., *January 20, 1862.*

On the 19th day of November last I arrested and brought to this place Levi Trewhitt, esq., of Cleveland, Tenn. This arrest was made under an order from Col. W. B. Wood, commanding the Sixteenth Alabama Regiment, who at that time was the commander of this post. The arrest was ordered because Mr. Trewhitt was suspected of a knowledge of the burning of the railroad bridges and the plans by which it was done. He was retained here for some weeks and then sent to Tuscaloosa by order of General W. H. Carroll, who succeeded Colonel Wood in command. There was no trial or investigation of the charges so far as I know or have understood.

JAS. W. GILLESPIE,
Colonel Forty-third Regiment Tennessee Volunteers.

His Excellency JEFFERSON DAVIS,
President of the Confederate States of America:

Your petitioners, the undersigned citizens of Bradley County, Tenn., humbly represent and show unto your excellency that Levi Trewhitt, who is now as they understand confined in Mobile as a prisoner of war, is one of the old, influential citizens of Bradley County, Tenn.; that he is about sixty-five years of age and has been for the past few years afflicted with paralysis and as they now understand is sick and in the hospital at Mobile. They further state that said Trewhitt was a very useful man at home. We therefore pray that said Levi Trewhitt be released from said confinement upon his becoming a loyal citizen and taking an oath to support the constitution of the Confederate States of America; and as in duty bound will ever pray, &c.

WILLIAM GRANT.
T. L. HOYL.
JNO. B. HOYL.
[And 31 others.]

We, the undersigned officers in the Confederate service, fully concur with the above petitioners.

D. M. KEY,
Lieutenant-Colonel.
[JAMES W.] GILLESPIE,
Colonel Regiment Tennessee Volunteers.
[And 16 others.]

STRAWBERRY PLAINS, TENN.,
December 16, 1863.

Brigadier-General SPEARS:

GENERAL: General Wagner arrived here last night with his brigade; now leaving to go to Blain's Cross-Roads. General Sheridan arrived this morning with another brigade. He says he is ordered to take charge or command of all the forces about here. I do not know what he is going to do. Palmer and the forces at Mossy Creek started for this point at 2.30 this morning, so he telegraphed. He expresses no alarm now.

Yours, truly,

D. C. TREWHITT,
Assistant Adjutant-General.

HDQRS. SECOND DIVISION, FOURTH ARMY CORPS,
Strawberry Plains, December 16, 1863.

Major-General FOSTER:

General Spears is at Blain's Cross-Roads, also Colonel Mott. Colonel Wagner, of my division, left here this morning for the same point. Colonel Harker will move out in a few minutes. There is no news here this morning. Colonel Palmer has been ordered here from Mossy Creek.

Respectfully, your obedient servant,

P. H. SHERIDAN,
Major-General.

HDQRS. SECOND DIVISION, FOURTH ARMY CORPS,
Strawberry Plains, December 16, 1863.

[General JOHN G. PARKE:]

GENERAL: I arrived here this morning with two brigades, and am now moving out to join you at Blain's Cross Roads. General Hazen is marching direct from Knoxville, and will also reach you to-day. Write to me all the news and your own impressions from your best information as to whether the enemy are making an advance or if it is a mere cavalry demonstration. General Elliott will move up the French Broad this morning with his cavalry division, so that by to-morrow or next day that flank will be well covered.

Respectfully, your obedient servant,

P. H. SHERIDAN.

Official Records - Union Correspondence. The signature on the first letter, D.C. Trewhitt, belongs to the son of Levi Trewhitt.

Reconstructed log cabin, located outside the Family History Center, LDS Salt Lake City, Utah.

Jackson Leonidas McCracken
1858-1934

Nancy Darthula Hampton McCracken
1860-1946

Fannie Jane McCracken Trewhitt
1887-1951

Mary Magdalene McCracken Wamsley
1889-1955

Bertha McCracken
1899-1957

Betty Jo McCracken Brown
1901-1975

David Franklin McCracken
1904-1948

Henry James (1893-1977), David and Fannie Jane McCracken.

Taken in early 1898, the Jackson McCracken family l. to r. Fanny, Jackson, Henry, Nancy holding baby Martha Mae (b.1897 d. 1898) Jackson's mother Fannie Mabry McCracken and Mary.

Jackson L. and Nancy McCracken with their children:

l. to r. Henry, Jackson, Mary, Bertha (holding doll), Fannie, David on mother Nancy's lap. Circa 1904

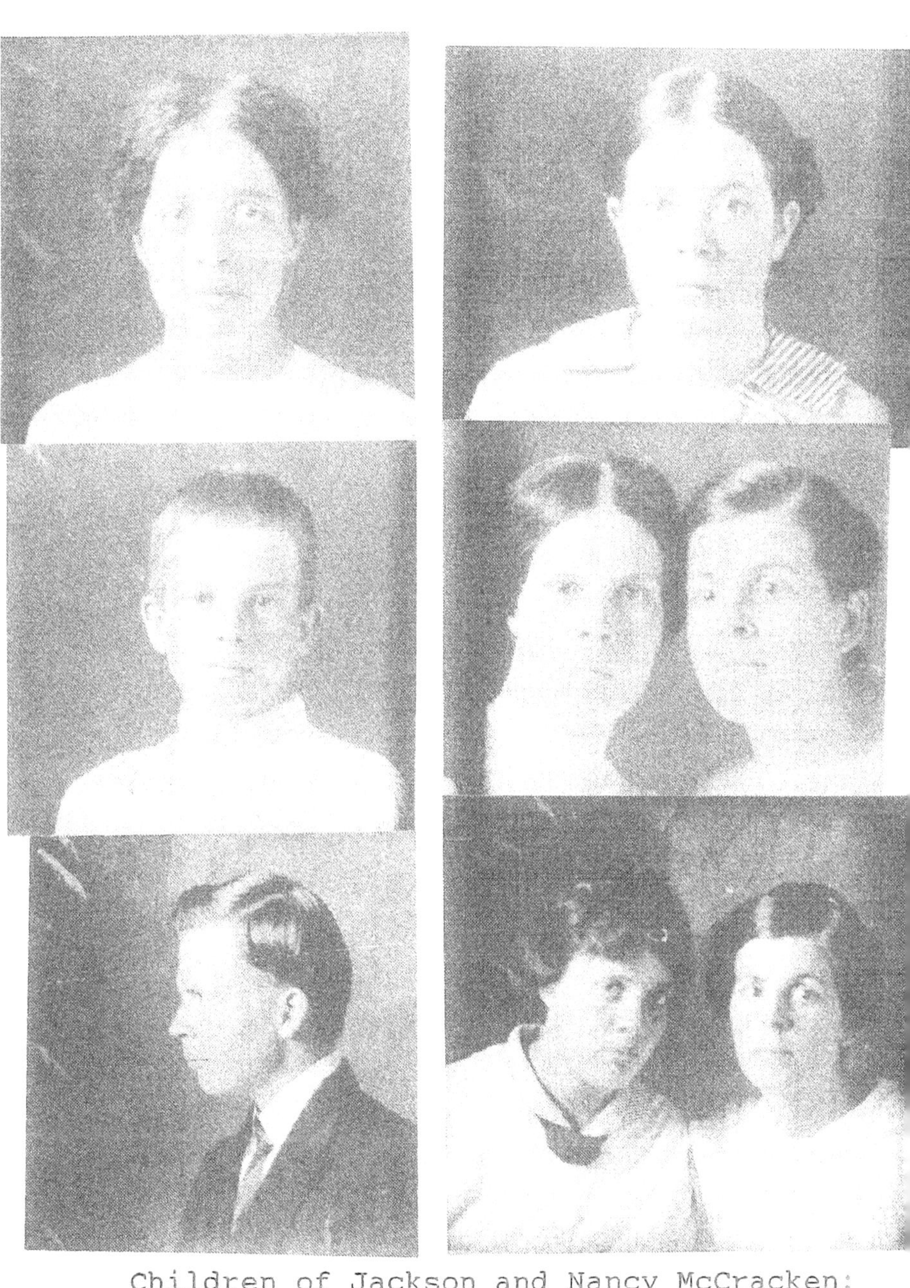

Children of Jackson and Nancy McCracken:
Upper l.to r. Fannie, Mary, Betty
Center l.to r. David, Bertha
Lower l.to r. Henry, Betty, Fannie

Fannie Jane McCracken Trewhitt
1887-1951

Fannie Jane McCracken and Daniel Coffee Trewhitt.

Fannie and Daniel Trewhitt

Mary
and
Bertha

School Teacher Mary McCracken and student.

Russell Wamsley husband of Mary (McCracken) Wamsley and r. David McCracken during 1920s.

Students of Gold School assembled in Fall of 1896 -- Gold School located in northeastern Bradley County east of the community of Charleston and about one mile southwest of the Union Grove Methodist Church, was consolidated with the Chilcutt School in 1922. The teacher William H. Sullivan, later studied medicine and practiced in Calhoun, Tasso and Cleveland for over 40 years, until his death in 1943.

Front row from left, Boyer, Arthur Boyer, Floyd Wilhoit, Bob Lawson, Porter Stevenson, Claude Hudson, Henry McCracken, (unknown) Will Cook, Lawson, Jim Lawson, Howard Lawson, Omas Pierce, Floyd Stevison, Grover Boyer, Harper Rice;

Second row, Pennington Goodner, Boyer, Effie Goodner, Iva Pierce, Bettie Pierce, Martha Parker, Gertie Hudson, Emma Lawson, Mamie Gibson, Pet Colley, (unknown) William H. Sullivan, teacher, Sallie Lawson, Bersie Cook, Maudie Stevenson;

Third row, Mrs. Martha Jane Boyer, and baby, Docia Colley, Mattie Gibson, Nora Cook, Lou Colley, Clarice Parker, Trula Ruth, Susie Pierce, Walter Pierce, Madie Pierce, Susie Lawson, Fannie McCracken, Mary McCracken, Ida Law, Melinda Rice, Rhode Rice;

Fourth row, Mrs. Isham Goodner, and baby Bertha, Mrs. Nancy McCracken, and baby Martha Mrs. Nancy Parker, and baby Ben, Beckie Parker, Alice Gibson, Easter Goodner, Lou Pierce, Rinda Pierce, Ollie Pierce, Mary Boyer, Ellen Stevenson, Zude Rice, Luther Boyer, Henry Ruth;

Back row, Mrs. F.M. Ruth, Nick Gibson, Lizzie Pursley, Willis Goodner, Wiley Gibson, Onie Lawson, Mary Pursley, Winston Goodner, Joe Rice, Phil Lawson, Luther Goodner, Lloyd Ruth, Noah Goodner, Frankie Stevenson, and Houk Lawson.

The students of Gold School assembled in 1907 along with their neighbors and posed for the picture on the opposite page.

Front row: Edward Goins, Ben Parker, John Hagler, Mark Lawson, Labe Boyer, Lake Barker, unknown, Frank Callahan, Henry Crane, Lake Helton, Vernon Rose, Ernest Lawson, Hobson Gregg, Elmer Goins, Ruick Bivens, William Goins, Everett Weiss, Sampson Lawson, Henry Helton.

Second row: Caswell Goodner, (teacher) Ona Mae McAlister, Emily Rose, Tiny Stevison, Nola Callahan, Sarah Lawson, Lillian Lawson, Chester Lawson, Frank Lawson, Mary Gregg, David McCracken.

Third row: Frances Orr, Vida Barker, Ida Callahan, Loma Stevison, Birdie Lawson, Beulah Barker, Dewey Boyer, Eunice Bivens, Leona Freeman, Bertha McCracken, Lennie Gregg, Florence Stevison, Betty McCracken, Paul Lawson, Walter Moore, Walter Pierce.

Fourth row: In window, Sosby Crane, unknown, Mary McCracken, Lou Callahan, Nola Boyer, Loma Callahan, Fannie McCracken, Iva Pierce, Lennie Callahan, Beulah Hudson, Frank Lawson, Andy Freeman, Grover Boyer, Dallas Moreland, Henry McCracken, Floyd Stevison, in window.

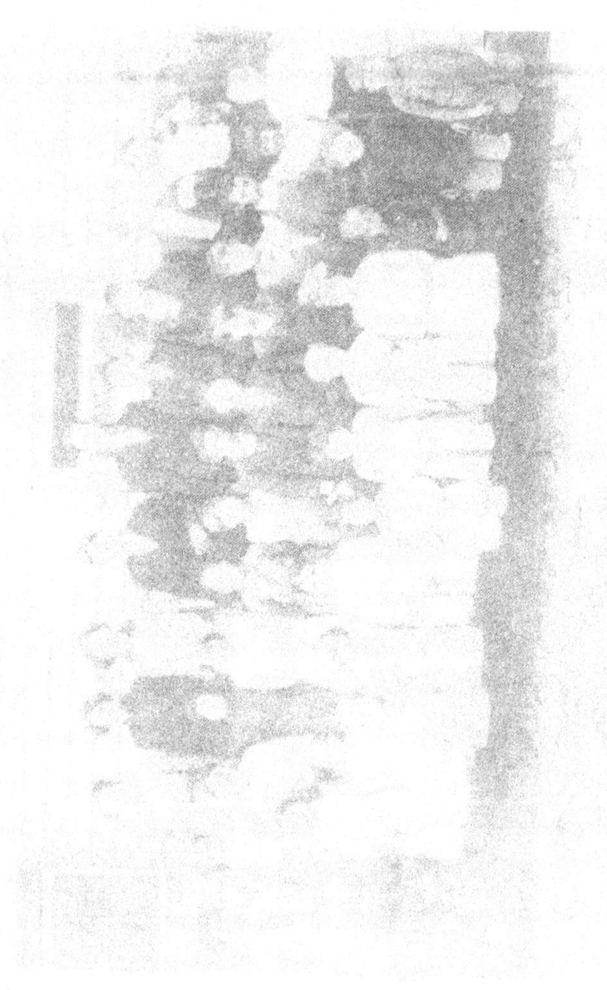

1913 school picture - back row far left Bertha McCracken, 3rd from left Betty McCracken; second row far right David McCracken

Graduation day: Henry and Fannie McCracken graduate from Teachers' College. Fannie back row second from left; Henry front row far left.

Betty McCracken received teachers'certificate from College in July 1925.

Henry L. and Sally McCracken with their children:

l.to r. small boy Isham, Henry L. McCracken holding picture of Charlie, Sally holding Mae, Sally's mother Jane (Rose) Sears

Early years on the farm in Kansas. Henry McCracken 1860-1939 and Sally Rose McCracken 1863-1933.

Cousins Anna Bell, David, Isham and Henry McCracken.

David Isham McCracken 1893 and Anna Bell (McCracken) McDaniel 1898-1983

Sally Rose McCracken and mother, Jane Blanche Gordon m. 1. Dowell Rose 2. Sears. Taken 1912.

Taken in the 1930s: l. to r. back row Henry L. McCracken, daughter Anna Bell McDaniel, wife Sally, Jessie T. McCracken (Henry L. uncle). Front row l. to r. Anna Bell's children Della Ray and Louis, Jessie T.'s grandson Donald Ray McCracken. Donald Ray's father is Walter T. McCracken.

Isham holding daughter Agailia, wife Theresa (far left), Henry L. McCracken wearing hat, wife Sally seated. Couple on right, Mae and husband Jim Richardson holding Louis. Seated far right husband of Anna Bell, Louis McDaniel, two children are theirs Della Ray and Louis. circa 1926

l. to r. Jessie T. McCracken b. 1847 d. 1938, son Walter and wife Maud, Henry L. McCracken, small boy Walter's son Donald.

CHAPTER 10

THE SOLDIERS

Serving on both sides of the War were soldiers from the related families of Griffith, Mabry, Liner, Hampton and McCracken. One such soldier was Samuel Hampton who served in the Confederacy. He is most probably a grandson of William and Hannah Hampton, however his parentage has not been established. He is listed, along with the widow Hannah, in the 1850 Census as a member of the Griffith household. At the time the census was taken Hannah gives her age as 83 and Samuel says he is ten.

Samuel was twenty-one years old when he enlisted into Company A, 2nd Calvary on November 2, 1861, at Loudon, Tennessee. From his military records he is described as having a freckled complexion, red hair, dark eyes and is 5 feet 8 inches tall. He served throughout the War and was discharged March 11, 1864. The Colonel of Company A was Henry M. Ashby and the Captain John H. Kuhn.

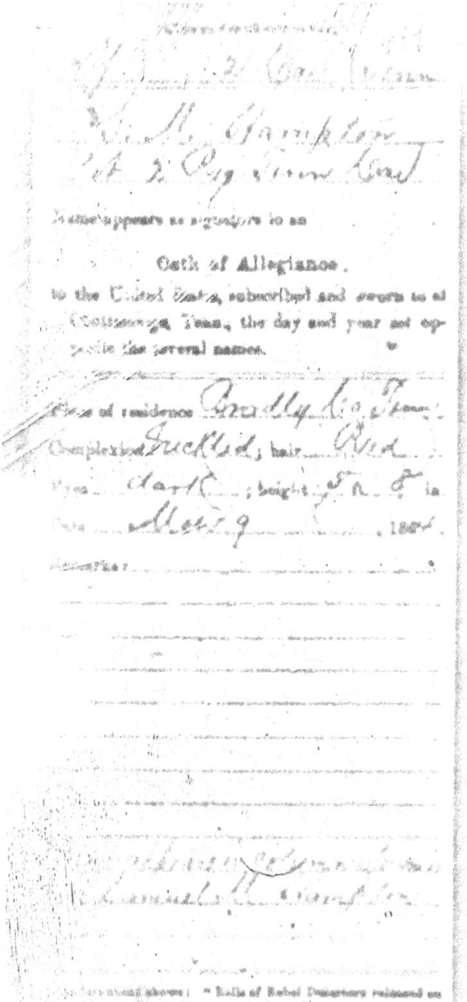

S. M. Hampton
Pvt. 2 Reg Tenn Cav.

Name appears as signature to an

Oath of Allegiance.

to the United States, subscribed and sworn to at Chattanooga, Tenn., the day and year set opposite the several names.

Place of residence [illegible]

Complexion freckled; hair Red

Eyes dark; height 5 ft. 8 in.

Date May 9, 1864.

Remarks:

Samuel M. Hampton

The document named above: "Rolls of Rebel Deserters released on oath at Chattanooga, Tenn."

Copyist.

Military record of Samuel M. Hampton.

The 2nd Calvary, from federal reports, seems to have moved about in northeast Tennessee engaging federal forces at Lead Mine Bend on the Powell River on June 30, 1862 and again at Cumberland Ford August 17. On August 29, the 600 strong Calvary, surprised the Federals at Rogers' Gap, killing six and taking 19 prisoner. By November 1862 Ashby's Calvary was detached to General Wheeler's Calvary. Operating in the rear of the Federal Army they attack along the Nashville Pike December 30, 1862, capturing a wagon train and several pieces of artillery. March 1863, it moved on a raid into Kentucky to gather cattle and supplies and participated in a raid through the streets of Danville on March 22, and in an engagement near Stanford March 29. It was here, in Kentucky, on March 30, 1863, Samuel was taken prisoner. Imprisoned at Louisville, Kentucky until April 13, 1863 when he is sent to Ft. McHenry, Maryland and then to City Point, Virginia where he was exchanged. The date of this exchange is not given on his military record. The final entry is the oath of allegiance taken March 9, 1864. He rejoined Captain Kuhn at Tunnel Hill, Georgia May 11, 1864. The fighting was between

Dalton to Atlanta. General Wheeler cited the 2nd Tennessee for "marked brilliancy" in the affair at Cass Station. The last record for the 2nd showed the brigade in the Calvary Corps of Lieutenant General Wade Hampton, which was surrendered at Durham, N. C.

Civil War Prisons:

A description of prison life is given in this account by a Confederate soldier who writes of his experiences in a prison near Alexandria, Virginia:[1]

"...arrived at the prison which was a large three story building set in the middle of a square... we were searched and relieved of everything we had that would help us to escape. We were placed in large tents on the open ground as the building was filled up with political prisoners. We were each allowed to talk to them in the evening. Four ladies and a gentleman came to the prison and inquired what state we were in from how we were off for clothing. Of course we had nothing but our uniforms. The man took our measure for everything. Next morning three large laundry baskets were

---

1. Questionnaires, Tennessee State Library, Nashville.

brought in with three suits of clothing for each man. Shoes, socks, collars, neckties, brushes of all kinds, combs and toothbrushes. God bless those ladies forever, and now let me state here that I have no complaint to make against any prison official. Major Wood treated us fine. We had plenty of the best to eat. Negroes to wait on us, polish our shoes and make up our beds. We played football, leap frog, run races, boxed and sometimes had a fight. Then we were locked up in the Guard House which consisted of the store house where everything to eat was kept, help yourself to anything you wanted. We were kept three months when the order came for us to be exchanged. We were put aboard a passenger train with plenty to eat and drink, arrived in Philadelphia at 1:30 a.m. A man and some women were walking on the platform. They asked if we were Rebel prisoners. One woman said 'you need not be afraid as we are all civilized up here.' Next day we were put aboard a steamboat...we put aboard the transport Merrimac and were taken for Fortress Monroe. Then we transferred to a steamboat and landed at Harrisons Landing in the James River where we met the men that were exchanged for us."

Another view:[1]

This Confederate soldier spent 16 months in an Illinois prison:

"...arrived Rock Island prison 11 December 1863 sick and worn out...sent to hospital next morning...treated very well... I was appointed nurse for a while...taken the small pocks...sent out to the pest hospital, stayed about a month with some where about one million or more cooties chasing each other up and down my spine and now and then stop to dig into the small pocks sores... it was awful...got back to prison pen and to my barracks near the middle of the prison. That was April or May. I could get letters from home once a week...gave me a heap of comfort... had plenty to eat at that time -- coffee, loaf bread, hominy, molasses, potatoes, rice vinegar, pickle beef or pork or mule sometimes bacon and sugar. Order came to cut some of the rations...was done...gave a call for volunteers for the Army. About 400 went out. At once they cut the rations off to 8 oz. of bread, about 2 oz. of green beef that

----

1. Questionnaires, Tennessee State Library, Nashville.

you could throw 25 feet against a wall and it would stick. No coffee, no potatoes, no hominy, nothing... only the bread and beef or mule. I got a piece of mule neck in my mouth and the hair in the meat scratched the roof of my mouth like it was briars. I have known men to give their meat rations for a bone when they would beat it up, put it in a cup with water and boil and boil when cold skim off the grease and enjoy it. I have seen prisoners get an old bone and such it just like I have seen children suck a candy stick... when they had starved us this way for a while they gave a call for volunteers to go to the frontiers... giving them 100 dollars bounty, 15 dollars per month feed and clothe them royally and for them never to have to fight the South... the result over 1700 went out the first call. 2 or 3 weeks after this they gave another chance to join them... 75 went... more calls... then no more calls... no more food were allowed. Guess they thought what remained were pretty true rebels... if the light in a stove flared up anytime of night Bang went a gun... 2 or three killed that way... if a soldier had to be punished they had the means right at hand for they had 2 posts about 6 feet from each other sunk in the ground. A 2 inch plank nailed to them with edge up... (made to shape a horse's head and tail) called Mulligins Filly... if prisoner had to ride and seemed sorta cowed he got off pretty easy but if he showed the least like it was fun they would tie a 6 lb. rock to each foot... bring tears to his eyes and curses to his lips... another mode were to tie them up by the thumbs... a spike driven into a post... a stout string secured prisoner... made to stand on a plank... hands high as he could reach... string fastened to his thumbs... blood run from the poor elbows to the ground... I get mad every time I think of these things... there were 12,000 prisoners arrived at Rock Island, 400 joined the Navy, 1,763 joined the frontier, 4,427 died, 45 killed or missing... 75 at another time joined the frontiers... we had 5,190 starved prisoners to come home and struggle for a living... while in prison we ate dogs, rats, mice and anything but a blue coat. I was released 24 March 1865."

The soldiers families living in Bradley and McMinn were caught in the chaos of war as well. The earliest period of the war brought the conflicts surrounding the

"Insurrection" and occupation by the Confederate troops, followed by the Union armies sweeping across their farms and homes. The descriptions found in the Official Record correspondence mentions sites and communities well known to these people and in some cases describes battle that took place nearby; Charleston, Benton, Riceville, Cleveland, Candy's, Chatata Creek and others. These letters give a glimpse back to late Fall 1863:

November 28, 1863, Lieutenant Edward Kitchell, Illinois Infantry to Colonel Eli Long, Commander (Union Forces): "In obedience to orders from Brigadier-General Crook, I reported to you with my regiment on the night of the 17th November, and moved with your command across the Tennessee River, and in obedience to your orders, on the night of the 24th instant, I tore up the railroad track at Tyner's Station, on the Chattanooga and Cleveland railroad, in some seven or eight places, and burned two caissons.

On the 25th, I was ordered to follow the road leading from Cleveland toward Chattanooga in search of the enemy's wagon train. I followed wagon tracks on the road for more than a mile until I ascertained that no wagons had recently gone in that direction, and then returned and struck the road leading from Ooltewah to Cleveland, driving in the enemy's pickets toward Cleveland, and capturing 25 prisoners.

On the 26th instant, with the Ninety-eight Illinois and a detachment of 100 men of the Seventeenth Indiana, I reported to Lieutenant-Colonel Seidel, Third Ohio, and with him proceeded to a point within one and one-half miles of Charleston. In compliance with his orders, I sent to his assistance two companies of the Seventeenth Indiana and eight scouts of the Ninety-eighth Illinois, and with the remainder of my command crossed the hills and struck the Knoxville and Cleveland railroad at a point about nine miles from Cleveland, and proceeded down the railroad track to the latter point, tearing up and burning the track in fifty different places, burning two cars and destroying two water tanks.

On the morning of the 27th instant, I moved out at daylight, and the command, being attacked by the enemy, consisting of infantry, artillery, and cavalry, when on the road leading to Harrison, in obedience to your orders, I ordered the Ninety-eighth

Illinois to dismount, and sent for the Seventeenth Indiana to return to its support. The Ninety-eighth Illinois dismounted and, under charge of Maj. D. D. Marquis, moved forward in line, and soon discovered the enemy, consisting of infantry, cavalry, and artillery, which he charged and drove, until ordered to fall back. The Ninety-eighth fell back to the gap in the hills, and I ordered it to take position on the hills on the right. The seventeenth Indiana, under command of Lieutenant-Colonel Jordan, by this time had arrived, and I ordered him to take position on the hills on the left of the road.....In the hurry of the retreat my pack train became separated from the command and the pack mules were abandoned. When ordered to mount horses, the Ninety-eighth Illinois and Seventeenth Indiana retired in good order, and arrived with balance of command in Chattanooga last evening."

Another report pertaining to the same engagement:

November 28, 1863, Report of Lieutenant-Colonel Henry Jordan to Indiana Volunteers Headquarters at Chattanooga (Union Forces): "...On the morning of the 27th, at

4 O'Clock, I was ordered to proceed to the north side of the town (Cleveland) and cover the front of the First Ohio Cavalry, while their horses were being groomed. At sunrise, under orders received the previous evening, I took my position in the column and took up line of march in the direction of Harrison, the enemy in the meantime having appeared in force on the east and north sides of the town and opened upon us a vigorous fire. Reaching and crossing Candy's Creek, about three miles from town. I received an order from the rear to return and cover the retreat of the First Ohio Cavalry, which was being hotly pressed by the enemy with cavalry and artillery. I recrossed the creek and returned about one mile to a point where the road passed through a gap in a line of hills, which crosses the road at right angles. Here I dismounted my command and formed line on the hill on the north side of the road, the Ninety-eighth Ilinois at the same time continuing the line on the south side. We at once opened fire on the enemy, while the cavalry, forming our rear guard, passed through the gap...."

December 5, 1863, Report of Colonel John C. Carter to Headquarters of Thirty-eighth Tennessee, Infantry (Confederate Forces): "I have the honor to report that on November 24, I was left in command at Charleston, Tennessee. The Thirty-eighth Tennessee Regiment, Lieutenant-Colonel Gwynne commanding, having an effective total of 215; portions of four companies of engineer troops, Captain McCalla commanding, have an effective total of 112; 17 effective cavalrymen, commanded by Major Shaw, and 14 effective men belonging to Captain Van Dyke's cavalry company, constituted the force under my command.

On the morning of November 26, Colonel Long's cavalry brigade of Federal troops were moved from Cleveland, Tennessee against our position. Our troops were formed on the north side of the Hiwassee River, for the purpose of protecting the bridges across the stream. After a struggle of more than an hour, the enemy were driven back, with slight loss. We did not suffer. The bridges were saved.

On November 29, I received from General Bragg an order to Lieutenant-General Longstreet. I forwarded this order immediately by telegraph and by courier to Lieutenant-General Longstreet. By this order Lieutenant-General Longstreet was ordered to fall back immediately upon Dalton, Georgia or to retire to Virginia. I immediately telegraphed to General Longstreet, stating that unless he intended to fall back upon Dalton, there was no necessity to hold my position longer. The dispatch was sent at 3 p.m. Had I been informed by General Longstreet that he did not intend to use the bridges at Charleston, I should have left for Dalton on the night of the 29th. I could have reached the place with safety. The enemy were at Cleveland in heavy force, yet by moving on the old Federal road, I should have left them far to the right. General Longstreet replied to my telegram, asking for information, and led me to suppose he might retire from Knoxville by way of Charleston. I immediately replied, giving him what information I could, and again stated that my position was becoming very critical and that unless he intended to use the bridges it was entirely unnecessary for me to remain longer at Charleston.

I received instructions from General Longstreet when the enemy was on all the roads between me and Dalton. I was ordered by him to destroy the bridges when I retired. I waited on the north side of the Hiwassee River until the enemy came up. Four thousand infantry, distinctly seen and counted, in two lines of battle, with cavalry on the flanks, were moved against us. Six pieces of artillery opened upon us a heavy fire, and I was informed that about 800 cavalry were crossing the river below. I immediately ordered the wagons and troops, preceded by a small cavalry force, to move rapidly on the Riceville road. I and my staff remained in Calhoun, on the north side of the River, until the skirmishers of the enemy reached the bridges. They found the bridges destroyed. The troops of the enemy were still passing through a defile in a range of hills on the opposite side of the river. I waited until I had seen about 6,000 soldiers debouch upon the plain before us. I then, with the remainder of the cavalry, followed our wagons and troops, leaving three men behind to watch the movements of the enemy. These men subsequently reported that the enemy were at least 15,000 strong, and that they had with them more than fifteen pieces of artillery. Our men reached Riceville a very short time before the enemy's cavalry did, having marched more than seven miles within an hour and a half.

We continued our march, moving as rapidly as possible, and at Sweet Water took the cars for Loudon. I reported to Brigadier-General Vaughn, commanding at that place.

I am glad to say that during the march we lost nothing. I started from Charleston with fifty barefooted men, yet only twelve of them were left behind."

The report continues with an account of difficulty had in removing the supplies of the commissary and failing this "...knowing that the supplies must necessarily fall into the hands of the enemy, I ordered them to be distributed among the citizens."

In the concluding paragraphs he commended several men for their services given. "...I take great pleasure in acknowledging the service performed by Captain Van Dyke and his company. With forty men he covered our entire front, and executed with promptness and efficiency every duty assigned him. There were eight roads leading from the southside of the river to our position. Under such circumstances it was unsafe to have the picket posts stationary. It was necessary that the whole cavalry force should be a constant patrol...To the soldiers I give all the praise. They manifested, as they have always done, unflinching courage and devoted patriotism."

December 23, 1863, Report of Lieutenant Jacob Bedtelyon, Fourth Michigan Cavalry (Union Forces): "...I was attacked yesterday at 3 p.m. by sixty rebel cavalry. They charged on my picket and drove him in, and followed him with a few rods where I am stationed; there we held them in check fiteen or twenty minutes until they flanked us and I was compelled to fall back; they held the place only half an hour...this post cannot be held with less than seventy-five men...I have only twenty-six and they are destitute..."

December 28, 1863, Report of Colonel Eli Long, Fourth Ohio Cavalry (Union Forces): "I have the honor to forward, for the information of the major-general commanding the department, report of attack made this a.m. upon this place (Calhoun) by the rebel General Wheeler. The attack was made at about 10 O'Clock by a force of from 1,200 to 1,500 cavalry and mounted infantry, led by General Wheeler in person. Brigadier-General Kelley, with his brigade, formed part of this force. Their object was evidently the capture of the supply train which arrived here last evening under charge of forces commanded by Colonel Laiboldt.

Colonel Laiboldt encamped on the Charleston side of the river and his skirmishers were at work with the enemy before I was apprised of their approach. I immediately mounted the small command which remained in camp not on duty (about 150 men), moved across the bridge, and found the infantry pretty sharply engaged, the enemy occupying position in the woods. The latter shortly after ward gave way, and I then started rapidly after them. Discovering a small portion of their force now cut off on the right, I ordered a saber charge, and followed a retreating column of several hundred which had taken out the Chatata road, running up the Hiwassee.

Our rapid pursuit and vigorous use of the saber completely demoralized this force, which was thrown into great confusion, and scattered in every direction, their men throwing away large numbers of arms, accouterments, etc. Several of the enemy were killed and wounded, and we captured 121 prisoners....Drove the remainder till I had arrived at a crek, which was scarcely fordable, and deemed it prudent to follow no farther....The main rebel column had fled out the Dalton road. I sent a small force out that road, who followed some five miles, and the enemy is still retreating toward Cleveland..."

This last report covers a period beginning November 17 and ending January 3, 1864. It was filed by Colonel Eli Long, Fourth Ohio Cavalry who was commanding the Second Brigade headquartered at Calhoun, Tennessee:

"...On the 24th received orders from Major-General Thomas to march to Cleveland, Tennessee and destroy as far as possible the enemy's lines of communication in that direction...On the night of the 24th I bivouacked 13 miles from Chattanooga and sent a party forward to Ooltewah, who found and destroyed some 4,000 pounds flour. On the following day I burned two freight cars, together with 100 cords of tan bark, belonging to the Confederate States of America. Nearing Cleveland, rebel pickets were encountered and driven in. The advance regiemtn (First Ohio) then charged into the town and drove out Colonel Woodward, with the Second Kentucky (rebel) Cavalry Regiment.

Next morning I sent a detachment...to go, if possible, to Hiwassee River and ascertain the enemy's strength at Charleston; also to tear up the railroad...Colonel Seidel went as far as Charleston and found Kelley's brigade stationed at Calhoun with artillery, and drove the cavalry across the river...Major Patton destroyed ten miles of the Dalton track, and considerable damage was done on the other road. In Cleveland I found a considerable lot of rockets and shells, large quantities of corn, and several bales of new grain sacks, all belonging to the rebel Government. Destroyed all that was not appropriated to use of my own command. Burned several railroad cars found here; also the large copper rolling mill--the only one of the kind in the Confederacy.

Early on the morning of the 27th I was attacked...the enemy pressing us closely and shelling vigorously. A strong line of skirmishers was kept up till we had passed Candy's Creek...I moved on to Chattanooga and reported at the headquarters.

On the 29th of November I again marched for Cleveland...from there took the road to Benton sending my ammunition wagons with the infantry column on Charleston road stiking the Federal road. I came upon a drove of about 300 hogs belonging to the Confederate Government...captured another drove of about 500 hogs.

December 1, I marched to Columbus on Hiwassee River; then returning to Benton... sent detachment to go back to Cleveland with captured hogs and prisoners...one regiment was sent to secure the boats at mouth of Ocoee and float them down to Charleston...I proceeded to Charleston. Orders from General Sherman directed me to move on immediately to Athens, and I reached there some two hours after midnight. From Athens I sent back 150 dismounted men...to garrison the town of Calhoun and hold the bridge at that place..."

CHAPTER 11

THE HAMPTONS

WILLIAM and HANNAH

William Hampton and Hannah Richardson were married in Greene County, Tennessee on November 15, 1788. The signature of Benjamin Richardson, father of Hannah, is at the bottom of the marriage bond.

"Benjamin Richardson and William Hampton are bound to his excellency Sam'l. Johnson, Esq. or his successors in office in the penal sum of five pound specie to be void on condition if there be no just cause or lawful impediment to obstruct the marriage of William Hampton to Hannah Richardson this hand, and seal the 15 day of November 1788.

The signature of Daniel Kennedy appears in the lower left of the certificate. Daniel who lived on the Nolachucky River four miles east of Greenville, was a pioneer of the State and served as clerk of the county court for several years.

Sometime between the date of this marriage and 1798, William and Hannah moved to Kentucky, first to Clay and then Madison County.

In Kentucky at this time, residences were designated by the nearest waterway. The Hamptons lived at Muddy Creek, located in the bluegrass section. Richmond, the county seat of Madison, was the nearest population center. It was a log village -- built near Dreaming Creek. Within the village was a courthouse with stocks, a pillory and whipping post, a log tavern, newspaper (Globe Register established in 1809) and a log hotel. For public transportation -- a stagecoach.

The Census taker, making his rounds in Madison County in 1810 recorded two adults and seven children in the Hampton household. (Five sons and two daughters.) Information gathered from public and private records suggest they were: William, James, John and Rebecca. No information on the other children has been found. James was born October 17, 1790 in Tennessee. He most probably was not the first born son as the tradition of the time was to name the first son to honor the father. This would suggest Wil-

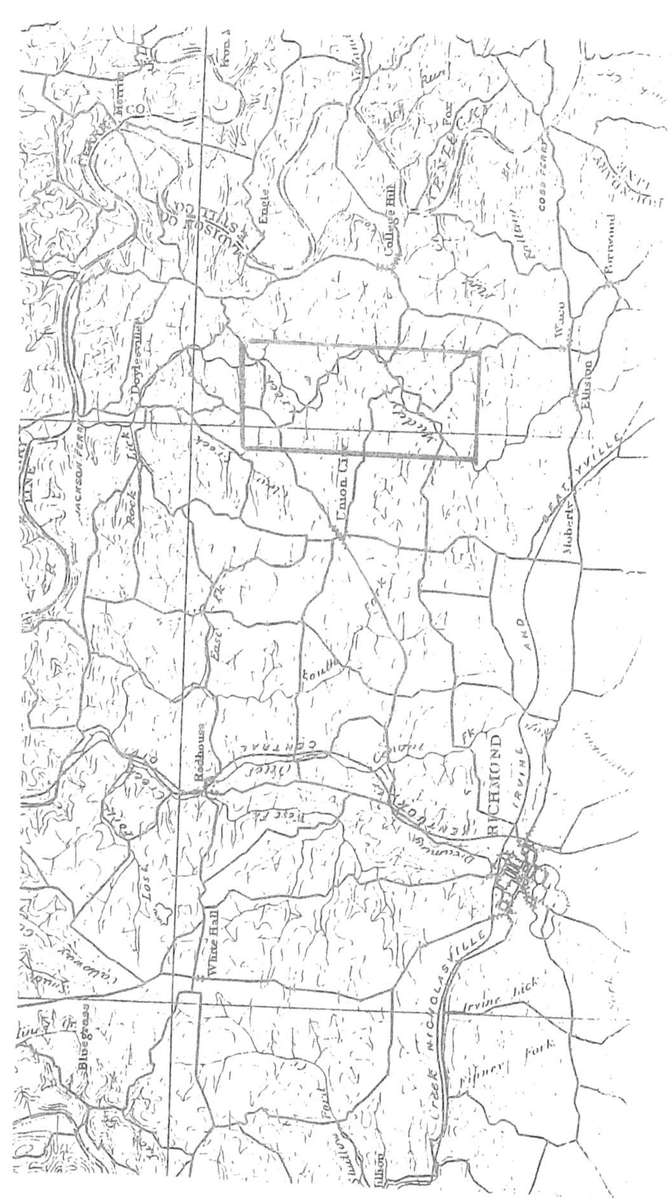

This section of a Kentucky map shows the relationship of Muddy Creek to Richmond.

liam was the older. Rebecca was born in Kentucky in 1798.

The information on the tax records of 1811 states that there is one male over 21, (William is now fifty years old), no slaves, and three horses. The amount of his acreage is illegible, however, the land was surveyed and patented. Living nearby on Drowning Creek, is Benjamin Richardson. This is possibly Hannah's father.

The Hamptons were Baptists and may have attended the Viney Fork Baptist Church. Located near their home on Muddy Creek, the Viney Fork Church began in 1779 when "...eighteen interested persons met in fellowship on January 22, 1779 and appointed a messenger to visit Tates Creek and Dreaming Creek Churches asking for help to build a new church. On February 26, 1797 Brothers Andrew Tribble and Christopher Harris from Dreaming Creek Church came and helped those eighteen persons to formulate a church Covenant and Rules of Decorum which were adopted on March 20, 1797."

Note (Picture of present day Viney Fork Baptist Church on page 65.)

In 1815 son James married Gemima Wells. Gemima's family also lived on Muddy Creek. Her father Henry, signed the marriage certificate.

By 1818 William and his family had moved to Montgomery County, Kentucky. Responding to a Congressional Act dated March 18, 1818, granting pensions to Revolutionary soldiers, William applied at the Montgomery County Court House: "...on this fifth day of October 1818, before me the subscriber, one of the Judges of the circuit court, in and for the state aforesaid, personally appeared William Hampton aged about sixty years... a resident in the county of Montgomery...." This pension was paid at the rate of eight dollars per month.

In the Fall of the year 1819, William and his family moved on, this time to Delaware County, Indiana. (In 1821 Delaware County was divided and the portion where the Hamptons lived became Bartholomew County.)

In October 1818 the United States bought from the Miami Confederacy seven and one-half million acres in central Indiana, in return for 120 horses and a perpetual annuity of $4,000. The land was opened for settlement. The first settlers came traveling along the Guthrie trace, the buffalo inter-state. A triangular shaped strip of land bordered by Haw Creek and Flatrock Creek, was the first area to be settled. This became known as the Hawpatch. The Hamptons were residents of Flatrock Parish, located within the Hawpatch.

The settlers cleared the land, built one room log houses, wrapped themselves in blankets and slept on the earthern floor. A county historian described them this way "They were a hardy breed, those first white settlers. If they were stubborn it was a necessary: manners could not fight malaria, culture could not uproot stumps. Besides the dense forests, swamps 'with rank gasses rising' abounded. The meeting place of rivers, Driftwood and Flatrock, Haw creek and Clifty, foretold trade and expansion, and the land at $1.25 an acre promised profit; but disease dissipated many a pioneer family. Only the most determined stayed."

The 1820 Census lists William's household with four boys and two girls in addition to William and Hannah. Son James lived nearby with two boys and one girl in his family.

June 17, 1824 daughter Rebecca married William Griffith "...be it remembered that on the 17th day of June 1824 a marriage license issued to William Griffith and Rebecca Hampton both of lawful age and residents of Bartholmew County and was joined together on the same day...." Lewis Singleton, J.P.

One year after the wedding the Hamptons gave up on Indiana and moved once more. Some time in July of 1825, 65 year-old William and 59 year-old Hannah entered McMinn County Tennessee. Traveling with them is son James and daughter Rebecca and their families. It is possible other children accompanied them also as early records in McMinn contain the names of Wade, Preston, Francis, William Jr., John and Zachariah Hampton.

At this time entry into McMinn was accomplished by waterway. Families loaded up their belongings, including livestock, farm tools, spinning wheels and such and floated down the river -- in this case a system of rivers to the Tennessee River and finally the Hiwassee River. The Hiwassee forms the boundary line between the two counties of McMinn and Bradley today. When the Hamptons entered McMinn however, it designated the southern boundary of the Hiwassee Purchase. The Hamptons and Griffiths planned to settle land in the newly formed County of McMinn. Across from the landing where they left the River was a Cherokee Village. Today this is the town of Charleston.

On October 29, 1825 James and John Hampton appear in McMinn County Tennessee Circuit Court and state "...William Hampton, private in the Army of the Revolution inscribed on the Pension List, Roll of the Kentucky Agency removed from the State of Kentucky to the State of Indiana in the fall of the year 1819 from which State he removed to the State of Tennessee, McMinn County in July 1825, where he now resides."

Throughout the history of this country taxation has been an ever certain fact of life and McMinn County was no exception. William is recorded for the year 1830 in the "taxable properties and polls taken in the bounds of Captain Lemon's Company..." he declares 160 acres and is carried the same for the year 1831.

The Hamptons are carried on the rolls of the Hiwassee Baptist Church. This church

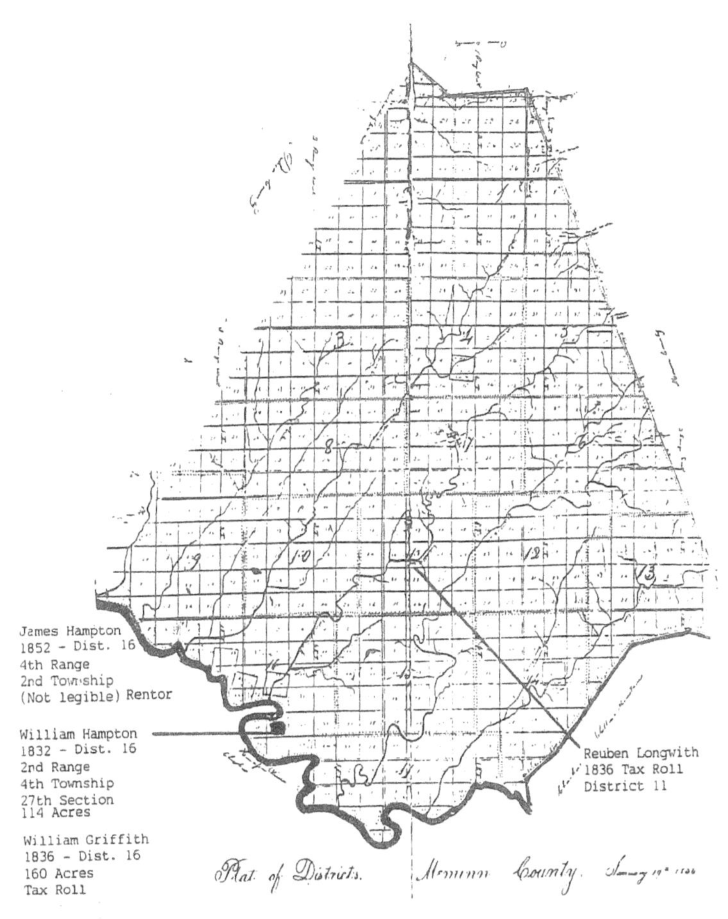

This early plat map of McMinn, County, Tennessee is dated January 19, 1836.

organized the 3rd Saturday in December 1824 in the house of Sterling Camp in its early time met in the homes of its membership. Beginning with the first entry in June 1829 "...received William Hampton and his wife Hannah by letter..." Members of the Hampton family and those descended from it continued to be recorded in its minutes until late in the Century. In addition to William and Hannah mentioned in these early minutes are James and Gemima and their children as well as the spouses of the children.

Other traces are found in the Court records: Monday, 5 September 1831 "...ordered by the court that Sterling Camp, Richard Hicks, Peter Hambright, William Hampton and Michael Scarberry be appointed a Jury of View...marker a road commencing at the corner of Sterling Camp's field on the Hiwassee River the most and best way to intersect a road at Jacob Cooks below Scarberry Mill and report to the next session of this Court."

The 1830 Census shows Simeon Oswalt, and William Jones living in dwellings adjacent to William Hampton. William Helms is enumerated 28 households away suggesting he lived at some distance. Living near Helms is the Reverend William G. "Parson" Brownlow, a figure who will gain prominence in the Civil War and as Governor of Tennessee during the reconstruction period. Brownlow, a minister in the Methodist Episcopal Church was described as "stepping into the pulpit, removing his gunbelt and pistol and preaching hell-fire and brimstone." In later years as the Civil War approached, he undoubtedly mixed in a liberal amount of politics as well as he became one of the leaders in the Unionist movement of East Tennessee.

On the 30th day of November 1832 the court records a land purchase made by William from Simon Oswalt:

"This indenture made and entered into this thirtieth day of November one thousand eight-hundred and thirty-two between Simon Oswalt on the one part and William Hampton on the other part all of the county of McMinn and State of Tennessee, witnesseth whereof I hereby acknowledge that the said Hampton hath paid the just and full sum of one hundred and seventy-five dollars to me in hand the receipt whereof is hereby acknowledged for a certain tract or parcel of land lying in the county of McMinn and State aforesaid in the second range west of the meridian fourth fractional township twenty-seventh section and the southwest quarter of said section beginning on the southwest line at a conditional... northwest with that line to the corner thence east with the section line to the corner, thence south with the section line to a small fraction sold off to William Hellems containing two and half acres thence with that line... to the conditional line made by the said Oswalt said William Jones, thence with that line to the beginning containing one hundred and eighteen acres together with the ...minerals... and appurtenances thereto belonging or in any ways incident thereto to have and to hold to him, his heirs and assigns forever and I do hereby these presents bind myself my heirs executors and administrators firmly by these presents to ...and forever defend the said land free from all lawful claims or demands of ...assigns forever. In witness whereof I have hereunto set my hand and fixed my seal this 30th day of November 1832, in the presence of James Hicks, Edom (sp.) Dixon Signed Simon Oswalt in the presence of Archibald R. Turk, Clerk of the County."

June 1833, William appears at the Circuit Court of McMinn County to make application for a pension in response to an Act of Congress passed June 7, 1832. This is the most personal statement in the pension file. He gives his age as 72 and recounts his war experiences. The application is also signed by Ezekial Ward, Sterling Camp and Peter Hambright. Ward, Camp and Hambright are neighbors.

State of Tennessee
McMinn County

On this 8th day of June 1833 personally appeared before Peter Hambright, an acting Justice of the Peace in and for the County of McMinn and State of Tennessee, William Hampton a resident of McMinn County and State of Tennessee aged about 72 years who being first duly sworn according to law doth on his oath make the following declaration in order to obtain the benefit of the provision made by the Act of June 7, 1832. That he enlisted in the Army of the United States sometime in the Spring of the year 1777 under Ensign Braden (his captain's name not recollected). His Cols. name he thinks was Smith but is not certain in the Second Virginia State Regiment in Chesterfield County in the State of Virginia for three years, rendevoused at Williamsburg in the State of Virginia remained there through the summer was called to the North. Joined General Washington's Army at Valley Forge and was put under the ...of General Mulinburg followed the British after they had evacuated Philadelphia and overtook them at Monmouth where he was in the Battle at Monmouth after that Declarant was taken sick and conveyed to Danbury Auspittle in Connecticut. Stayed there until after the army to which he belonged took up Winter quarters at Middlebrook after Winter quarters were broken up ... on the North run at some distance from Stonypoint until after Stony Point was taken by Gen Wayne. Then marched toward New York and took a place called Fowlers Hook from there the Regiment to which he belonged marched to Philadelphia and from there to Alexandria from there was furlowed for three months to go home. Met at Williamsburg in Virginia and was discharged by his officer some time in the Spring of 1780 having served out his full three years which discharge has been long since lost or misplaced.

In a few weeks after the Spring of the year 1780 he enlisted in the Army of the United States at Williamsburg in the State of Virginia for two years the names of his officers he cannot recollect and marched... under the Command as in Company with a Col Gass (sp) who had a company of Indians and marched to the Eastern Shore of Virginia and in his marches passed Little York and Guinea Island and several other places not recollected. Remained in that section of the country until sometime in the Summer of 1781. Marched to Little York from there to Jamestown from these to a place called Sleepy... then to Petersburg. Stayed there until sometime in the Winter and was called up to the South. Joined General Greene's army at the Cheraws then marched back near Guildford Courthouse and was put under the command of Col Greene. Was at the battle of Guilford Courthouse under General Greene in the faul of the same year. Was discharged by his officer which discharge has been lost or mislayed long since after having served out his two years of enlistment he was discharged he thinks in Guilford County in the State of North Carolina.

Declarant William Hampton further states upon oath that he has been previously on the pension roll and that he has been struck from the same for some cause he knows not without it was on the account of property or some other reason that he resided in Montgomery County in the State of Kentucky when he then applied for the three years... as a private soldier... in the Second Virginia State Regiment (the officers mentioned above) that the certificate he received at that time he gave or sent by mail to a member of Congress then at Washington City to get it renewed if possible but never has heard from it since. That he is the identical William Hampton who applied from Montgomery County Kentucky for three years service as a private listed soldier, enlisted in the year 1777 as aforesaid. Declarant states that his memory has failed him much with regard to names that he cannot recollect the names of many of his officers that he has no documentary evidence nor does he know of any person by whom he can prove his services in the revolution. He is acquainted with Generals Washington, Wayne, Greene, Dram, Lafayette and other officers of the regular line but has forgot their names.

He has never seen a record of his age nor does not know where there ever was one. He was born according to the best information he can get on the subject in the year 1761 in the County of Henrico in the State of Virginia and moved to Chesterfield County same state where he lived during the war. From there he moved to Gracen County Virginia then to Washington County Virginia and from there to Greene County Tennessee then to Clay County Kentucky then to Madison County Kentucky then to Montgomery County Kentucky where he applied for and obtained a pension as stated above. From there to Bartholomew County Indiana then to McMinn County in the State of Tennessee where he now resides and has resided for 7 years. That he never made but two draws of the pension he obtained when he drew before, before it was discontinued as above stated. Declarant also states that he is so inform from age in body that he is not able to attend at Court of the County to make his declaration but has went before a Magistrate agreeable to one of the regulations of the department. Declarant also states that he is acquainted in his present neighborhood with Ezkial Ward a clergyman and Sterling

Camp who can testify as to his character for veracity and their belief of his services as a soldier of the Revolution.

He hereby relinquishes every claim to a pension or annuity except the present and declares that his name is not on the pension roll of the agency of any state but that his name was on the pension roll but has been stricken off on some account he knows not what as stated above.

Sworn and subscribed before me this 8th day of June 1833
/s/ Wm Hampton
Peter Hambright
Justice of the Peace for McMinn

We Ezekial Ward, clergyman residing in the County of McMinn and State of Tennessee and Sterling Camp residing in the County and state aforesaid hereby certify that we are well acquainted with William Hampton who has subscribed and sworn to the above declaration and statement that we believe him to be 72 years of age that he is respected and believed in the neighborhood which he resides to have been a soldier of the revolution and that we concur in that opinion.

Sworn to and subscribed before me
this 8th day of June 1833
Peter Hambright
Justice of the aforesaid County
/s/ Ezekial Ward
Sterling Camp

William's last entry in the Church record was made on the 3rd Saturday in April 1836 when the Church met at Hiwassee and "...after Divine service proceeded to business..." The third item on this business agenda was Brother Wm Hampton and wife requested letters of dismission and was granted." He died the following February. In a pension application for Hannah made in May 1839 Hannah gave the following information "...married William on the 16th day of October 1788 and he died February 24, 1837 of chills and fever..."

During November of 1839 in the Open Court of McMinn County, Hannah again applies for a pension. Part of the document states: "...personally appeared in open court William Hampton and William Griffith and made oath that the family record (hereto attached) of the marriage of William Hampton and Hannah Hampton is the true family record and that the same is in the handwriting of William Hampton deceased."

It seems the Acts of Congress granting pensions were limited to a period of one or two years at a time and Hannah would have to return to Court to make a new "Declaration" for each one. The "Declaration" was mainly that she was who she said she was and things had not changed. She returned to Court in August 1844, May 1848, April 1855 and finally in 1856 when she received 160 acres of Bounty Land. This land was located in Minnesota. She immediately sold it to John E. Baskin.

Hannah's last entry in the Church minutes came in January 1845 when she was granted a letter of dismission. As she is enumerated with daughter Rebecca Griffith in the 1850 Census in Bradley County she must have moved about this time. She would have been seventy-seven years old in 1845.

By the time the Civil War began in 1861 Hannah had been living in her daughter Rebecca's household for several years. Rebecca and her husband William lived on property described as Township 12, Range 1 East in the First Civil District. They were neighbors of the Trewhitt family.

An account written by A.J. Trewhitt,[1] son of Levi, depicts the hostility in Bradley County between the Unionists and the Confederates, and tells the story of Hannah:

"At the commencement of the rebellion I was following the profession of law... I considered it my duty as a citizen of the United States to espouse the cause of the Union of all the states under the Constitution ...thus affairs rested between me and the rebels, with the exception that I occasionally heard that they cursed and threatened me, swearing that I ought to be shot, hung, etc., until the 26th of April 1863... early in the morning of this day I went to my business... that same morning, with a view to procure some tobacco, I started to go about three-fourths of a mile with my gun on my shoulder, hoping to shoot a turkey or some other wild game for my wife, in the woods by the way. On the trip I happened to fall in with a brother-in-law, two of his brothers, and three other neighbors, all good Union men, and all rebel conscripts. (At the time Tennessee entered the Confederacy, the previous June, all men 16 to

----

1.Hurlburt, History of the Rebellion

1850 - All of Bradley County is described as "26th SubDivision" by the Census Records. Levi Trewhitt with son A.J. are household number 47; Joseph and father Samuel McCracken 155; Henry and Rebecca McCracken 685; William Griffith 691 and Reps Mabry 693.

1860 - The 13th Civil District has been established and the above families are recorded with the exception of Reps Mabry. John B. McCracken, son of Henry is added, shown living near his parents.

A.J. Trewhitt, now married and living in a separate household is listed in District 5, adjacent to District 13.

By 1866 Henry and Rebecca McCracken move to a farm near the Gum Spring Meeting House in the 9th District. Their property located near Georgetown, borders Meigs County on one side. Daughter-in-law Fanny mentions living "out the Georgetown Road" in her pension papers.

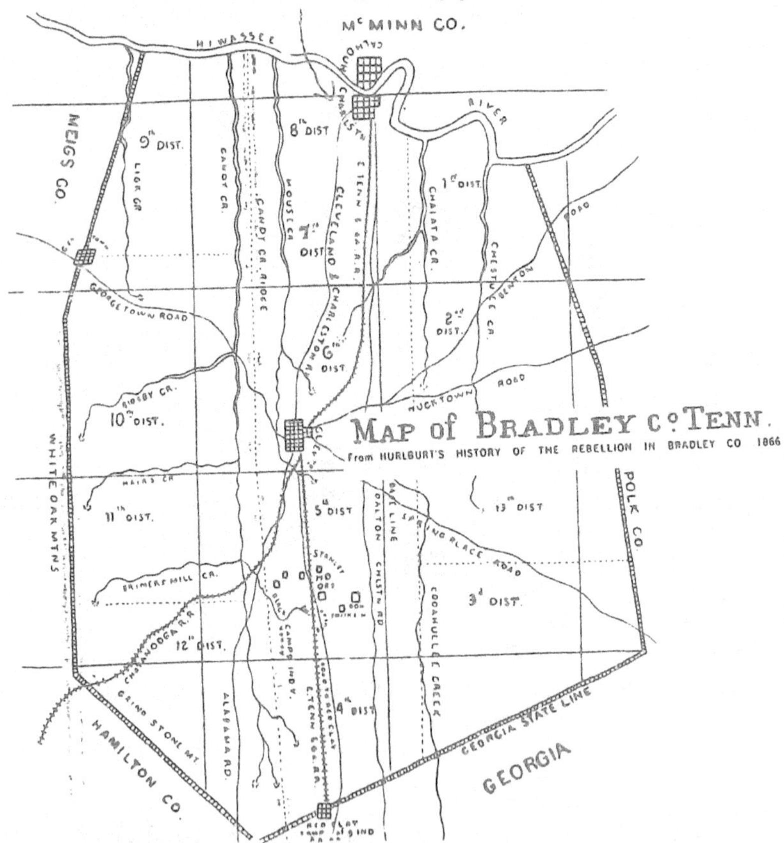

Bradley County, Tennessee Civil Districts, 1866.

forty-five were subjected to conscription. Andrew, the following April had still not reported. He, like many Union men felt this conscription was illegal.) Soon after meeting these men, on a sudden I heard some one cry halt! All but myself fled to the bushes. On looking around I saw five or six armed and mounted men about fity yards from me. I immediately went to them, three of whom I knew -- Captain May, Jathan Gregory and Springfield May. Captain May ordered me into the custody of Gregory, and after cursing me a few times, he and the others started after the other boys, leaving me to be guarded by Gregory. As I was going up to the rebels after hearing the word halt, when within about twenty yards of them I heard the report of a gun or pistol, fired by some one of their party either at me or some of those fleeing... but the shot was harmless. Very soon after the rebels left me and Gregory, I heard twelve or fifteen shots, mostly in the direction they went. In about ten minutes after these shots were fired they all returned, having captured none of my friends, but stating that they had shot one of them through the shoulder; and Springfield May stating that he was shot by one of them. Both statements, however, were false. They shot none of the men who were with me, nor was Springfield May shot by any of them; for I subsequently saw the entire company and got the facts in the case.... thus returned Captain May and his son Springfield, expended a few minutes in again cursing and abusing me in a manner that would have shamed the imps of Satan themselves. They took me to a house where a man lived by the name of Griffith. Here they had about fifteen infantry rebels belonging to Captain Foster's company of the 3rd Georgia regiment. Here, also, Captain May, feeling himself re-enforced, his cub Springfield joining his father in the game, showed themselves brave and patriotic men. Armed as they were, and backed as they were, they could curse me as a tory, a bushwhacker, a dammned liar, and using towards me every other epithet of abuse, could also coolly inform me that I would never get to Cleveland alive. Brave men, they could not only curse a solitary prisoner, but could take the last morsel of bread from a lone woman and three children; curse and whip a granny woman not under one hundred years of age; and rather than be particular, if necessary could rob the old lady of her shroud after she was dead."

This "hundred year old granny" is undoubtedly ninety-five-year-old Hannah. A. J. is taken prisoner and placed in jail at Knoxville. His imprisonment ended in 1864.

JAMES and GEMIMA

The first entry in the Family Bible is a record of James' birth "...was born 17 October 1790." He was born in Tennessee, most likely in Greene County the county in which his parents were married the previous 1788. The second entry is Gemima's birth date "...was born February 15, 1795." Gemima was born in Kentucky, probably Madison County. This Bible published in 1850 belonged to their granddaughter Nancy Darthula (nee Hampton) McCracken. It is likely however, that it was passed to her by a preceding generation. In any event, the entries were made after the publishing date of 1850 with the last entry made in 1904. Gemima's father was Henry Wells, whose signature appears on the marriage certificate dated September 14, 1815.

At the time of the marriage James and Gemima lived with their parents on Muddy

Memo: The age of the within named James Hampton sworn to by Joseph Simmons & the age of Gemimah Wells sworn to by Henry Wells this 14th Sept 1815

Attest [illegible]

James Hampton and Gemima Wells are wed September 14, 1815.

Creek, Madison County Kentucky. The Bible recorded the birth of their first child Peter, on the 18th, month illegible, 1816 and a second child named Hannah in 1818. Sometime in 1819 James and his family along with his parents and brothers and sisters moved to Delaware County, Indiana. James and his father William are recorded in various tax records that indicate they lived close together. The next four children were born in Indiana: Dulseana April 6, 1821; an illegible entry; William Everest March 13, 1819; and Rebecca Adaline November 27, 1824. Two sons James M. and John were born later in McMinn; James M. on April 2, 1833; John on May 15, 1838; Levi circa. 1840; Thomas c. 1842 and Martha c. 1845.

James and Gemima entered McMinn County in 1825, traveling with James' parents. James and Gemima have at least five children at this time. With them is Rebecca, James' sister and her husband William Griffith. They were married in Bartholmew County, Indiana. (Bartholmew was created from Delaware in 1821).

The tax record of 1830 lists James Hampton in the "...taxable property and polls of Captain Ewing's Company." In 1831 he is carried in the "...taxable properties and polls of Captain Walling's Company..." He has 80 acres of land and pays one poll. In this same list is William Hampton Jr., and brother-in-law William Griffith. The record for 1832 is the same. Brother-in-law William appears in the Court Records for March 5, 1832, Monday -- "...ordered by the Court William Griffith be appointed overseer of the road from the corner of Sterling Camp's field to intersect a road below Jacob Cooks etc."

In addition to the tax and property records the Hamptons are carried on the rolls of the Hiwassee Baptist Church. For the next thirty years beginning in the late 1820s the minutes of the Church contain entries for James, Gemima, their children and their children's spouses.

1832 received by letter ...Jemimah Hampton...

February 1836 ...Jemima Hampton dismissed by letter...

On July 11, 1837, five months after his grandfather William's death, James' oldest son Peter, enlisted in the Tennessee Mounted Volunteers at Fort Cass. This fort was located at Calhoun. He mustered out July

10, 1838. As a soldier participating in the Cherokee removal he would have spent this year traveling to Oklahoma along the "Trail of Tears."

Returning to the church records -- November 1839, "...received by experience Rebecca Hampton." This is James' fifteen-year-old daughter.

March 1843, Rebecca's name is erased from the roll "...on the account of having neglected the duties of a Christian..."

On the 7th of February, 1849 daughter Jane married John W. Liner. One month later, on the 14th of March, Rebecca married William F. Melton.

In July 1849 the newly married couples of Jane and John and Rebecca and William are entered in the Church Record. John joins the Church, Rebecca, Jane and William are baptised. At this same meeting sixteen-year old brother James M. Jr. is also baptised. James M. died 12 years later in the Civil War.

The 1850 Census records list 60-year-old James as a miller, Gemima 55 and sons James 18, John 13. Also in the household is daughter Rebecca and her husband William Melton; Levi 10, Thomas 8, and Martha 5.

This Hiwassee Baptist Church record dated Saturday in July 1849, states in part "...received by Baptism Jane Liner ...Wm. Melton and Rebecca Melton...and James Hampton Jr."

7629

Liner, John W.

Co. H, 43 Tennessee Inf.

(5 East Tenn. Vols.
Gillespie's Reg't.)

Reg't mounted about Dec., '63, and served as mounted infantry until paroled at Washington, Ga., in May, '65.

(Confederate.)

Drummer | Drummer

CARD NUMBERS.

1 50699713

Number of medical cards herein 0

Number of personal papers herein 0

Book Mark:

See also

H | (Confederate.) 43 (Mounted.) | Tenn.

John W. Liner

Drummer, Capt. W. L. Lafferty's Company, Gillespie's Regiment Volunteers.*

Age 39 years.

Appears on

Company Muster-in Roll

of the organization named above.

Roll dated Riceville, Tenn.,

Nov. 16, 1861.

Muster-in to date Nov. 16, 1861.

Joined for duty and enrolled:

When Nov. 16, 1861.

Where Riceville, Te.

By whom Jas. W. Gillespie

Period 12 Mos

Remarks:

Entry cancelled.

*This company subsequently became Company H, 43d Regiment Tennessee Mounted Infantry.

The 43d Regiment Tennessee Infantry (also known as the 5th Regiment East Tennessee Volunteers and Gillespie's Regiment Tennessee Volunteers) was organized December 14, 1861, and reorganized May [illegible], 1862. When the 35th Regiment Tennessee Infantry was disbanded, about June [illegible], 1862, some of the men were assigned to Companies F, I and M of this regiment. About December, 1863, the regiment was mounted and served as mounted infantry until paroled at Washington, Ga., in May, 1865.

Book mark:

J. W. Boyd
Copyist.

(068)

Military record of John W. Liner, husband of Jane Hampton.

On December 16, 1851 James Liner bought property from John Scarbrough. Contained with this deed is a clue to the location of the residence of the James Hampton family. The purchased property is "...in the fourth range, second West of the meridian in the Hiwassee District...adjoining James Hampton's lease..." (Map on page 189.)

Again from the Church Record -- November 1858, Case of Wm. Melton referred to next meeting...

December 1858,"... Wm. Melton did not give satisfaction so he was not restored to fellowship." Reason for this action not given.

June 1859, "...granted letters of dismission to John W. Liner and wife, also for Sister Jemima Hampton..." At the same meeting resolutions pertaining to the "evils of intemperance" are part of the agenda.

June 7, 1859, son James M. married Nancy Jane Longwith. Their only child Nancy Darthula was born April 10, 1860. James died in the Civil War March 1861.

The 1860 Census described the senior James' residence in the 16th Civil District. Living with him and Gemima is "married within the year" son John H. who is now 22 and Mary Jane 16.

The last entries from the Church Record were during 1863.

March,"... J. W. Liner came forward and gave his hand, there being some reports in circulation relative to the separation of him and wife which the church considered ought to be enquired into...appointed J.M. Miller, W.B. Carr and Thomas M. Swaffar as enquiring committee..."

April, "...John W. Liner and wife both excluded for withdrawing from this Church and joining the Cumberlands..."

July, John W. Liner came forward and was restored to fellowship.

Gemima's death on April 21, 1865 was recorded in the Family Bible. No record of James' death has been found.

JAMES M. and NANCY JANE

James M. and Nancy Jane Longwith were married June 7, 1859. Their only child Nancy Darthula, was born April 10, 1860. The 1860 Census lists 31 year-old James, wife Jane 23 and three-month-old Nancy living in District 1 of Bradley County. Parents Gemima and James live just across the county line in the neighboring county of McMinn. James' sister Jane and her husband John Liner live nearby.

When Nancy D. was one year and eight months old, James was conscripted by the 36th Regiment, Tennessee Volunteers of the Confederate States of America. It is not known whether the description "volunteer" is an accurate one as this Regiment was surrounded by controversy as the following military history will show:

Charges of illegal conscription were heard from its' very beginning. There were many desertions to the enemy and the general character of the regiment was described in a military report as one for disloyalty. By April (1862) a report from Major General E. Kirby Smith[1] stated 'Morgan's Regiment is disloyal and has been ordered down from Cumberland Gap to be sent out of the department.'" Another official letter regarding the 36th, dated May 11, 1862 relaying a message from Major General Smith to Colonel Morgan states "...owing to the pecular circumstances under which your regiment was

----

1.Official Records, Union and Confederate Armies.

36 | Tenn.

James M. Hampton

Capt. Moses H. Purvines' Company
Tennessee Volunteers.

Company Muster-in Roll

of the organization named above.

Copyist.

Military record of James M. Hampton.

(CONFEDERATE.)

36 Tenn

Jas M. Hampton
Private C C 36 Regt

Name appears on a

Register

of Claims of Deceased Officers and Soldiers from Tennessee which were filed for settlement in the Office of the Confederate States Auditor for the War Department.

By whom presented M. H. Purdines atty

When filed Nov. 29, 1862

Where born

Where died

Comptroller:

When reported to , 186

When returned , 186

Number of settlements:

Certificates

Report

Amount found due

To whom paid

No. of Paymasters' Settlements

Abstract and No. of Voucher

Confed. Arch., Chap. 10, File No. 27, page

J. B. Hyatt
Copyist.

Military record of James M. Hampton.

organized and the evil influences surrounding it, some unfaithful members have been received into it. Removed from the disloyal element of Eastern Tennessee and to a purer political atmosphere, no longer arrayed against relations who have joined the Federal Army in Kentucky and with examples of true patriotism about them, these men will become good and loyal soldiers. For these reasons your regiment is ordered to Savannah, Georgia." And so the regiment ended after only four months. Captain Moses Purvines, Captain of Company C, James' Company, returned home to McMinn.

Purvines lived at the confluence of Big and Little Chatata Creeks in McMinn County until his death in 1889. William A. Camp was the Major and Companies A-G were known as Camp's Battalion. The first reference to Camp's Battalion found in the Official Records was in a letter dated March 7, 1862 from D. Leadbetter, Colonel, Provisional Army to General S. Cooper, Inspector General, in which he stated: "On receiving your order by telegraph to re-enforce Cumberland Gap, I proceeded to that point with the 29th North Carolina Regiment, and the 3rd Georgia Battalion. Major Camp's Battalion, Tennessee Volunteers had already been sent forward. Camp's Battalion, should be withdrawn to Morristown to make up a regiment." Continuing from the Official Records. "On March 22, 1862 Colonel James E. Rains (11th Tennessee Infantry) commanding the post at Cumberland Gap, reported that one man of Colonel Morgan's Regiment (Morgan was the Colonel and ranking field officer of the 36th) was mortally wounded in a skirmish with Federal troops on that day."

Another soldier who joined Company C, of the 36th was John Varnell.[1] John signed up at Cleveland on December 16, 1861, the same day as James. On March 2, 1863 Captain Purvines makes the following statement:

"State of Tennessee
Bradley County

I Moses H. Purvines do certify that John Varnell was a private in my Company mustered into the service of the Confederate States of America in the town of Cleveland, Tennessee on the 16th of December 1861 and died at the Post Hospital at Tazewell Tennessee on the 9th of March 1862 and never

---

1.Military Records, Confederate Soldiers, National Archives, Washington, D.C.

had drawn any pay for his services from the Confederate States is not in arrears to the Confederate States given under my hand this March 2nd, 1863.
Moses H. Purvines
Captain of Company C
36 Regiment Tenn."

Did James who also died in March of '62 die at the Post Hospital at Tazewell? No record has been found.

After the death of James, Nancy Jane and daughter Nancy return to the household of her widowed mother, Tabitha. The 1870 Census describes their household as number 106 in the 1st Civil District of Bradley County. In addition to Nancy Jane there are two sons remaining at the home of Tabitha -- 18 year-old John and 16 year-old Joseph Greenberry. Nancy Jane was the oldest of twelve children.

"Yesterday there was an alarm—the report came that the Yankees were closing in upon us. We could see them distinctly; they looked like there were two or three thousand. The stars and stripes could be plainly seen—they looked very natural to one who has always been taught to love and reverence them, next almost to the Supreme Being. When I saw them floating in the breeze, feelings ran through my mind which will be forgotten only when this body of mine is laid beneath the clods of the valley. I could have stood there and gazed at them till the next day, without eating or sleeping.

"The time I have yet to serve the Confederacy as a volunteer is nine months from this good day; then I will again be a free man, and once more be permitted to speak the sentiments of a freeman, without the fear of any. Then, probably, I can the better appreciate what freedom is.

"I have understood that there is a great deal of excitement in and around Cleveland. If such is the case I wish you to remain at home; do not become alarmed, you have done nothing for which you need to run; therefore I charge you particularly to stand your ground; no difference who runs or who does not. If I am in the Southern army it will not hurt you; there are plenty of witnesses in Cleveland who are friends of ours, who know my condition, and know what placed me in my present situation."

The above letter was written on March 12, at Cumberland Gap near Knoxville by Fantroy Carter to his wife at Cleveland. Carter who was forced into rebel service describes events taking place in camp. The feelings and thoughts he expresses were undoubtedly shared by his fellow soldiers who were nearly all like himself, Unionists forced into the Confederate army, James M. Hampton among them. According to the Family Bible James died a few days later on March 26. Many of these unwilling "soldiers" were harshly treated, poorly clothed, overworked, starved easy targets for illness and disease.

CHAPTER 12

THE LONGWITHS

The surname Longwith appears in new world records as early as 1623. George Longwith departed London during this year and arrived in Barbados where he is documented as a resident. By late 1700 several Longwiths are given as residents of Warren County, North Carolina.

REUBEN and NANCY

The Warren County, North Carolina Court Records contain the following marriage bond in the amount of $500 -- an obligation on the part of Reuben Longwith:

"...there is a marriage shortly to be solemnized ...between ...Reuben Longwith and Anna Capps."

Perhaps Reuben lost his money, no marriage record was found. Later in the same court, the year 1796, another bond was issued between Reuben and Nancy Hathcock.

It is this Reuben and this Nancy who are the most likely candidates for the

Know all Men by these presents that we Reuben Longwith of the County Warren & Henry Capps of the County afore are held and firmly bound unto Richard Dobbs Spaight Esqr. Governor &c in the sum of Five hundred Pounds to which payment well and truly to be made to the said Richard Dobbs Spaight Esqr. Governor aforesaid or to his Successors in office we bind ourselves our heirs Executors and Administrators jointly and severally firmly by these presents sealed and dated this 3rd Day of Jany. Anno Dom. 1793

The Condition of the above Obligation is such that whereas there is a Marriage shortly to be Solemnized and had between the above bound Reuben Longwith & Anna Capps now if there be Lawfull Cause to Obstruct the said Marriage then the above Obligation to be Void or Else to Remain in full force & Effect

Signed Sealed &c In presence of

Richd. [illegible]

Reuben his mark Longwith (Seal)

Henry Capps (Seal)

This 1793 marriage bond, posted in Warren County, North Carolina, bound Reuben Longwith and Henry Capps, most probably Anna's father.

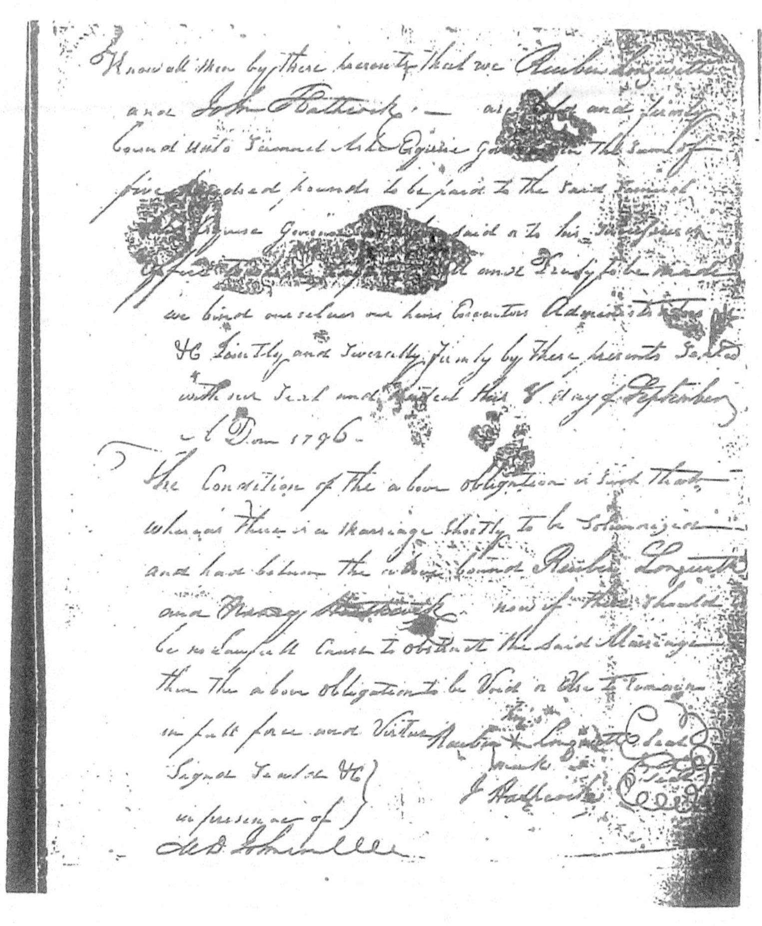

Know all Men by these presents that we Reuben Longwith
and John Hathcock — are held and firmly
bound unto Samuel Ashe Esquire Governor in the sum of
five hundred pounds to be paid to the said Samuel
[illegible] Governor [illegible] said or to his successors in
office [illegible] and truly to be made
we bind ourselves our heirs Executors Administrators
&c Jointly and Severally firmly by these presents Sealed
with our Seal and dated this 8 day of September
A Dom 1796

The Condition of the above obligation is such that
whereas there is a marriage shortly to be solemnized
and had between the above bound Reuben Longwith
and Nancy Hathcock now if there should
be no lawfull Cause to obstruct the said Marriage
then the above obligation to be Void or else to remain
in full force and Virtue

Reuben his x mark Longwith (Seal)
J Hathcock (Seal)

Signed Sealed &c
in presence of
[illegible]

In September 1796 Reuben Longwith and John Hathcock to secure the marriage of Reuben and Nancy Hathcock. Court record of Warren County, North Carolina.

parents of Reuben Longwith who is recorded in the McMinn County records.

The 1800 Census of Warren County states that Reuben Longwith's household consists of four children the oldest less than sixteen and two adults between the ages of 26 and 45. They have one slave. If these two are the parents of Reuben who lived in McMinn and Bradley County, Tennessee, they moved to Tennessee shortly after this Census was taken as Reuben was born there ca. 1808. The 1840 Census records list Nancy Longwith in Knox County, Tennessee. She is between 60 and 70 years of age.

The earliest tax record of Reuben, age 21, was found for the year 1829 in McMinn County when he was carried on the taxable property of Rickers Company. He was assessed and paid one poll in the amount of 31 cents. By 1832 he is listed in the "...taxable property and polls in the No. 8 bounds of Captain Stephenson's Camp..." The 1836 records place him in District 11.

(McMinn County map showing location of Longwith household on page 189.)

REUBEN and TABITHA

About 1830 or so Reuben married Tabitha Hardin. Tabitha was born February 3, 1815, records variously say in North and South Carolina. McMinn County tax lists of 1829 list Joseph, Solomon and Hardy Hardin. (Hardy had a daughter named Tabitha, but she was not the same person who married Reuben Longwith). Tabitha's relationship to these men has not been established nor is it known who her parents were.

Reuben and Tabitha's first child Nancy Jane was born February 18, 1832. In addition to Nancy Jane there are eleven other children: William Franklin 1834; Reuben Christopher 1836; James W. 1838; Rachael Catherine 1840; Isaac Lafayette 1842; Mary A. 1844; Azel M. 1846; Rebecca 1847; Sarah Elizabeth 1848; John Steven 1850 and Joseph Greenberry 1853.

When the 1850 Census was taken the Longwith family lived in the 7th Civil District of McMinn County, fairly close to the center of present day Athens.

Sometime in the Spring of 1852 Reuben died tragically. The court record reproduced on the following page, tells the story.

This McMinn County record described as County Court July Session 1852, states in part "...Ordered by the court that certificate issue to the County Trustee for fifty cents each the following named persons a Jury of inquest over the body of Reuben Longwith who was burned to death (to wit) John Williams, J. P. Williams, Daniel Pearce, Jessee Tunnel, David Grunway, Benjamin Franklin, H. J. Eaton, B. M. Smith, S.M. Thomas, E. A. Eaton and Elijah Williams."

Tabitha was expecting their 12th child, Joseph Greenberry, at the time of his death.

It is unclear where Reuben died. Though the court records are from McMinn, information contained in the probate at the time of Tabitha's death indicate he died in Bradley County. This could be explained by the fact that the McMinn County Courthouse was used in the early developmental period of Bradley County.

The most probable explanation for Reuben's death was a murder by the Cherokee Indians of Bradley or McMinn County. The way in which he died would seem to indicate that this would be the best explanation. Many Indians stayed behind after the removal of 1838-39. One resident of McMinn, Jerome King, talked about his early childhood in the 40s and 50s "...there were still many stray Indians who were left behind and were a common sight...for several years after the main bulk of the tribe had gone. They were wanderers through the forest being in groups of from two to five... when seen by white men they would be strolling noiselessly through the woods like ducks or geese, one behind the other, each one carrying his bow and arrow, quiver and a deerskin pouch containing a quantity of parched corn and a hunk of dried venison."

Tabitha purchased land in Bradley County in the Fall of 1858:

"This indenture made and entered into this 2nd day of September 1858 between Wm. A. Weatherly of one part and Tabitha Longwith of the other part both of the State of Tennessee and Bradley County. (Note that Tabitha is described as a resident of Bradley). Witnesseth, that the said William A. Weatherly doth bargain and sell to the said Tabitha Longwith a certain piece or parcel of land situated in Bradley County, State of Tennessee, for the sum of four hundred dollars said sum of money has all been paid the receipt where of is hereby acknowledged bounded as follows beginning at the North East corner of said land of the 2nd fractional township it being a part of the School section in said fractional township fifty-five acres adjoining the Camp farm it being a part of the North East quarter of said section with its appurtenances. To have and hold the said tract or parcel of land with appurtances to said Tabitha Longwith her heirs and assigns forever. In witness whereof I set my hand and seal this 29th day of September eighteen fifty-eight."

Signed William A. Weatherly Attest: John Pearce, R. T. Weatherly and A. J. Parker.

The following year on June 7, 1859 Tabitha's oldest child Nancy Jane, married James Hampton.

It was here on this land that Tabitha died May 27, 1896. She was buried in Chilcutts Cemetery.

The court appointed an administrator for her estate:"It appearing to the Court that Tabitha Kyle alias Tabitha Longwith, late a citizen of Bradley County has died leaving no will, and came John Longwith, son of the said Tabitha Kyle and made application to the Court that W. C. Day public administrator be appointed to administer upon said estate. Therefore the Court is pleased to order that W.C. Day be appointed administrator of the estate of Tabitha Kyle deceased, and therefore the said W. C. Day appeared in open court. A bond was duly qualified and Letters of Administration issued."

The inscription reads "Tabitha Longwith, born February 3, 1815, died May 27, 1896.

246

Final Report and Settlement of W.C. Day Administrator of the estate of Tabitha Longwith deceased made to J.S. Harrison, Clerk, October 23, 1900.

Said Administrator is chargeable as follows:

Amount of sale of personal property	176.30	
" notes that came to my hand	120.00	
" Interest received	[illegible]	
" Received for corn	14.50	
" " cotton	7.59	
Said Administrator is entitled to the following credits:		
Paid Dr. B.H. Cate		27.50
" Clerk for appointment and Report		4.00
" J.S. & W.S. [illegible] acct		14.50
" E.P. Knox " burial		27.63
" Taxes for 1896		1.29
" for Tombstones		17.00
" Johnnie McCollister acct		.60
" Taxes for 1897		[illegible]
By credit of note on [illegible]		22.00
Paid [illegible] account		[illegible]
The following amounts were paid to the following named heirs of said estate:		
Paid Ellyzabeth [illegible] heirs		12.00
" John Hampton		[illegible]
" W.B. Longwith		12.00
" Reuben A. Longwith		[illegible]
" James Longwith		12.00
" Catharine Nichols		12.00
" Lafayette Longwith		12.00
" Mary A. Dawson's heirs		12.00
" A.M. Longwith		12.00
" John F. Longwith		12.00
" Rebecca Petty		12.00
" Joseph T. Longwith		12.00
" Clerk for this settlement		1.00
By amount allowed Admr for his services		[illegible]

Sworn and subscribed to before me, this October 23, 1900.

J.S. Harrison
Clerk

W.C. Day
Administrator

This final Report and Settlement of W.C. Day, Administrator of the estate of Tabitha Longwith is from Bradley County Court records.

CHAPTER 13

THE MABRYS

JOSHUA and LUCRETIA

A list of inhabitants in Captain Twiley's District, state Census of Warren County, North Carolina 1784, contains the name of Joshua Mabry. Living in the household is one male, white, between 21 and 60 years of age; four white males, either under 21 or over 60; two white females of all ages; three black 12 to 50; 8 blacks under twelve or over 50, for a total of 18 persons.

Joshua is the father of seven sons -- Charles, Reps, Joshua, Stephen, Gray, Daniel and Jordan. These sons all served in the Revolutionary War in what was known as the Battle of King's Mountain.

Joshua's Will was entered in the Warren County May court of 1791:

"In the name of God Amen I Joshua Mabry of the County of Warren and State of North Carolina being weak in body but sound in mind and memory, praise be God for the same do make and ordain this my last Will and Testament in manner and form following, first principally I recommend my soul into the hands of almighty God and Saviour hoping through the meritorious death of Jesus Christ my Saviour to receive free pardon for all my sins past and my body to be buried at the discretion of my executors, hereafter mentioned... my will is that my just debts be paid.

Item, I give unto my dearly beloved wife, Lucretia Mabry during her natural life my land and plantation also five negros Shaff? Nurrow? Ted? Yo? and my stock of horses excepting Euling? cold, cattle, hogs, sheep and geese with one half of the profits ...are missing from the whole also ...the household furniture. Exceptions are bed and ....

Item, I give and bequeath unto Richard... on negro boy by the name of Will.

Item, I give and bequeath unto George Walker (sp) my son-in-law one negro man named Jacob.

Item, I give and bequeath unto my son Reps Mabry after the death of his beloved mother one negro woman by the name of Mary.

Item, I give and bequeath unto my son

Charles Mabry one Negro by the name of James.

Item, I give and bequeath unto my grandson Joshua Mabry son of Charles Mabry one negro girl named...

Item, I give and bequeath unto my grandson H. P. Mabry, son of Charles Mabry sixty three acres of land that I purchased of John Denton.

Item, I give and bequeath unto my son Gray Mabry one negro girl named Sil...and one negro boy named ... also one bay colt and after the decease of his mother I give unto the said Gray Mabry all the stock, horses, cattle, hogs, sheep and geese also one feather bed bedstead and furniture and the land where I now live.

Item, I give and bequeath after the death of my dearly beloved wife Lucretia Mabry, I give unto my son Joshua Mabry one negro man by the name of Ska....

Item, I give and bequeath after the death of my dearly beloved wife Lucretia Mabry I give unto daughter Fannie Lightfoot one negro woman named Tab...

Item, I give and bequeath unto my granddaughter Fannie Walton one feather bed and furniture.

Item, I give and bequeath after the death of my dearly beloved wife Lucretia Mabry, I give unto my son Gray Mabry all my household... furniture also my plantation...

Item, I give and bequeath after the death of my dearly beloved Lucretia Mabry unto my son Stephen Mabry one negro man named Norrow... I appoint Gray Mabry... Executor of this my last Will and Testament revoking... and making... all other wills and testaments before made in... I have hereunto set my hand this day of November 1790 and... also appoint that there shall be no inventory of this my estate returned to court.

Wt Gray Mabry
Richard Proctor
Francis Walton

Joshua Mabry

Warren County May Court 1791

This last Will and Testament of Joshua Mabry deceased was proved in open Court by the above three witnesses oaths and therefore were ordered to be recorded and Gray Mabry the Executor named in the said Will qualified as such to whom Letters of Testamentary were granted.

....Johnson

REPS (RIPS, REPPS, ZREPTS) and MATILDA

During the early 1800s, Gray and one or two other sons moved to the State of Georgia. Gray is recorded in the Census of Green County, Georgia 1820. Reps however, remained in Warren County and died there in the year 1819. Reps' Will was filed in the May Court of 1819. Unfortunately, this will mentions "older children" but does not name them. However, because of so many corresponding bits of information it would seem that Joshua Mabry's family is the antecedent of Reps Mabry of Bradley County, Tennessee, who gives his place of birth as North Carolina and the date of birth 1794. He is most probably a grandson of Joshua.

Reps appears in Bradley County court records as early as 1839 when he makes three separate land purchases totaling 480 acres. On the 5th of August at the Entry Taker's Office of the Ocoee District he is granted 160 acres situated in the First range East of the basis line in the First Township, thirty-fourth section, Southeast quarter of the section; on December 1, 1839 in partnership with Morton Grey he enters 160 acres located in the Southwest quarter of the same parcel. On April 19, 1852 Reps sells a portion of this land, the East half to David Norman "...in consideration of the sum of three hundred dollars..." The third and final purchase was dated December 29, 1839 in partnership with Absalom Carson (both Grey, Carson and Mabry as well as others with the surname Grey, are involved in court proceedings during the mid 1840s as they variously sue, charge and counter charge each other -- at issue are property disputes, trespass and such difficulties) same range, same township, twenty-seventh section Southwest quarter. All three entries are signed by James K. Polk, Governor of Tennessee. In 1845 Polk became the eleventh President of the United States.

Information from the 1850 Census: Reps gives his age as 56 and states he was born in North Carolina. His wife Matilda, age 43 was born in Tennessee. Their children are Eliza 20, Fanny 18, Mary 16, Caroline 15, John 12, Riley 10, Stephen 8, Archibald 7 and Francis M. 2. By the time the 1860 Census is taken Reps had moved to Polk County. His children are Riley 21, John 18, Harry 16, Archibald 14, Franklin 12, and Prier 10. The 1870 Census shows Matilda living with son Harry and his wife Juliet

THE STATE OF TENNESSEE. No. 1295

To all to whom these presents shall come greeting:

KNOW YE, That in consideration of an ENTRY made in the Entry Taker's Office of the Ocoee District, of No. 1386 dated the 5th day of December 1839 by Absalom Carson & Reps Maberry, as general enterers,

there is GRANTED by the said State of Tennessee, to the said Carson & Maberry and their heirs a certain TRACT OR PARCEL OF LAND, CONTAINING one hundred & sixty acres, lying in the county of Bradley in the said District, situate in the first RANGE East of the basis line First TOWNSHIP Twenty seventh SECTION, being the South West QUARTER of said section: beginning at the North East corner of said quarter; with its appurtenances, TO HAVE and TO HOLD the said TRACT or PARCEL of LAND, with its APPURTENANCES, to the said Carson & Maberry and their heirs FOREVER.

In Witness whereof James K. Polk GOVERNOR of the State of Tennessee, hath hereunto set his hand and caused the GREAT SEAL of the State to be affixed at NASHVILLE, on the 7th day of July in the year of our Lord one thousand eight hundred and forty and of American Independence the sixty fifth. James K. Polk

By the Governor,

John S. Young

Secretary,

Absalom Carson & Reps Maberry

One of several land purchases made by Reps Mabry.

with new baby Ulysses Grant.

Fanny, the second daughter of Reps, married John B. McCracken October 29, 1857.

Sometime in December 1861, Stephen born in 1842, and Archibald born 1843, joined Company K, 43rd Regiment of the Confederate State of America.

The 43rd Regiment Tennessee Infantry (also known as the 5th Regiment East Tennessee Volunteers and Gillespie's Regiment Tennessee Volunteers) was organized December 14, 1861 and reorganized May 10, 1863. When the 36th Regiment Tennessee Infantry was disbanded about June 23, 1862 some of the men were assigned to Companies F, I and K of this regiment. About December 1863 the regiment was mounted and served as mounted infantry until paroled at Washington, Georgia in May 1865.

VICKSBURG, MISSISSIPPI, JULY 15th 1863.

To all Whom it may Concern, Know Ye That:

I A. Mabry a Privat of Co. K 43 Reg't Tennessee Vols. C. S. A., being a prisoner of War, in the hands of the United States Forces, in virtue of the capitulation of the city of Vicksburg and its Garrison, by Lieut. Gen. John C. Pemberton, C. S. A., Commanding, on the 4th day of July, 1863, do in pursuance of the terms of said capitulation, give this my solemn parole under oath—

That I will not take up arms again against the United States, nor serve in any military, police, or constabulary force in any Fort, Garrison or field work, held by the Confederate States of America, against the United States of America, nor as guard of any prisons, depots or stores nor discharge any duties usually performed by Officers or soldiers against the United States of America, until duly exchanged by the proper authorities.

A. Mabry

Sworn to and subscribed before me at Vicksburg, Miss., this 15th day of July 1863.

John C. Fry 20th Reg't Ohio Vols.
Major and Paroling Officer.

VICKSBURG, MISSISSIPPI, JULY 15th 1863.

To all Whom it may Concern, Know Ye That:

I S. H. Mabry a Privat of Co. K 43 Reg't Tennessee Vols. C. S. A., being a prisoner of War, in the hands of the United States Forces, in virtue of the capitulation of the city of Vicksburg and its Garrison, by Lieut. Gen. John C. Pemberton, C. S. A., Commanding, on the 4th day of July, 1863, do in pursuance of the terms of said capitulation, give this my solemn parole under oath—

That I will not take up arms again against the United States, nor serve in any military, police, or constabulary force in any Fort, Garrison or field work, held by the Confederate States of America, against the United States of America, nor as guard of any prisons, depots or stores nor discharge any duties usually performed by Officers or soldiers against the United States of America, until duly exchanged by the proper authorities.

S. H. Mabry

Sworn to and subscribed before me at Vicksburg, Miss., this 15th day of July 1863.

John C. Fry 20th Reg't Ohio Vols.
Major and Paroling Officer.

Military records of Archibald and Stephen Mabry.

(Confederate.)

M | 43 (Mounted.) Tenn.

A. Mabry +

Pvt, Co. K, 43 Reg't Tennessee Infantry.

Appears on

Company Muster Roll

of the organization named above,

for May & June, 1862

Enlisted:

When Dec. 12, 1861.

Where

By whom Jas. W. Gillespie

Period 12 mo

Last paid:

By whom A. C. Day

To what time Apl. 31, 186

Present or absent Present

Remarks: Joined by transfer 36 Regt June 23.

Name appears on roll of name above as Arch Mabry +

(Confederate.)

M | 43 (Mounted.) Tenn.

Arch. Maybery +

Priv., Co. K, 43 Reg't Tennessee Infantry.

Appears on

Company Muster Roll

of the organization named above,

for July & Aug., 1862.

Enlisted:

When 12 Dec., 1861.

Where Cleaveland

By whom Jas. W. Gillespie

Period 12 mos.

Last paid:

By whom A. C. Day

To what time 30 June, 186

Present or absent Present

Remarks:

Name appears in list of names present as Arch Maybery

Military record of Archibald Mabry.

(Confederate.)

M | 43 (Mounted.) Tenn.

A. Maberry

Pvt., Co. K, 43 Reg't Tennessee Infantry.

Appears on

Company Muster Roll

of the organization named above,

for Sept. & Oct., 1862.

Enlisted:

When Dec. 12, 1861.

Where Ooltewah

By whom J. W. Gillespie

Period 12 m

Last paid:

By whom

To what time , 186

Present or absent Present

Remarks:

Mayberry Step[illegible]

Co. K, 43 Tennes[illegible]

(5 East Tenn. Vols.
Gillespie's Reg't.

Reg't mounted about Dec., '63, and ser[illegible]
infantry until paroled at Washington, G[illegible]

(Confederate.

Private | Pr[illegible]

REFERENCE SLIP.

Cards filed with

Mayberry [illegible]

(Confederate.)

M | 43 | Tenn.

Stephen H. Mayberry
Pvt. 43 Reg. Tenn. Inf.

Name appears as signature to an

Oath of Allegiance

to the United States, subscribed and sworn to at Chattanooga, Tenn., the day and year set opposite the several names.

Place of residence Polk Co. Tenn.

Complexion florid; hair dark

Eyes hazel; height 5 ft. 10 in.

Date Mar. 10, 1864.

Remarks:

[illegible]

Indorsement shows: "Rolls of Rebel Deserters released on Oath of Amnesty at Chattanooga, Tenn."

Number of roll: 73 sheet 8

(666) E. C. Simons

Copyist.

Military record of Stephen Mabry.

CHAPTER 14

THE McCRACKENS

JOHN and MARGARET

The following was filed in Washington County, Tennessee Will Book, Volume 1, page 214: (The name McCracken is variously spelled McCrackin.)

"In the name of God Amen. I John McCrackin of Washington County and State of Tennessee being sound in mind, memory and understanding thanks be to Almighty God for the same, being mindfull of my mortality do make and constitute this my last will and testament. As to my worldly estate wherewith it hath pleased God to help me I give and dispose as follows:

Item 1. It is my will that my loving wife Margaret have the house and lot we live on in Jonesborough with all the household and kitchen furniture and as much of the personal property as she shall have in need of living her life and also the lot of land adjoining John Kennedy and Samuel Bayles and the remainder of the personal estate I have to be sold and the money coming from the sale to be put out on interest and the interest to be for the use of my wife if she should have need of it during her natural life.

Item 2. It is my will that my son, John McCrackin, have that part of the plantation that he now lives on as it was laid of by John Wilson, surveyor, with all the bonds and notes I now hold on him.

Item 3. It is my will that my son Samuel McCrackin, have the other part of that plantation adjoining the land given to my son John, as it was laid of by John Wilson, surveyor.

Item 4. It is my will that my son, Robert McCrackin, have the land on plantation that he now lives on, also all the notes and bonds that I now hold aginst him.

Item 5. It is my will that my son Henry McCrackin, have the house and lot that he now lives on by paying two hundred dollars to be paid fifty dollars per year. After my death to be paid in to the hands of my executors.

Item 6. It is my will that my daughters, Mary Kelsey and Catherine Greer, that no charge be made aginst them for what I have given them. But that my daughter Mary Kelsey have my old woman Jennie, at such time as my wife, Margaret shall think proper to give her up.

Item 7. It is my will that my grandsons, John M. Kelsey have ten dollars out of my estate; John McCrackin, son of Samuel have ten dollars; John McCrackin son of Robert have ten dollars; and John B. McCrackin, son of Henry have ten dollars and William McCrackin, son of John have also ten dollars.

Item 8. It is my will that my granddaughter Mary B. McCrackin have at her marriage or the death of my wife Margaret one horse worth sixty dollars and saddle and bridle worth fifteen dollars and also a good bed and furniture. To come out of the money to be paid by my son, Henry McCrackin.

Item 9. It is my will that my negro man Lock, be set free at the death of my wife Margaret, if he can give such surety as will be agreeable to law.

Item 10. It is my will that my negro girl Spice, be set free at the age of thirty-five if my wife Margaret should die before that time, if not to serve to her mistress' death and then to be free by giving support security and if Spice should have any children they are to be free at the age of twenty-one.

Item 11. It is my will that at the death of my wife Margaret, that all my estate real and personal not heretofore disposed of by me, be sold and equally divided among my children and my granddaughter, Mary B. McCrackin have an equal share with the rest of my children, and that all debts levied on in the State of Pennsylvania coming from the estate of Alexander Adams, deceased, be equally divided in the manner I have stated. I do appoint and nominate my son, John McCrackin and my wife, Margaret McCrackin executor and executrix of this my last will and testament.

I publish and declare this to be my last will and testament in witness whereof I have hereunto set my hand and seal this eighth day of January, one thousand eight hundred and twenty." John McCrackin's signature appears as does witness Jennie. John Patton and Samuel Chilton also witnesses, sign with an X.

[illegible]

[illegible] McCracken [illegible] Washington Co. Tenn.
[illegible]-1820

Records of Washington Co. Tenn.
Wills - Vol 1 - p 214

Will of John McCracken, of Washington Co. Tenn.
wife Margaret McCracken, house & lot in Jonesboro.
son John McCracken - part of plantation where he now lives
son Samuel McCracken other part of sd plantation
son Robert McCracken - plantation whereon he now lives
son Henry McCracken - house & lot where he now lives
dau Mary Kelsey. slave "Jenny"
dau Catherine Greer.
grand son John M. Kelsey. $10
Grandson John McCracken, son of Samuel, $10
" John McCracken " " Robert, $10
" John B. McCracken " " Henry, $10
" William McCracken " " John $10
grand dau Mary B. McCracken at marriage horse worth $[illegible].
out of Henry McCracken's part -
grand dau Mary B. McCracken to share with my [illegible]
"all debts due me in the State of Pennsylvania "coming
from the estate of Alexander Adams, dec'd" -
exr John McCracken & wife Margaret -
8 Jan. 1820.
Wm Patton
Saml G. Smith } wit
Proven Feb. 2, 1820
[illegible]

This abstract of John McCracken's Will dated February 2, 1820 is on file at the Lawson-McGee Library, Knoxville, Tennessee.

John McCracken died January 8, 1820, leaving as heirs his wife, four sons and two daughters.

The date of his youngest child Catherine's birth in Pennsylvania during 1785 and the earliest record in Tennessee, the birth of a grandchild in 1802 in Washington County located in northeast Tennessee, sets the period of time in which this family moved from Pennsylvania to Tennessee.

No record of the family's residence in Pennsylvania has been found. However, by using the 1790 Census for Pennsylvania some traces appear. This Census contains the names of John McCracken and Alexander Adams, residents of Chester County. The McCracken Will mentions Alexander Adams "that all debts levied on in the State of Pennsylvania coming from the estate of Alexander Adams, deceased, be equally divided..." By linking these two names from the Census record McCracken in Vincent Township and Alexander Adams in West Marlborough Township, it is probable that the McCrackens of Chester County are the McCrackens of Washington County.

The surname McCracken is found in Chester County records as early as 1725 when

John McCracken paid taxes at New London, a town named for the London Trading Company, the same company that brought the Jamestown residents in 1609. This part of Pennsylvania represented a portion of their holdings in the State.

Samuel, the second son mentioned in the Will is the line of descent of the McCracken family in Bradley County.

Born about 1780, Samuel married Alice Mercer the daughter of Joseph. Both Samuel and Alice are mentioned in Joseph's Will filed in Washington County, October 9, 1828:

"This indenture made and executed between Thomas Mercer, Rachel Mercer, Samuel McCracken and Ailse his wife, Abner Mercer, Joseph Mercer, Elbert Mercer, Rebecca Green and Malinda Mercer, heirs of Joseph Mercer dec'd of the one part and Thomas W. Mercer of the County of Washington and State of Tennessee of the other part witnesseth that the said Thomas, Rachael, Samuel McCrackin and his wife Ailse, Abner Mercer, Joseph, Elbert, Rebecca Green, and Malinda Mercer, heirs as aforesaid for and in consideration of eight hundred dollars to them paid the receipt whereof is hereby acknowledged doth grant bargain sell release and relinquish unto the said Thomas Mercer all the right title claim and interest that we or others of us have in and to a certain tract of land lying and being in the county of Washington and state of Tennessee and bounded as follows. Beginning at a chestnut near a field on Henry Bottles line thence north of said Bottle lines that thence following courses and distances: South 36 W 78 poles to a black oak thence 56 East thirty poles to two hickories, thence S 36 W 30 poles to a large post oak, thence N 59 W30 poles to a white oak and hickory standing on Mercer dist. line hence with said line S 36 W 67 poles to a stake thence S 20 W 28 poles and white oak, thence South 99 E 20 poles to a stake near a white oak, on John Mathes' line, thence with said line S 19 1/2 poles to a stake near a white oak thence East 184 poles to a stake on Rueben Bayles line thence with said line North fifty three poles to a stake a white oak sassafrass sourwood D Bayles' corner thence with his line East 12 poles to two Spanish oaks thence North one hundred and seventeen poles to a red oak thence with McCracken's line West 39 poles to a stake near a white oak thence with another line of said McCracken's North 18 E 61 poles to a

Hornbeam on the other bank of a branch thence down the meanders of the said branch the six following courses and distances N 93 W 15 poles to a stake thence S 72 W 2 poles to a stake, South 5 poles to a stake N 65 W 10 poles to a stake N 16 W 11 poles to a stake N 55 W 21 poles to a stake Henry Bottles corner thence with his line S 22 W 62 poles to a stake near a poplar on a field said Bayles corner then with his line N 52 W 18 poles to the beginning containing two hundred and four acres to which tract or parcel of land we have and do hereby release and relinquish our undivided respective shares in said land for the consideration aforesaid to the said Thomas W. Mercer and his heirs and assigns forever and hereby warrant and defend the same unto the said Thomas against claim or claims of either of us or our heirs forever.

In witness whereof we have hereunto set our hands and seals this 9th day of October, 1828. Attest: E. L. Mathes, Michael Byerly Signed: Thomas Mercer, Rachel Mercer, Samuel McCracken, Alsey McCracken, Abner Mercer, Martha M. Mercer, Elbert F. Mercer." Martha M. Mercer and Elbert Mercer sign and acknowledge the written deed. The following statement was made by Alsey: "We do certify that Alsey McCracken was examined on the signature of the written deed in open court by us and says she done it without fear of her husband and of her own free will." April session 1829. The deed was recorded and registered on the 11th of June 1829.

Samuel and Alice had at least four children: John born 1808; Joseph born in 1810; Margaret in 1813; Henry in 1814 -- there were other children, perhaps a Martha for which no birth dates are available. The same year Henry was born thirty-five-old Samuel enlisted at Jonesboro for service in the War of 1812. He served from 13 November to 18 May 1815.

Samuel's oldest son John married Dicey Oliver in Jonesboro October 22, 1835. Three others, Joseph, Henry and Margaret married three Wood family members, the marriages taking place in neighboring Hawkins County. Margaret married Jesse Wood December 28, 1831; Henry to Rebecca Wood October 25, 1832 and brother Joseph to Sarah Wood the following December. Joseph married a second time to Eliza Mitchell in 1835.

Church Minutes of Washington County recorded the withdrawal of Rebecca, wife of

Henry in the year 1848. It is possible this was done in preparation for the move to Bradley County.

When the 1850 Census was taken Samuel, Alice and three of their children, Henry, Joseph, and Margaret, were enumerated in Bradley County. Samuel and Alice live in the household with son Joseph and his family. Their dwelling is number 155. Henry and Rebecca are at 685 and Margaret and her husband Jesse Wood at 1296. Living near Henry is Reps Mabry at dwelling 693 (Reps daughter Fanny will in the future become Henry's daughter-in-law when she marries son John B). William Griffith is 691. All of Bradley County is described as the 26th SubDivision with Charleston the only town listed separately. The 1860 Census lists these families in the 13th Civil District. (See Bradley County map on page 202.)

It is possible to estimate the location of the McCrackens' households by using the description of land purchased by their neighbor Reps Mabry in 1839 remembering the Census tells us Reps at dwelling 693 is near Henry at dwelling 685. Reps land is located in Range 1, Township 1. He owns two parcels, one in section 27 and the other in 34.

In 1852 he purchased another parcel in Section 34.

On the 12 of June 1851, Samuel went to the Courthouse in Cleveland to make application for bounty land as provided for by the U. S. Congress. The previous September legislation was passed granting Bounty Land to soldiers who served in the War of 1812, as other wars in the past, in payment for their services.

Appearing before the Justice of the Peace, Samuel makes the following statement:

"...personally appeared before me, a Justice of the Peace within and for the County and State aforesaid Samuel McCracken aged 71 years, a resident of Bradley County in the State of Tennessee, who being duly sworn according to law declares that he is the identical Samuel McCracken who was a private in the Company commanded by Captain Bacon in the Regiment of East Tennessee Militia commanded by Col Bailes in the War with Great Britain declared by the United States June 18, 1812. That he was drafted at Jonesborough, Tennessee on or about the first day of November A.D. 1814 for the term of six months and continued in the actual service in said War for the term of six months and more and was honorably discharged at Jonesborough, Tennessee on or about the first of May A.D. 1815. As will appear by the muster rolls of said company. That he received a discharge but let one McKee have said discharge to enable him to draw the pay due to affiant as a soldier thence he cannot present the same. He makes this declaration for the purpose of obtaining the Bounty Land to which he may be entitled under the act granting Bounty Land to certain officers and soldiers who have been engaged in the military service of the United States passed September 28, 1850. Affiant further declares that he has not received nor is not entitled to Bounty Land under any former act of Congress.

Signed Samuel McCracken

A. J. Parker, Justice of the Peace for Bradley County, Tenn.

The following letter was written by J.B. Collins and sent to the Commissioners of Pensions at Washington, D.C. on Samuel's behalf:

19 May 1851: "In his former declaration the applicant stated that he served in

Capt. J. Waddle's Company by a mistake when in fact he served in Captain Bacon's Company as stated in the above. But the name of Capt. Waddle was suggested to his mind at the time of making his former declaration by the fact that he was permitted by his officer to do duty with that Company that he might be in the company of relations who belonged to it. But he states that he was not regularly transferred..." Samuel was granted 80 acres of land, under Warrant 33217, April 1, 1852.

The mention above "...might be in the company of relations..." most probably is a reference to brother Robert who was a private in Captain Jonathan Waddles Company, Regiment commanded by Col. Samuel Bayles. Robert was drafted at Jonesboro, Tennessee for six months on November 1, 1814 and discharged at Jonesboro the last day of April 1815. By 1830 Robert had moved to Rhea County, Tennessee and from there to Madison County, Arkansas where he died in 1855.

March 3, 1855 Congress again enacted legislation granting additional Bounty Land in the same manner. On the 16th of March, Samuel "...personally appeared before me a Justice of the Peace within and for the

County and State aforesaid Samuel McCracken aged 75 years a resident of Bradley County in the State of Tennessee...declares that he is the identical Samuel McCracken commanded by Captain Bacon in the Regiment commanded by Samuel Bailess in the War with Great Britain...he had made application for Bounty Land under the Act of September 28, 1850 and received a land warrant for eighty acres...which he has since legally disposed of and cannot now return. He makes this declaration for the purpose of obtaining additional Bounty Land to which he may be entitled to under the act approved the 3rd day of March 1855." He was granted eighty acres, Warrant No. 48553. This Warrant was mailed to John Hambright at Calhoun, Tennessee. Reproduced on the following pages are various letters and statements contained in the military records of Samuel on file in the National Archives.

HENRY and REBECCA

According to the 1850 Census taken in Bradley County, Henry and Rebecca had the following children: Mary A. (Margaret) 23, James 9, Sarah A. 7, Eliza M. 5, Jesse T. 3. John B. age 18 does not appear with the

pvt. Tenn. Mil.
Cap. Bacon
Col. Baily
En. 13 Nov 14. dis. 18 May 15
War of 12.
3 Mc Lee [illegible]

Land office
22 March 1852
Samuel McCracken
service under Captain
Bacon from 13 November 1814 to 18 May 1815

R Crane
[illegible]

Warrant 33.217
Iss. & sent Apl. 1/52

J. B. Collins Cleveland Tenn.

Vol 95 - 115

From Samuel McCracken's military record War 1812 on file National Archives, Washington D.C.

letter of the 19th of May 51.

In his former declaration the applicant states that he served in Capt. S. Waddle's Company by a mistake when in fact he served in Capt Bacon's Company as stated in the above. But the name of Capt Waddle was suggested to his mind at the time of making his former declaration by the fact that he was permitted by his officer to do duty with that Company that he might be in the Company of relations who belonged to it. But he states that was not regularly transferred. You will therefore please accept this as supplemental to or in lieu of the former declaration

Respectfully
Your obt Servt
J. B. Collins

110562 June 23/51
Samuel McCracken

Commissioner of Pensions
Washington

May 19, 1851 letter sent by Samuel McCracken to Commissioner of Pensions, Washington, D.C.

State of Tennessee
Bradly County }
On this 12th day of June
A.D. one thousand Eight hundred and
fifty one personally appeared before
me a justice of the peace within &
and for the County and State
aforesaid Samuel McCracken
aged 71 years a resident of Bradly County in the State of Tennessee
who being duly sworn according
to law declares that he is the identical Samuel McCracken who
was a private in the Company
commanded by Captain Bacon
in the Regiment of East Tennessee
~~Volunteers~~ commanded by Col
Booth in the War with Great Britain declared by the United States
June 18th 1812 that he was drafted
at Jonesborough Tennessee on
or about the first day of November A D 1814 for the term of six
months and continued in the
actual service in said War for
the term of six months and more
and was honorably discharged at
Jonesborough Tennessee on or
about the first of May A D 1815
as will appear by the muster rolls
of said Company. that he received
a discharge but he [illegible] have
said discharge to enable him to
draw the pay due to affiant

June 12, 1851 letter sent by Samuel McCrack-
en to Commissioner of Pensions, Washington,
D.C.

as a soldier hence he cannot present the same

He makes this declaration for the purpose of obtaining the Bounty land to which he may be entitled under the act granting Bounty Land to certain officers and soldiers who have been engaged in the military service of the United States passed Sept 28th 1850

Affiant further declares that he has not received nor is not entitled to bounty land under any former act of congress

Samuel McBracken

Sworn to and subscribed before me the day and year above written And I hereby certify that I believe the said Samuel McBracken to be the identical man who served as aforesaid and that he is of the age above stated

A. J. Parker
Justice of the peace
for Brady County Iowa

Second page of letter dated June 12, 1851.

State of Tennessee }
Bradley County }
I John H. Robertson Clerk
of the County Court for the County
of Bradley aforesaid do certify that
A. F. Parks Esqr whose name is
signed to the foregoing attestation
as a certificate is and was
then & there [illegible] the time of
a Justice of the Peace within and
for the County aforesaid duly
commissioned and sworn that
his commission is dated the
[illegible] day of [illegible] 18[illegible] and
will expire the [illegible] of [illegible]
1854 [illegible]
In testimony whereof
I have hereunto set my
hand and affixed the
seal of my office at
office in Cleveland
this 12th June 1851
John H. Robertson Clerk

Cleveland Tenn
June 14th 1851
Sir the above declaration of
Samuel McCracken for Bounty
Land is filed as supplemental
to the declaration heretofore filed
by him and which was taken
[illegible] as you notified me by your

Affidavit of John Robertson, Clerk of Bradley County, accompanied Samuel McCracken's letter of June 12, 1851.

State of Tennessee } On this 16th day of March 1855
Bradley County } personally appeared before me
a Justice of the peace within and for the County and State
aforesaid Samuel McCracken aged 75 years a
Resident of Bradley County in the State of Tennessee
who being duly sworn according to law declares
that he is the Identical Samuel McCracken who
was a private in the Company Commanded by
Captain Bacon in the Regiment Commanded by
Samuel Bailiss in the war with Great Britain
declared by the U.S. on the 18th day of June 1812
for the term of six months and continued in
actual service in said war for fourteen Days
and that he has heretofore made application for
Bounty Land under the act of Sept. 28th 1850
and Received a Land warrant for Eighty Acres no.
not Recollected which he has since Legally disposed
of and cannot now return he makes this declaration
for the purpose of obtaining additional Bounty Land
to which he may be entitled to under the act approved
the 3rd day of March 1855 he also Declares that he
has never applyed for nor Received under this or any
other act of Congress any Bounty Land warrant Except
the one above mentioned } Samuel his x mark McCracken

We John Hambright & John S Freeman Residents of this
neighbourhood in the State of Tennessee upon our oaths
declare that the foregoing Declaration was signed and
acknowledged by Samuel McCracken in our presence
and that we believe from the appearance and statements
of the applicant that he is the Identical person
he represents himself to be } John Hambright
John S Freeman

March 16, 1855 communication sent by Samuel McCracken to Commissioner of Pensions, Washington, D.C.

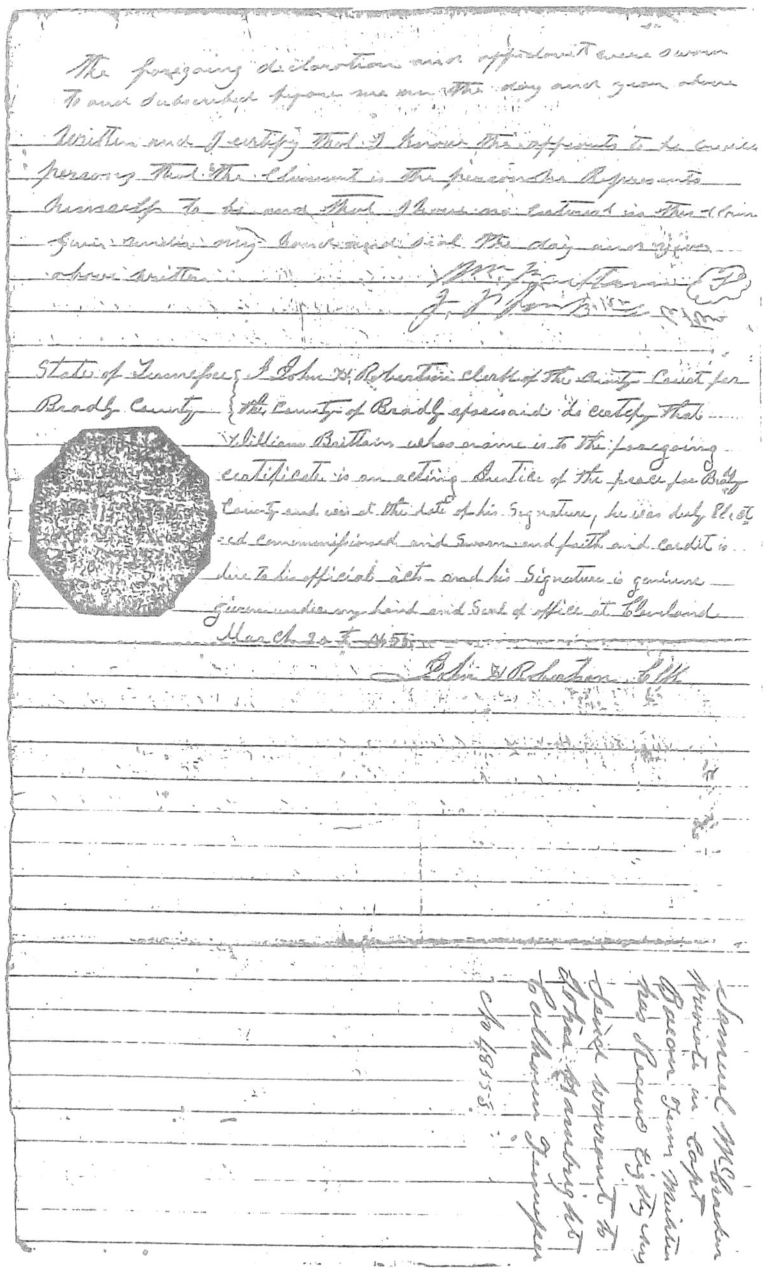

The foregoing declaration and affidavit were sworn to and subscribed before me on the day and year above written and I certify that I know the affiants to be credible persons that the Claimant is the person he represents himself to be and that I have no interest in this claim. Given under my hand and seal the day and year above written

Wm Brittain (Seal)
J. F. [illegible] (Seal)

State of Tennessee } I John H. Robertson Clerk of the County Court for
Bradley County } the County of Bradley aforesaid do certify that William Brittain whose name is to the foregoing certificate is an acting Justice of the peace for Bradley County and was at the date of his Signature, he was duly Elected commissioned and Sworn and faith and credit is due to his official acts and his Signature is genuine. Given under my hand and Seal of office at Cleveland March 20th 1855

John H Robertson Clk

Samuel McCracken
private in Capt
Bacon Tenn Militia
[illegible] Eighty [illegible]
Land Warrant to
John Cambright
Cherokee [illegible]

No 48555

Second page of March 16, 1855 letter.

family. Family tradition placed John B. in this family in that Jesse was known by succeeding generations as Uncle Jess. A newspaper article printed in the early 1930s supports this tradition. In this article Jesse is identified as the uncle of H.L. McCracken necessitating the explanation that Jesse and John B. were brothers.

In addition to the children named in the Census, Henry and Rebecca were the parents of Lucretia J. born in 1838 and Richmond in 1850.

According to Bradley County records, on September 25, 1866 Henry purchased 102 acres of land described "...bounded as follows ...commencing at the corner between Arch Fitzgerald and the said Davis G. Foster on the Spivy line and thence in West direction with said line to the Meigs county line, thence in South direction to a stake thence in South direction to the Willson line thence... being in the Ocoee District first township, second range... being a part of the tenth and eleventh section...." Further description puts it near the Gum Spring Meeting House.

On November 9, 1869 Henry sold 87 acres to Thomas Rains. The land is described as

J. T. McCracken Made 89er Run in Oklahoma

A clipping from an old paper was placed in our hands recently, giving a little of what those went through who made the 89'r run to settle in Oklahoma when the Cherokee strip was opened. J. T McCracken, the principal character, is an uncle of H. L. McCracken of this city.

McCracken and a few neighbors living near Purcell decided to make the run and were directed by some Indians to good land along the Little River just southeast of Oklahoma City. McCracken said the Indians had no way of estimating distance by miles but they gave perfect directions to the land by sand hills.

The group set out from Purcell on April 22, noon, the men mounted on fast horses to go ahead to stake their claims and left the women and children to drive the covered wagons through. Upon arrival the men found the land had already been settled. Some had already marked his land off while some had even started their plowing. The soldiers camping near advised the McCracken party to take the land because the possessors had staked early claim but they were immediately confronted by men with heavy rifles During the argument one fellow noticed the horses of the late arrivals were all sweated so he rushed his horse to the river and poured water over it to give the appearance of a hard ride.

The tired party nearly decided to return home but as their wagons were already in the new land they decided to travel toward Oklahoma City. At Hog Creek they came to a swamp that even the horses could not even cross so the party built one of the first bridges in the new land

On his claim near Mishak McCracken built the first frame house in the state. Later this same party erected the first school house in the state. Mr. McCracken and Mrs. Mary Jo Shirley, both of Oklahoma City, are the only survivors of the original party who made the run.

This story was carried by an Argonia, Kansas newspaper some time in the 1930s.

120 DEED BOOK, BRADLEY COUNTY, TENN.

DATE.	Hour. A.M. P.M.	GRANTOR.	GRANTEE.	Bradley County.	ACRES.	FEES.

State of Tennessee }
Bradley County }
I certify that the foregoing deed was received this day at 10 o'clock A.M. and noted in Book A page 40 and with the Clerks certificate is duly registered in My Office in Book A Pages 119-20 February the 1st 1867
A. B. Foster
Register

DEED
Davis C. Foster
to
Henry McCracken

State of Tennessee }
Bradley County }
September the 25th day 1866 This Indenture Made by and between Davis C. Foster of the first part and Henry McCracken of the second part all of the county and State aforesaid Witnesseth that I Davis C. Foster have this day bargained and sold to the said Henry McCracken a certain tract of land for the consideration of Two hundred Dollars One hundred Dollars paid in hand and the said Henry McCracken has secured his promissory Note for two hundred Dollars Bounded as follows to Wit Commencing at the Corner between Nich Fitzgerald and the said Davis C. Foster On the Spring line and thence in West direction with said line to the Meigs County line thence in South direction with the County line to James Youngs line Corner thence in East direction to a stake thence in South direction to the [illegible] line thence [illegible] direction to a conditional line [illegible] thence in North direction with the top of the Ridge to a Post Oak tree thence east to a popular thence North to a Hickory tree thence east direction to a Rock Corner thence [illegible] line in North direction to the beginning corner supposed to be One hundred and Twenty acres More or less it being in the Ocoee District first Township second Range West of the [illegible] of the tenth and eleventh Districts [illegible] the title of the above described land [illegible] a piece of land [illegible] the Spring Meeting house stands, On which piece [illegible] Marked Out near the center of the South East quarter in the tenth [illegible] which piece of land with its appurtenances is reserved [illegible] and Myself My heirs and Representatives to Warrant the title [illegible] to the said Henry McCracken his heirs or assigns forever in testimony whereof I set my [illegible] the day and year first above written
Davis C. Foster

[illegible]
Thomas H. Gilbreath
Jesse Word

State of Tennessee }
Bradley County }
Personally appeared before Me Samuel Hunt Clerk of the County Court aforesaid Thomas H. Gilbreath and Jesse Word the subscribing Witnesses after being duly sworn depose and say that they are well acquainted with Davis C. Foster the bargainer in the foregoing deed and that he acknowledged the execution of the same for the purpose therein contained, Witness My hand at Office in Cleveland this 2d day December 1867
Samuel Hunt Clerk

Bradley County Deed Book records purchase of 102 acres by Henry McCracken.

February 11th 1870 [illegible]

DEED

Henry McCracken

To

Thomas Rains

State of Tennessee Bradley County

November the 9th day 1869 This Indenture made by and between Henry McCracken of Bradley County and Thomas Rains of Meigs County of the State of Tennessee Witnesseth that I Henry McCracken [illegible] sell and convey to the said Thomas Rains a certain lot of land for the consideration of five hundred Dollars to me paid the receipt of which is hereby acknowledged bounded as follows, beginning at the corner between Lewis Griffin and the said McCracken on the Spring line thence in west direction with said line to [illegible] corner thence south said line to Austin Shipetts line thence with said line to the Wilson line thence East 56 poles to a conditional line on the top of the ridge thence with the top of the ridge to a post oak tree thence East to a [illegible] thence North to a Hickory thence East to the Griffin line thence North with said line to the beginning corner witnessed to be eighty seven acres and a half more or less in the Ocoee District first Township second range west of the basis line being a part of tenth and eleventh section [illegible] and will ever defend the title to the said forever to the said Thomas Rains his heirs or assigns [illegible] Whereof I set my hand and seal the day [illegible]

Witness

[illegible]

Henry McCracken [illegible]

Bradley County Deed Book dated November 9, 1869 describes sale of land.

in the Ocoee District, first township, second range west of the basis line, part of tenth and eleventh section a portion of the original purchase.

Henry and Rebecca loaded up the wagon and moved West. Leaving behind the devastation and ruin of the Civil War and the widow of son John B., Fannie Mabry McCracken with her two little boys, Jackson Leonidas and Henry Love.

In the Township of LeCompton, County of Douglas, Kansas, July 23, 1870 with the post office at Clinton the Census Taker records household number 6: Henry, wife Rebecca and the following children Jane 31, James 29, and Sarah 25. At household number 7 is Jesse and his wife Melinda with children Mary J. eight months, and two of Jesse's siblings, sister Eliza 20, Richmond 18 and one additional child John age 1 who was born in Tennessee suggesting the move from Tennessee to Kansas most probably was after the child's birth in 1869. The 1880 Census reports Jesse and his brother with their families living in Aubrey Township, Johnson County Kansas. Henry and Rebecca do not appear and it is not known when or where they died.

WALTER THOMAS McCRACKEN

1884-1957

Walter Thomas McCracken, prominent pioneer, civic leader and Churchman of Oklahoma City, died at Polyclinic hospital, Oklahoma City, August 24, 1957, at the age of seventy-three years. Funeral services were conducted at the Capitol Hill Methodist church with the Reverend Grady Ross and J. Frank Graham, former pastors, officiating.

Walter McCracken was born March 23, 1884, on the Smith Paul farm near Pauls Valley, Oklahoma. The only son of J. T. McCracken and Malinda Wilson McCracken.[2] His parents with six little daughters made the trip by covered-wagon from Eureka Springs, Arkansas, and settled on the farm in February, 1884, one month before Walter's birth. His father made the run in 1889 and staked a claim southeast of Oklahoma City known as Clear Springs; he returned to his home on the Smith Paul farm for his family, leaving one of the little girls buried in the old Cemetery in Pauls Valley.

Mr. McCracken was born and reared by Christian parents. His father donated an acre of ground for a church but the permanent building was never built. The acre remained virgin soil and while waiting for the church building a brush arbor was erected where church services were held by the Methodist circuit-riders. His father helped build the first school at Clear Springs, Oklahoma, (later called Mishak) where his son and two daughters attended school, Walter finishing the seventh grade.

Ambitious and wanting to go on with his education, he enrolled in the public schools in Oklahoma. Walter was a charter member of the Jeffersonian Debating Society at Irving High School, and had the distinction of being a member of the first graduating class of old "Irving High," having completed his studies under the direct leadership of Judge Edgar S. Vaught, then Superintendent of Oklahoma City schools and now (1958) retired United States District Judge of Western Oklahoma. Later, after continuing his education, Mr. McCracken was principal of public schools at Jones, Choctaw, Harrah and Moore.

On September 1, 1909, Mr. McCracken was united in marriage to Dollie May Brown, daughter of Reverend E. J. Brown, one of the Methodist circuit riders who had served Clear Spring, Sunny Lane and other little Methodist churches in the Methodist Conference of Oklahoma Territory. To this union was born four children: Mildred McCracken Crossley, Oklahoma City; Wilson Walter McCracken, Guthrie; and the twins, Lawrence McCracken, Oklahoma City and Laurene McCracken Needham, Tulsa. On November 30, 1914, Mrs. Mc-

Jesse T. McCracken's son Walter is the subject of this biography reproduced from the 1958 Spring issue of The Chronicles of Oklahoma.

Cracken died at the birth of the twins. Mr. McCracken soon gave up his teaching in the public schools and entered into a new career.

On December 24, 1916, he was united in marriage to Miss Maude Hill, who was also a public school teacher. Three children blessed this union. Edmond Clarence, Thomas Creal and Donald Ray. Edmond and Thomas died in infancy. Donald lives in Oklahoma City.

Mr. McCracken was Superintendent of Sunny Lane Cemetery for more than a quarter of a century. In his capacity as superintendent and presiding over burials, he really lived the philosophy of Sam Foss: "Let me live by the side of the road and be a friend to man." His church, Capitol Hill Methodist, took priority. He ably served in every capacity in the Church open to a layman, twice elected delegate from the Oklahoma Methodist Conference to represent the State at the Methodist Jurisdictional Conference.

For many years, he was an active member of the Capitol Hill Chamber of Commerce, serving in 1933 as president. His advice and counsel were especially valuable to the group when it staged the big 89'er parade every year. He was in charge of the 89'er section of the parade, and rounded up the old timers and the old-time pieces such as surreys, chuck-wagons, buggies and the hearse. He was also the Master of Ceremony at the Chamber's annual dinner for 89'ers whose ranks diminished every year.

On April 23, ~~1958~~ 1957, at the 89'er Day observance by the Chamber of Commerce, Mr. McCracken was honored for the work he had done in this community. His pastor, Dr. Alva R. Hutchinson, was chosen to pay tribute to Walter McCracken, the mutual friend of all present. He received many words of praise and gifts at this meeting. He was also an honorary member of the Capitol Hill Junior Chamber of Commerce.

The McCrackens lived in the house at the Sunny Lane Cemetery, of which he was in charge until just a few months before his passing. During his last illness, the family moved back to their home in Capitol Hill. He was laid to rest in Sunny Lane Cemetery in the McCracken family plot. Walter Thomas McCracken has left his host of friends with memories of a good life well spent for us and the future generations to observe and follow. Besides his widow, children and grandchildren, he leaves three sisters, Mrs. Jessie Hogan, Mrs. Mary Jane Shirley and Mrs. Frank Trosper all of Oklahoma City.

—E. M. Sellers

Capitol Hill Beacon
Oklahoma City

Here's what the County Clerk gave me pertaining to the records about the J. T. McCracken homestead. I prepared a map showing the juxtaposition of Tinker Field.

Talked with Almire Hogan, 528 S. W. 26, a daughter of the Carpenter shown on the plat. She's a mine of information. Recalls that McCracken and Braden 'traded places' at an early day altho records presently at the courthouse don't show it. Said that there were three 'living' 'springs' in the area, which showed why the settlers chose the land. Her father did not make the run, she said, but bought the right to the quarter-section for $175. A Mr. Berge, who owned the land where Clear Springs school was located, bought out someone for a horse and saddle, and later proved up and got the patent in his name. Mrs. Hogan remembers four territorial schools in Boone Township as being Clear Springs, Round Top, Harmony and Log (or Boston).

QUARTER SECTIONS BORDERING AND CORNERING NE¼ of Section, Township 11 North, Range 2 West showing names of persons to whom U. S. Government issued Homestead Patents and Dates of same.[1]

JOHN B. and FANNY

At the time of John B.'s enlistment in the Union Army he lived with his wife and young sons near Charleston, Tennessee. He married Fannie Mabry, daughter of Reps, on October 29, 1857. Their first child was a boy William, who died before the age of five. Their second son Jackson Leonidas, was born September 25, 1858 followed by Henry Love on April 5, 1860.

Many years later, an elderly Henry remembered this experience that occurred when he was a three year-old "...father and mother walked slowly down the road together... then they parted... mother came back alone..."

At its beginning the 8th Tennessee Calvary Regiment was part of the 5th East Tennessee Calvary. The company records show that John B. was on the muster roll when the regiment was organized at Indianapolis, Indiana June 11, 1863. Francis McFall was captain of Company A, 28 year-old John's Company.

On June 30, the 5th Calvary was reported in the 2nd Brigade, 4th Division, Twenty-third Army Corps, Department of the Ohio. On July 5, 1863, at the time of

Brigadier General John H. Morgan's raid into Ohio, Major General George L. Hartsuff, Commanding at Lexington, Kentucky reported: "The 5th Tennessee Calvary have no sabers or pistols. Can they be sent immediately, about 300 each?" On July 29, at the time of Colonel John S. Scott's raid into Kentucky with a brigade of Confederate Calvary, McFall's Company and others left Lexington as part of the troops under Colonel Sanders and took part in the fighting which resulted in Scott's repulse and withdrawal into Tennessee. July 31 they were again reported in the 2nd brigade.

August 6, 1863... the 2nd Brigade was ordered to rendezvous at Glasgow, Kentucky. Those men fit to march from the four companies under Major Sawyers arrived at Glasgow on August 14; at Celina, Tennessee, August 21; those men unfit to march when this battalion left for Glasgow, remained at Camp Nelson (Ky.) under Captain McFall of Company A. On August 24, Colonel DeCourcy, writing from Crab Orchard, Kentucky reported: "The 8th Tennessee Calvary will probably be here tonight. The Calvary and infantry are principally composed of raw, undisciplined troops; "skirmished near Montgomery, Tennessee August 30; as a part of Maj. General Burnside's forces, they entered Knoxville September 1, 1863. They arrived at Cumberland Gap September 8, where they were joined by the men who had been left with Captain McFall at Camp Nelson; took part in the operation which resulted in the capture of Cumberland Gap on September 9; and joined Sawyers' battalion at Greeneville, Tennessee on September 14, 1863. They were placed in Colonel Foster's 4th Brigade.

The regiment was reorganized from the 5th East Tennessee Calvary to the 8th Tennessee Calvary on August 31, 1863 consisting of four companies A, B, C and E under Major John M. Sawyers. The report from Colonel DeCourcy quoted above makes reference to this change in the first sentence "The 8th Tennessee Calvary..."

September 17, 1863 -- a detachment from the regiment under Captain McFall and Kenner were sent on an expedition to attempt to cut the East Tennessee and Virginia Railroad near Carter's Depot. It returned to Greeneville September 25 after some skirmishing with the Confederates near Jonesboro. The remainder of the regiment was engaged for about four hours at Halls Ford on the Watau-

KNOXVILLE, TENN.,
September 13, 1863.

Colonel FOSTER,
Greeneville, Tenn.:

Please send me by telegraph a full and detailed report of the condition of affairs with you. Keep the country well scouted to the front and avoid any possibility of surprise. It is reported that the enemy are shipping a large body of troops from Virginia to Bristol. The Fourteenth Illinois Cavalry and the Eighth Tennessee (formerly the Fifth) will report to you to-day, if they have not already done so. Morristown should be kept secure. Mail train coming by way of Cumberland Gap. Make no general movement till I have consulted with you, as other movements are pending having reference to the same end.

A. E. BURNSIDE,
Major-General.

Official Records - This report places John B. McCracken's Eighth Tennessee enroute to Greeneville.

ga River, near Blountville, on September 22 and returned to Greeneville on September 25. From Greenville the regiment moved to Knoxville and was a participant in several expeditions out of Knoxville during October, including an engagement at Rheatown on October 11, 1863. On October 29, the regiment went into camp at Henderson's Station near Greeneville. Here, on November 2, 1863, Brig. General Shackelford advised General Burnside: "I would suggest that the horses belonging to the 8th Tennessee Regiment, about 250, be turned over to one of the brigades; and that the regiment, or that part of it that is left (for want of field officers a large number have deserted and absented themselves from the regiment and the balance are demoralized and inefficient) be sent to Morristown or some other point and be placed in camp of instruction under efficient field officers." The regiment was dismounted on November 2 and sent by rail to Knoxville, where it remained on duty during the siege of Knoxville by Confederate General Longstreet. During this time the regiment was commanded by Major Sawyers. On December 15 it left Knoxville and marched to Camp Nelson, Kentucky, in charge of prisoners captured during the siege of Knoxville. It arrived at Camp Nelson December 27, after marching 185 miles. The regiment was transferred to Nashville during January 1864, where on February 6, 1864, by order of Governor Andrew Johnson, they were consolidated with the 10th East Tennessee. The consolidated regiment bore the name of the 8th Tennessee Calvary Regiment.

John's military record indicates that he died in Knoxville February 15, 1864. It is not known whether he was returned from Nashville or had perhaps been ill and remained at Knoxville until the time of his death.

Many Union soldiers are buried in the Knoxville National Cemetery. More than 1500 graves are unidentified. There are three identified graves of men from the 8th Calvary; G. P. Wilson of Company M, who died one day prior to John on February 10. He was originally buried at Columbus, Tennessee and was sometime later moved to the Knoxville Cemetery; John Conner of Company G, who died April 7, 1865 at Wytheville, Virginia; Newton Howard of Company M, died December 20, 1864 at Moccasin Gap, Virginia.

Widow's Application for Army Pension.

This Army Pension Declaration must be executed before a Judge or Clerk of a Court of Record, and if before the Judge, the Clerk thereof will certify and Judge's official capacity and signature, and attest the same under the seal of the Court. A Justice of the Peace must not authenticate this paper. If he does the work is utterly useless, and must be all done over again before a Judge or Clerk of a Court of Record, as first stated.

State of Tennessee County of Bradley SS.

On this 22nd day of September, A. D. 1865, personally appeared before me (1) Joseph H. Davis Clerk of the (2) County Court, a Court of Record, within and for the County and State aforesaid, Mrs. Fanny M. McCracken a resident of the (3) County of Bradley in the State of Tennessee, aged 30 years, who, being first duly sworn according to law, doth on her oath make the following declaration, in order to obtain the benefit of the provision made by the act of Congress approved July 14, 1862: That she is the widow of John B. McCracken deceased, who was a Private in company (A) commanded by Capt. Mansfield in the 8th regiment of (4) Tennessee Cavalry commanded by Col. Capp in the war of 1861, and who died (5) whilst in the service aforesaid, at Knoxville in the State of Tennessee on or about the 15th day of February A. D. 1864, from (6) Small Pox incurred in the service aforesaid and whilst in the line of his duty, (7)

She further declares that she was married to the said John B McCracken on the 29 day of October in the year 1857: that her husband the aforesaid John B McCracken died on the day above mentioned, and that she (8) has Remained a widow Ever since that Period

as will more fully appear by reference to the proof herewith accompanying or to be hereafter filed.

She also declares that she has not, in any manner, been engaged in, or aided or abetted, the rebellion in the United States. She appoints John Hambright of Charleston Bradley County, Tenn, her attorney with full power of substitution and revocation in her said behalf, and authorizes him to receive the Pension Certificate when issued. Her Post Office is at Charleston in the County of Bradley in the State of Tennessee That her domicile or place of abode is (9) five miles from Charleston on or near the wagon Road leading to Georgetown She says she has had Two Children by her said husband John That (10) B. McCracken (to wit) Jackson L McCracken born September 25th 1858 Henry L McCracken born 5th day of April 1860 She says there is no Public Record of her marriage for Reason the Records are all Burned up in Cleveland where the marriage License were destroyed to the County seat when of this county

If applicant makes her mark, let two persons who can write their names attest her signature, the officer administering the oath must not be one of the attesting parties.

ATTEST:
J. W. Hicks
A. P. Miller

Fanny M her X mark McCracken Applicant.

Sworn to, subscribed and acknowledged before me, the day and year first above written, and also personally appeared Samuel McCracken and Elizabeth McCracken residents of the (3) County of Bradley in the State of Tennessee persons whom I certify to be respectable and entitled to credit, and who, being by me duly sworn, say that they were present and saw Mrs. Fanny M McCracken (11) make her (12) mark to the foregoing declaration; and they further swear that they have every reason to believe, from the appearance of the applicant and their acquaintance with her, that she is the identical person she represents herself to be, and that they have no interest in the prosecution of this claim.

If the witnesses, or either of them, make their mark, let two persons who can write their names attest the signature. The officer administering the oath must not be one of the attesting parties.

ATTEST:
J. W. Hicks
A. P. Miller

Two witnesses.
Samuel his X mark McCracken
Elizabeth her X mark McCracken

Sworn to and subscribed before me, this 22nd day of September, A. D. 1865

John B. McCracken's military record on file at the National Archives, Washington, D.C.

Widow's Declaration for Increase of Pension.

State of Tennessee,
Bradley County. } ss.

ON THIS 29 day of April, 1867, before me, Joseph H. Davis, Clerk of the County Court, in and for the County and State above named, personally appeared Mrs. Fanny M. McCracken, aged 32 years, who being duly sworn according to law, declares that her Post Office address is Charleston, in the county of Bradley and State of Tennessee, that she is the widow of John B. McCracken formerly in the service of the United States, and that by reason of the service and death of her said husband, she is a pensioner of the United States on the roll of the Knoxville Tennessee Agency at $ Eight per month—as will appear by her pension certificate herewith presented.

She further states that she has now living the following named children, under the age of sixteen years; the said children being also the children of her late husband named above, and are of the ages respectively named:

Jackson L McCracken was born Sept. 25th 1858
Henry L. McCracken was born April 5th 1860

That the soldier left no children by any former marriage.

She avers that she has not married since the death of her husband, nor abandoned the support of any one of their children under sixteen years of age, nor permitted any one for whom increase is claimed to be adopted by any person or persons, and that they are the only legitimate children of herself and her deceased husband now living.

She makes this declaration for the purpose of obtaining the increased pension to which she is entitled under the provisions of the Act approved July 25th, 1866, and hereby constitutes and appoints John Hambright her Attorney to prosecute her claim and procure her pension certificates, and revokes and countermands all former authority that may have been given for the above specified purpose.

Witnesses: S R Routh
David Norrene

Fanny M. her + mark McCracken

Sworn to, subscribed and acknowledged before me, and also personally appeared Sary J. Norman, a resident of The County of Bradley, and Michola Routh a resident of The County of Bradley, persons whom I certify to be respectable and entitled to credit, who, being duly sworn according to law, declare that they are personally acquainted with Mrs. Fanny M McCracken, widow of John B McCracken, who has made the foregoing declaration, and know that she is in receipt of a pension as stated in said declaration, and that her statement of the names and ages of her children are true. That their knowledge of her identity as the pensioner named, and of the names and ages of her children is derived from personal knowlege by being present at Their Births and been well acquainted with Them Ever since and the above are Their true names and ages

John B. McCracken's military record on file at the National Archives, Washington, D.C.

Parole Proof of Marriage.

JOINT AFFIDAVIT.

We, Eliza R. Brewster and Sarah P. Norman residents of the County of Bradley in the State of Tennessee upon our oaths declare that we are personally well acquainted with Mrs Fanny M McCracken widow of John B McCracken deceased, and who is a resident of the County of Bradley in the State of Tennessee and who by virtue of the military services of her said husband, the said John B McCracken deceased, is now applying for Army Pension We were likewise personally well acquainted with the said John B McCracken now deceased, which fact we know by general repute, and his said wife, the said Fanny M McCracken during the lifetime of the former, and know that they lived together as husband and wife, and to be so reputed, without any question to the contrary. We also further state, that we were present at the marriage of the above named John B McCracken with the said Mrs Fanny M McCracken whose name before her said marriage was Fanny M Mabry That we were eye-witnesses to said marriage, and saw the same take place. That it occurred in the County of Bradley in the State of Tennessee on or about the 29th day of October A.D. 1857 That Gilmore Randolph a Minister of The Gospel administered the rites of marriage between said parties, and pronounced them man and wife. That we make this affidavit as a simple act of justice, and nothing further, having no interest in so doing whatsoever. They further swear that the Public Record of marriages which is kept in this State at the county seat was burnt up at Cleveland the county seat of Bradley county during the late war. That the said Fanny M McCracken has a family Record which shows the above facts

Sarah P. Norman, her mark

Eliza R. Brewster

Attest: John P Campbell

Chas. A. Cath Hughes

If the witnesses, or either of them, make their mark, let two persons who can write sign their names as witnesses to the mark. The officer administering the oaths must not be one of the attesting parties.

Two Witnesses.

wrongfully signed
Fanny M McCracken, her mark

Sworn to and subscribed before me, on this 7th day of June 1866 A. D. 18 : and I hereby certify, that I know the affiants to be credible persons; that the foregoing affidavit was read over and fully explained to, and understood by them, before the signing and execution thereof, and that I have no interest in this matter.

Wm. I. Campbell
Justice of the Peace in and for the County of Bradley
State of Tennessee

John B. and Fannie nee Mabry McCracken's marriage affidavit.

John was survived by his widow Fannie and two sons. In her pension application dated September 22, 1865, Fannie states that her domicile is "...five miles from Charleston on or near the wagon road leading to Georgetown." John's parents purchased land bordering on Meigs County in 1866. Inasmuch as Georgetown is located partially in Bradley and partially in Meigs the description of Fanny's residence and the holdings of her in-laws suggest they may have lived near each other.

On August 11, 1886 Fannie and son Henry purchased fourteen and one-half acres. This land is described as "...out of the Northwest quarter of Section 21, range 1, East of the basis line Ocoee District..." The following transcription is from Bradley County Court Records: "Simm Mee and Wife to Fanny and H. L. McCracken: For and in consideration of the sum of ninety-five dollars cash in hand paid the receipt of which is hereby acknowledged, we Simm Mee and wife Jane Mee have this day bargained, sold and by these presents do hereby transfer and convey unto Fanny M. McCracken and H. L. McCracken equally the following piece or parcel of land to wit 14 and 1/2 acres out of the northwest quarter of section 21 range one east of the base in the Ocoee District, Bradley County... The southeast corner of the land transferred from Simm Mee to H. B. Hennegar thence south with the said east side of said H. B. Henegar land 20 poles. ...to have and to hold to the said McCrackens and assigns forever warrant and defend the title of said real estate to the said McCracken their heirs and assigns against the claims of all persons whatsoever. We further covenant with the said McCracken that we are lawfully... to convey the land given under our hand and seal this August 11, 1886."

HENRY and SALLY

Twenty-seven-year-old Henry married Sally McCullough Rose May 2, 1883. They were the parents of nine children: Charley 1886; H. Bartley 1891; Isham 1893; Sally May 1896; Anna Bell 1898; and four others; only three survived childhood.

In 1902, Henry L. with his wife and children: Anna Bell, Isham and May moved to Kansas and settled near Argonia.

SERVICES FOR H. L. McCRACKEN

Funeral services for H. L. McCracken were held at the Pilgrim Holiness church Friday, September 1, at 5:00 p. m., in charge of Rev. Wayne R. Plummer.

Misses Faye and Alethea Pearce sang "Safe In The Arms of Jesus", "This World Is Not My Home", and "On That Morrow". They were accompanied by Mrs. Argus Pearce.

Pall bearers were Louis Isgrigg, Earl Isgrigg, Willie Pearce, Forrest Pearce, Hubert Phillips, and Erby Phillips.

Interment was in the Argonia cemetery in charge of the Argonia Undertaking Co.

Henry Love McCracken was born near Charleston, Tennessee, April 5, 1860 and departed this life August 30, 1939 at the age of 79 years, 4 months, and 25 days.

He was united in marriage to Miss Sally McCullough Rose, May 2, 1883. To this union nine children were born, six of whom preceded him in death. In 1902 Mr. McCracken, with his wife and three children, came to Kansas and settled near Argonia, living for many years in what is known as the Frog Pond community.

On May 2, 1933, just eight days before his wife's death, he and Mrs. McCracken celebrated their Golden Wedding anniversary. After her death, he left the farm, finally moving into Argonia where he lived until a short time before his death at the Wellington hospital.

A touching incident occurred in the early life of Mr. McCracken at about the age of three years when his father left to be a soldier in the Union army during the Civil War. He remembered his father and mother walking slowly down the road together. Then they parted--the mother coming back alone--the father never to return.

Mr. McCracken is survived by three children, Rev. D. I. McCracken of Milroy, Pa., Mrs. May Richardson of San Angelo, Texas, and Mrs. Anna Belle McDaniel of Argonia; three grandchildren, Della Ray and Louis McDaniel and Agallia McCracken, other relatives, and a host of friends.

Mr. McCracken was a man of his word, a good neighbor, a loving father, and a friend to all. His passing was made easier by the hope he had of seeing little Lee McDaniel, a grandson who preceded him in death nearly a year. Lee was always a source of joy to him, bringing sunshine and cheer in the last years of his life.

Among Mr. McCracken's last sayings was the assurance to his family that he was ready to go.

Obituary-McCracken

Sally McCullough Rose, daughter of Dowell and Jane Rose, was born March 20, 1863, near Berryville, Benton Co., Arkansas, and departed this life May 10, 1933, aged 70 years, 1 month and 20 days.

One week before her birth her father was called to the Civil war, never to return. Later with her mother she moved to Charleston, Tenn., where she grew to womanhood. She was united in marriage to Henry Love McCracken, May 2, 1883. To this union nine children were born, six of whom preceded her in death. In 1902, she with her husband and three children, came to Kansas and settled near Argonia. With the exception of two years which the family spent in Comanche, Okla., she spent the remaining years of her life in what is known as the Frog Pond community, where she has drawn to herself a large circle of friends. In her early wedded life she was converted at Union Grove church, near Charleston, Tenn., and became a member of the Methodist church. October 12, 1907, her membership was transferred to the Argonia Methodist church. She was active in the Christian work of her community until in latter years when she became an invalid and unable to attend services. While not privileged to attend she always manifest a keen interest in the Lord's work. And though she was not present in the Sunday school and church services held near her home the influence of her prayers was a blessing and inspiration to the workers. She was a loyal neighbor, a true friend and her affliction seemed to increase her faith and draw her nearer her Master. She became a wise counselor, an understanding consoler and many came to know the blessing of strength and encouragement her words could give. She will be missed from her chair by the window more than words can tell. One of her last enjoyments was the celebrating of her Golden Wedding anniversary with her husband, daughters, grandchildren and a few friends.

Those left to mourn her going are her faithful husband, one son David Isam of Clinton, Penn. two daughters, May Richardson of Corsicana, Texas, Anna Belle McDaniel who, with her family, lived in the home and tenderly cared for her mother during the years of her affliction, three grandchildren Della Ray and Louis McDaniel and Agalia McCracken, one brother W. J. Sears Comanche, Okla., a sister Mrs L B Ruth of Port Lavaca, Texas, a host of other relatives and friends.

Funeral services were conducted at the Friends church with Rev. Bertha Sumpter in charge assisted by Rev. H. E. Stipe and Rev. L. B. Brady. The sermon text was "Thy Servant will go a Little Way Over Jordon with the King." Ruth and Faye Pearce sang "On the Morrow," Lauren Martin, John Isgrigg, Everett Bland and Tom Baird sang "Shall We Gather at the River," and "When They Ring Those Golden Bells," accompanied by Mrs. Ruth VanWinkle. Pall bearers were Erby and Hubert Phillips, Earl and Louis Isgrigg, Boyd Stephens and Forrest Pearce. The body was laid to rest in the Argonia cemetery. Argonia [illegible]

H. L. and Sally McCracken obituaries.

JACKSON and NANCY

Nancy Darthula Hampton and Jackson Leonidas McCracken were married September 5, 1886 in Bradley County, Tennessee.

Three years after their marriage the McCrackens purchased land in the first Civil District of Bradley County. This purchase is followed in 1908, when they enlarge their farm by thirty-two additional acres. (Bradley County Court records of both transactions are reproduced on pages 284 and 285.)

The court records contains in addition to the land purchase, Jackson's entry into political life. In 1896 he was appointed Road Commissioner for the First District "...be it ordered by the Court that Road Commissioners for the several road districts of Bradley County, Tennessee be elected. ballot was had and Jack McCracken receiving a majority of the votes of the court, the chairman announced that Jack McCracken was duly elected Road Commissioner of the First Road District of Bradley County Tennessee."

Nancy and Jack had nine children born between the years of 1887 and 1904. Three of the children died before the age of five, James Bartley, Martha May, and Rufus Pledger the twin of Betty. The other children were in order of their births: Fanny Jane (1887); Mary Magdalene (1889); Henry J. (1893); Bertha (1899); Betty Jo (1901); and David (1904).

Jack and Nancy were residents of Dare, according to their testimony given on August 16, 1897 when they appeared at the Bradley County Courthouse in Cleveland on behalf of Nancy's mother Jane. This transcription is from a Bradley County Deed Book, August 1897: " Jane Hampton et al To John S. Long-with. This indenture made and entered into by and between Jane Hampton widow James Hampton, Jackson L. McCracken and wife Nancy McCracken heirs at law of Nancy and James Hampton of the first part and J.S.Longwith of the second all of Dare, Bradley County Tennessee. Witnesseth; that for and in consideration of the sum of $20.00 twenty dollars in hand paid by the said J.S. Long-with the receipt whereof is hereby acknowl-edged, we the parties of the first part have this day bargained and sold and by the presents do bargain sell and convey unto J. S. Longwith his heirs and assigns the fol-lowing tract or parcel of land situated and lying in the first civil district of Bradley County, Tennessee, described and bounded as

D B & D.

J. L. Lawson + wife
To
J. L. McCrackin

Know all Men by these presents that I J. L. Lawson and wife in Consideration of (250.00) Two hundred and fifty dollars Cash in hand paid the receipt of which is hereby acknowledged. do Sell. deed. + transfer and Convey in fee Simple unto J. L. McCracken and his heirs forever the following land to wit (40) forty acres more or less in the 1st Civil district of Bradley County Tenn. and bounded on the North by Chillcutt & Swafford. East by M. Lawson. South by Thomas Lawson. West by Chillcutt. We warrant that the above land is not encumbered and that we have a good and legal right to Convey the same and we waive all right to homestead or dower in and to the above described land. In Witness Whereof we hereunto Subscribe our names this Oct. 19" 1889

J. L. Lawson.
Rebecca her X mark Lawson.

State of Tennessee
Bradley County.

Personally appeared before me F. A. Frazier Clerk of the County Court of Said County, the within named J. L. Lawson and wife Rebecca Lawson the bargainors, with whom I am personally acquainted. and acknowledged that they executed the within instrument for the purpose therein expressed. And Rebecca Lawson wife of the Said J. L. Lawson having personally appeared before me privately and apart from her husband. the Said Rebecca Lawson acknowledged the execution of the said instrument to have been done by her freely Voluntarily and understandingly without Compulsion or Constraint from her said husband and for the purpose therein expressed.

Witness F. A. Frazier Clerk of Said Court at office this 19 day of October 1889

Deed Book, Bradley County records purchase by Jackson L. McCracken in 1st Civil District, of 40 acres, October 19, 1889.

D E E D

T. A. Lawson & E. L. Gibson To J. L. McCracken

For and in Consideration of the Sum of two hundred and Forty Dollars, to be paid as follows, five promissory notes, to wit one note for Forty eight dollars due the 11 - Dec. 1909. One note for Fortyeight dollars dew 11 Dec. 1910. one note for Fortyeight dollars dew 11. Dec. 1911. one note for Fortyeight dollars dew 11 Dec. 1912. And one note for Fortyeight dollars dew 11 Dec. 19-13. Said notes are given for the following described real estate and to secure the payment of said note when the same becomes dew with interest and is a spesific lein on said real estate, and a failure to pay eny one of said notes at maturity shall operate to render the whole indetness due and collectible and the lin infars ahell. We T. A. Lawson, and E. L. Gibson have this day bargand sold transferd and conveyd to J. L. McCracken, a certain tract of real estate it all lying in the first Civil District of Bradley County Tennessee, and is bounded as follows. on the North by F. G. Pearce, on West by S. F. Stevison on the South by J. L. McCracken and East by Mrs. N. J. Lawson, Containing 32 acers to have and to hold for ever unto the said J. L. McCracken in fee simple and we covnant with said J. L. McCracken that we are lawfuly possest of said real estate and have a perfect and legal right to sell and convey the same and said real estate is unincumbered, and we further covnant to for-ever warrent and defend forever, the titel to said real estate against the lawfull claims of all persons whomsoever. In testamony where unto we subscribe our names this 11. Dec. 1908

E. L. Gibson.
Nettie Gibson
T. A. Lawson.
Sarh Lawson.

State of Tennessee } Bradley County. } Personaly appeared before me F. M. Rawlty a Notary Public for Bradley County Tennessee T. A. Lawson and E. L. Gibson The within named bargnors with whom I am personaly acquainted who acknowledg the exection of the within deed and for the purposes thaire in expresed And allso appeared before me Sarah Lawson and Nettie Gibson Wives of T. A. Lawson & E. L. Gibson privatly and a parte from thair said husbands T. A. Lawson & E. L. Gibson who acknowledg that the execu-

Deed Book, Bradley County entry for 32 acres in the 1st Civil District purchased by Jackson McCracken on December 11, 1908.

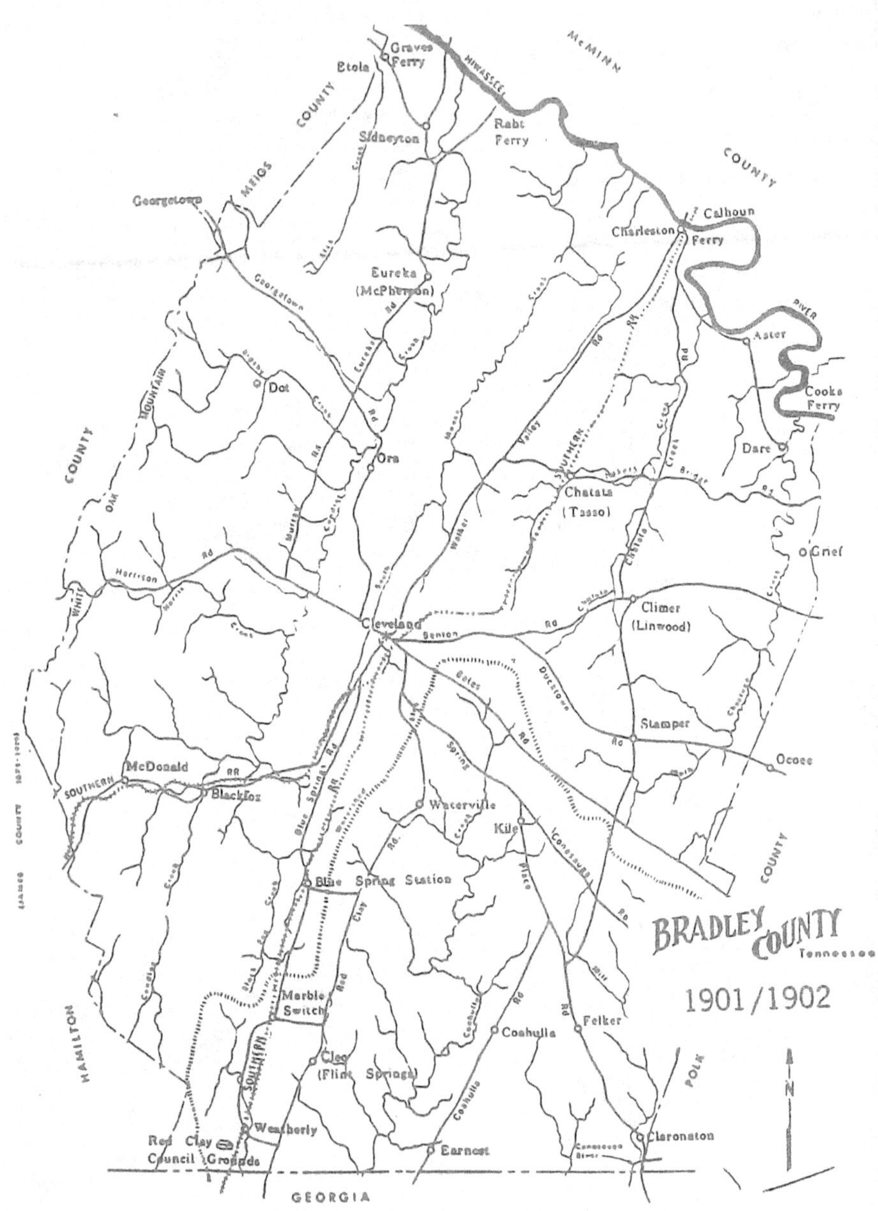

During 1897 Jackson and Nancy McCracken lived at Dare located in northeast portion of county.

follows to wit being a child's part one twelfth (12) of the 55 fifty-five acres of land homestead of Reuben and Tabitha Long-with and bounded by Hambright heirs on the west by W.A. Denton on the East, by Workman and Moore on the North, and by J. S. Long-with on the South. Said boundary of land said to contain (55) fifty-five acres more or less of which this deed is to convey a one-twelth part and interest we have in said lands estate of Reuben and Tabitha Longwith deceased. The property where the parties died. And we convenant with J.S. Longwith that we are lawful heirs of Reuben and Tabitha Longwith and Jane Hampton and that we have lawful right to sell and convey the said land or child's part in said estate together with all appurtenances thereunto belonging mineral and mineral substances. That we the parties of the first part bind our selves heirs and assigns to forever warrant and defend the title to the one-twelfth (12) part of said described tract or parcel of land against the lawful claims of all persons whomsoever, and that we have a just right to convey the same unincumbered in fee simple. Signed sealed and delivered in presence of attesting witnesses - August

16, 1897." Signed Jane Hampton, and J. L. McCracken

W. F. Duncan, Notary Public makes the following statement: "Personally appeared before me a Notary Public in and for County and State, Jane Hampton, Jackson McCracken and wife Nancy McCracken bargainors with whom we are personally acquainted and acknowledge that they signed executed the within instrument deed for the purposes therein expressed Jane Hampton having said division or part of land from her father's estate and being a widow executes this deed with her children. Also Jackson L. McCracken, son-in-law of Jane Hampton acknowledged that he executed the within deed for purposes therein expressed. Also personally appeared before me Nancy McCracken wife of Jackson McCracken separate and apart from her said husband and acknowledged that she executed the within deed for purposes therein expressed freely voluntarily and knowingly without force, restraint or persuasion from her said husband or any one else. That she and her husband Jackson L. McCracken joins with our mother and sign this deed with our mother because she is partially demented to make a good and lawful deed.."

From the Register T. M. Caldwell: "I certify that the foregoing deed was received this day at 11:30 a.m. and noted in book B page 51 and with the accompanying certificate is duly registered in my office in Deed Book T pages 393-394 this September 16th 1901.

The 1900 Census taken in June, lists living in the household with Jackson and Nancy, their four children: Fanny Jane 12, Mary Magdalene 10, Henry James 6 and baby Bertha who is six months. In addition to the children, Jackson's mother and Nancy's mother are included in the listing. Fanny Mabry McCracken born April 5, 1834, gives her age as 66 years. Nancy Jane Longwith Hampton, born in 1832, gives her age as 68 years. Both women died the following year, Fanny on March 13 and Nancy Jane on October 10, 1901.

In 1910 at the time of the Census, Jackson is 51 and Nancy 50 years of age. Fannie now 22, is still in the household as is Mary 20, Henry 16, Bertha 11, Bettie 9 and David 5. Henry is working as a farm laborer and is attending school as are Mary, Bertha, Bettie and David.

Jack and Nancy lived in a log cabin that contained just two rooms and a kitchen.

Their farm produced food for the table and livestock as well as income for store bought goods. The Old Gold School near Union Grove was the closest elementary school and several of the children appear in early pictures of the student body. An employment record for Betty states she attended the Polk County High School, at Benton. Four of their children, Fannie, Mary, Henry and Betty became school teachers. Fannie's and Henry's graduation picture appears in the photo section, however the school has not been identified. Henry, fluent in Latin taught the langugage to high school classes. His teaching career ended when he became hearing impaired during his military service in World War I. Betty graduated from State Teachers College at Johnson City, Tennessee in July of 1925. Mary's college record has not been found.

On April 20, 1934 Jackson, who had lived in Bradley County all his life, died. He was survived by his wife and six adult children: Fannie, Henry, Mary, Bertha, Betty, Henry, and David.

In the early forties Nancy went to live with her oldest daughter Fannie, where she died in 1946. Nancy and Jackson long time members of the Union Grove Methodist Church are buried in the church's cemetery along with several other family members and relatives.

The family farm was run by son David until his death April 15, 1948 when he was tragically killed in a mill accident. McCracken descendants continue to live on the farm.

CHAPTER 15

THE WELLS

HENRY and ANNA

Henry Wells, the father of Gemima, is entered on the tax rolls of Madison County, Kentucky in the year 1811. He is assessed tax for seventy-five acres of land on Muddy Creek and two horses. The Wells family are neighbors of the William Hampton family. Four years after this tax record was made in 1815, daughter Gemima married William's son James. Henry died in the year 1822.

Sometime after Henry's death the following inventory was recorded in the County court. The three page list of household items, farming tools and livestock gives a very interesting look into the life of the Wells' household. However it is difficult to read, therefore some illegible entries have been omitted.

"Pursuant to the order of the Madison County Court at their October term 1822 with the commissioners appointed by said court met on the premises of Henry Wells dec'd. on the ...and after being sworn did inventory and appraise the estate of the dec'd as follows to wit:

one cupboard	15.00
one set cups and saucers and cream mug two wine glasses	1.50
one quart bottle and pint cup and coffee pot and pt bottle	1.00
five plates, dish and 2 bowls and 1 pitcher of earthern ware	2.50
eleven plates, 1 dish of pewter 7 spoons 8 knives and forks	8.00
one funnel has two prongs and tumbler and four tin cups	1.25
one looking glass and water (?)	2.50
six chairs and dining table	3.00
one big wheel and little wheel	4.00
one wheel	3.00
one bedstead and furniture	25.00
one do do	20.00
one do do	25.00
one bureau	12.00
one... and iron square	3.00
two pols one oven ...one skillet two pair hooks	8.50
one kettle one oven and ...	5.00

two flat irons two pails and 3...	2.75
one jar and old drawing knife	
two augurs and...	1.50
two hogshead and ...meal...	3.50
one man's saddle	3.00
one pair...(this may be guns)	
two baskets and one tray	4.00
one grindstone	1.00
one bearshear plough, cradle and	
stock	4.00
three hoes and two axes	3.75
one paid of... and stillyards (?)	4.50
one trunk, one iron wedge, one	
whiskey barrel and tea pot	3.75
one pair sheep shears and one pair	
saddle bags	2.00
one...tub two... and ...	2.75
one red cow	12.00
one brindle cow and calf	12.00
one red heifer	5.50
one bell and collar	1.25
one brindle heifer	7.00
one muly heifer	7.00
one red bull calf	4.00
one black heifer	3.00
one... and one black...	7.00
one... 5 pigs and two shoats	6.00
four choice hogs	14.00

eight hogs and ten shoats	28.50
2/3 of oats in the barn	3.50
the whole of the flax	3.50
one bay filly	30.00
one mare and colt	60.00
8 small stacks of hay	5.00
2/3 of eleven acres of corn in the field	40.00
Eleven...	20.00
2/3 of one oat stack	3.00
2/3 of the crop of tobacco supposed to be 1600 pounds	32.00
2/3 of eight acres of corn in the field	40.00
one little barshear plough and...	2.50
cash on hand in specie	84.00
one receipt on Richard French for the collection of a note on M.H.Winn for $100 due 26th December 1818 with one years interest, paid. Received by said French August 16th, 1820. Also received of M.H. Winn in part of the above debt 80 dollars 18 August 1822	
one sythe and cradle	2.50
one bridle	2.25
one reap hook and shovel plough	2.00
one pair double traces and two...	2.00

one sorrel horse	65.00
one half bushel	.50

Signed Colby Queshenberry, William Asher, John Jones

"At a county court held for Madison County on Monday the 2nd day of December 1822 this inventory and appraisement of the Estate of Henry Wells dec'd was returned and ordered to be recorded and the same has been done accordingly. Attest David Irvine, Clerk Madison County Court."

On the 15th of October 1822 the Bill of Sale was recorded. Among the buyers are Anna Wells, William and Richard Wells. William Wells served as administrator. One third of the estate sale was set aside for a widow's dower in the amount of $238.38.

BIBLIOGRAPHY

Allen, Penelope Johnson. Leaves from the Family Tree. Chattanooga Times, 1933-37.

Berg, Fred Anderson. Encyclopedia of Continental Army Units. Stackpole Books

Boatner, Mark M. Landmarks of the American Revolution. New York: Hawthorn Books, Inc., 1975.

Boyer, Reba. Wills and Estate Records of McMinn County Tennessee 1820-70. Boyer, 1966.

Byrum, C. Stephen. McMinn County, Tennessee County History Series. Memphis: Memphis State University Press, 1984.

Dorris, Jonathan and Maud. Glimpses of Historic Madison County Kentucky. Nashville: Williams Printing Co., 1955.

Drake, Daniel. Pioneer Life in Kentucky. Henry Schumann, Inc., 1948.

Goodspeed, Weston A. History of Tennessee. Nashville: Goodspeed Publishing Co., 1887.

Harrower, John. The Journal of John Harrower, An Indentured Servant in the Colony of Virginia 1773-76. Colonial Williamsburg Inc. 1963.

Hurlburt, J. S. History of the Rebellion in Bradley County, Tennessee. Indianapolis: Downey and Brouse, 1866.

Lillard, Roy G. Tennessee County History Series, Bradley County. Memphis: Memphis State University Press, 1980.

Lossing, Benson J. Pictorial Field Book of the War of 1812. New Hampshire Publishing Co., 1976 reprint of 1868 edition.

Manarian, Louis H. and Dowdey, Clifford. History of Henrico County. Charlottesville: University Press of Virginia, 1985.

Matloff, Maurice. American Military History. Army Historical Series, U.S. Army, Washington, D.C., 1973.

Nuckolls, Benjamin F. Pioneer Settlers of Grayson County Virginia. Genealogical Publication, 1982.

Rankin, Hugh F. The American Revolution. New York: G. P. Putnam's Son, 1964.

Sanchez-Saavedra, E. M. A Guide to Virginia Military Organizations in the American Revolution, 1774-1787. Virginia State Library, 1978.

Savage, Henry. Seeds of Time. New York: Henry Holt, 1959.

Snell, William R. Cleveland, The Beautiful. Nashville: Williams Printing Company, 1986.

Sullins, David. Recollections of an Old Man, Seventy Years in Dixie. Bristol: King Printing Co., 1910.

Thatch, T.E. Brief Sketch of a County Neighborhood, Laurel Hill. 1894

Thwaites, Reuben. The Colonies. Longman, Green and Co., 1890.

Trabue, Daniel. _Westward into Kentucky. The Narrative of Daniel Trabue._ edited by Chester Raymond Young, The University Press of Kentucky, 1981.

Wilder, Minnie S. _Kentucky Soldiers of the War of 1812._ Baltimore: Second Edition, Baltimore Genealogical Publishing Co., 1969.

NEWSPAPERS

Cleveland Banner. Cleveland, Tennessee, est. 1854.
Cleveland Dispatch. Cleveland, Tennessee, est.1854.
Hiwassean, & Athens Gazette. Athens, Tennessee, est. 1827.
The Athens Union Post. Athens, Tennessee, est. circa. 1862.
The Kentucky Gazette. Lexington, Kentucky, 1787.
Valley Freeman. Athens, Tennessee, 1824.

PUBLIC RECORDS

Land, tax, military, marriage and estate records on file:

Indiana State Library, Indianapolis, Indiana. Kentucky Public Records Division, Frankfurt, Kentucky.
National Archives and Records Service, Washington, D.C.
Tennessee State Library and Archives, Nashville, Tennessee.
Virginia State Library and Archives Division, Richmond, Virginia.

SELECTED RECORDS

MARRIAGES, BIRTH AND DEATH DATES

Hampton Family Record (William-Hannah):
William b. 1761 d. February 24, 1837 m. November 15, 1788 Hannah Richardson b. circa 1767 d. after 1861
Hampton Children-
1. James b. October 17, 1790 (died after 1860)
2. John
3. Rebecca b. 1798 (died 1860-70)
   At least four other children.

Hampton Family Record: (Rebecca-William)
Rebecca daughter of William and Hannah m. June 17, 1824 William Griffith b. 1800 d. July 3, 1880
Griffith Children -
1. James A. b. 1827
2. John H. b. 1829 d. January 28, 1879
3. Larkin N. b. 1831 d. April 22, 1879 m. November 21, 1865 Margaret Davidson d. October 1883

4. Leander J. b. 1833 m. Julia B. Gallaway December 24, 1882
5. Iva b. 1835
6. Uriah b. 1835 m. Mollie Carson April 13, 1885
7. Malissa b. 1837 m. Davidson
8. Hannah M. b. 1839

Hampton Family Record: (James-Gemima)
James son of William and Hannah m. September 14, 1815 Gemima Wells b. February 15, 1795 d. April 21, 1865

Hampton Children -
1. Peter b. (illegible) 18, 1816
2. Hannah b. 1818 d. June 16, 1856
3. Dulseana b. April 6, 1821
4. William Everest b. March 13, 1819
5. Rebecca Adaline b. November 1824
6. Jane B. b. April 19, 1827
7. James M. b. April 2, 1833 d. March 26, 1862
8. John b. May 15, 1838
9. Levi b. 1840
10. Thomas b. 1842
11. Martha b. 1845

Hampton Family Record: (Rebecca-William)
Rebecca daughter of James and Gemima m. March 14, 1849 William F. Melton

Hampton Family Record: (Jane-John)
Jane daughter of James and Gemima m. February 2, 1849 John W. Liner

Hampton Family Record: (John H.-Mary Jane)
John H. son of James and Gemima m. 1859-60 Mary Jane

Hampton Family Record: (James M.-Nancy Jane)
James M. son of James and Gemima m. date unknown Nancy Jane Longwith b. February 18, 1836 d. October 10, 1901

Hampton Child -

1. Nancy Darthula b. April 10, 1860 d. July 29, 1946

Hampton Family Record: (Samuel-Rachel)
Grandson of William and Hannah, Samuel born 1840 died after 1890 m. July 5, 1877 Rachel Skelton

Longwith Family Record:(Reuben-Tabitha)
Reuben son of Reuben and Nancy Hathcock (most probable parents) b. 1808 d. 1852 m.

circa 1830 Tabitha Harden b. February 3, 1815 d. May 27, 1896

Longwith Children -

1. Nancy Jane b. February 18, 1836 d. October 10, 1901 m. James M. Hampton June 7, 1859
2. William Franklin b. 1834 m. Amanda
3. Reuben Christopher b. 1836 m. Mary Ann Lawson February 15, 1866
4. James M. b. 1838 m. Florence Williams November 5, 1875
5. Rachael Catherine b. 1840 m. Nichols
6. Isaac Lafayette b. 1842 m. Angeline Pascall
7. Mary A. b. 1844 m. Isham Lawson
8. Azel N. b. 1846 d. July 17, 1919 m. Sarah Chamblin, November 10, 1868
9. Rebecca b. 1847 m. James Petty September 11, 1865
10. Elizabeth b. 1848 d. prior to 1896 m. Repier
11. John Steven b. February 8, 1850 d. September 5, 1935 m. Martha McAlister, August 22, 1866
12. Joseph Greenberry b. April 15, 1853 d. February 9, 1919

McCracken Family Record: (John-Margaret)
John b. prior to 1850 d. January 8, 1820 m. Margaret b. unknown - d. after 1820
McCracken Children -

1. John b. December 10, 1777 (Pa.) d. April 9, 1859
   m. Ann Kelsey
2. Samuel b. 1779 (Pa.) d. 1854-60 m. Alice Mercer
3. Robert b. August 29, 1783 (Pa.) d. December 14, 1855 m. Nancy McClure
4. Henry b. unknown d. 1851 m. 1. Nancy Barclay 2. Katherine Hamilton
5. Mary b. unknown d. unknown m. John Kelsey
6. Catherine b. 1785 (Pa.) m. Samuel Greer

McCracken Family Record: (John Jr.-Ann)
John Jr. son of John and Margaret m. Ann Kelsey daughter of William Kelsey, b. February 13, 1778 d. December 10, 1856.
McCracken Children -

1. Margaret b. July 4, 1802 m. August 22, 1834 William Greenway
2. Agnes Kelsey
3. William K. b. 1804 m. October 28, 1838 Jane Patton

4. Elizabeth b. 1807
5. Mary A. b. 1815 m. 1837 William L. Shields
6. Susan B. b. 1818 m. November 16, 1846 John A. May
7. Catherine K. b. 1824 m. December 25, 1845 Matthew Hundly

McCracken Family Record: (Samuel-Alice)
Samuel son of John and Margaret m. Alice Mercer b. 1790 d. after 1850
McCracken Children -

1. John C. b. 1808 d. after 1850 m. Dicey Oliver, October 22, 1835
2. Joseph b. circa 1810 d. after 1850 m. 1. Sarah Wood, December 19, 1832. 2. Eliza Mitchell, April 15, 1835
3. Henry b. 1814 d. after 1870 m. Rebecca Wood, October 25, 1832
4. Margaret b. unknown d. unknown m. Jesse Wood, December 28, 1831
5. Martha b. unknown d. 1870 m. Gilbreath

McCracken Family Record: (Robert-Nancy)
Robert son of John and Margaret m. May 8, 1810 Nancy McClure daughter of John and Rebecca (nee Ewing) McClure b. 1792 at

Lynchburg, Virginia d. ca. 1857 Madison County Arkansas.

McCracken Children -

1. John b. April 15, 1811 m. 1. Nancy Henry 2.Mary B. K. Henderson 3. Lisa Mashler
2. Mollie
3. Ewing b. December 23, 1817 m. Emaline J. Brown
4. Minerva
5. Robert b. 1823 m. Elizabeth
6. William M. b. 1825 m. Elizabeth Jane Doak
7. Margaret b. 1828
8. James b. 1830 m. Theresa Boren
9. Dave m. Liza Mashburn
10. Campbell G. "Sam" b. January 6, 1832 m. Bethina Boren
11. Nancy Jane b. 1835 m. James Monroe Doak

McCracken Family Record: (Henry-Nancy)

Henry son of John and Margaret m. September 25, 1811 1. Nancy Barclay m. October 22, 1816 2. Katherine Hamilton b. 1786 d. April 29, 1874. The 1870 Census shows Mrs. McCracken living in the home of David K. McCracken, Washington Co. This May 7, 1874 newspaper obituary states"...Mrs. Catherine

McCracken, aged 88 years died April 29, 1874 near Telford's Depot at home."

McCracken Children -

1. John Barclay b.July 21, 1812
2. Mary Barclay b. March 24, 1814 m. John Asten 1832
3. Catherine Greer b. April 2, 1817 m. David Kelsey 1836
4. James Henry b. July 16, 1818 m. Sarah Byerly 1841
5. Samuel Greer b. May 26, 1820 m. Sally Greenway
6. Nancy Barclay b. February 8, 1822 m. John L. Williams 1846
7. William Franklin b. September 3, 1823 m. Jane Patton 1839
8. David Kelsey b. April 18, 1825 m. 1. Jane Ellis 2. Julie Ekiss 1850
9. Ebenezer Barclay b. March 17, 1828 m. Nancy Caroline Williams 1849
10. Margaret Patton b. September 27, 1828 died single
11. Hetty Greer b. April 14, 1830 m. William J. Williams 1846

McCracken Family Record: (John-Dicey)

John C. son of Samuel and Alice m. October 22, 1835 Dicey Oliver d. October 13, 1865

McCracken Children -

1. Mary Jane b. 1837 m. Abraham Early June 17, 1854
2. D. John C. Jr. b. 1840 never married
3. Samuel b. 1841 1. Rachael Letterman 2. Martha Clowers
4. James b. 1842 m. Sarah
5. Eliza b. 1845 m. August 18, 1865 Pleasant Little
6. Thomas b. 1848 m. September 7, 1875 Amanda Ivester
7. Annie b. May 13, 1854 m. February 15, 1868 James Smith
8. Julia b. April 29, 1856 m. February 8, 1870 Winfred Taylor Raulston

McCracken Family Record: (Henry-Rebecca)
Henry son of Samuel and Alice m. October 25, 1832 Rebecca Wood b. 1813 d. after 1870
McCracken Children -

1. Mary A. b. 1827
2. John B. b. 1832 d. February 15, 1864
3. Margaret b. 1833
4. Bunthony b. 1835
5. Lucretia J. b. 1838
6. James A. b. 1842 m. 1. Nancy Wilson, October 13, 1867 2. Betsy A. b. 1855 d. unknown

7. Sarah A. b. 1844
8. Eliza M. b. 1845
9. Jesse Thomas b. February 1, 1847 d. November 10, 1938
10. Richmond W. b. November 10, 1850

McCracken Family Record: (Jesse T.- Malinda)
Jesse Thomas son of Henry and Rebecca m. March 23, 1869 Malinda Wilson b. March 10, 1846

McCracken Children -

1. Mary Jane b. September 19, 1869 m. O. D. Shirley, December 27, 1885
2. Martha b. January 21, 1872 m. W.W. Walker
3. Elizabeth b. February 28, 1873 m. C.E. Fario
4. Sarah b. July 15, 1874 m. 1. Thomas Cunningham, January 27, 1905 2. Otis Hogan
5. Pearl b. February 11, 1876 m. Frank Trosper
6. Walter Thomas b. March 23, 1884 d. August 24, 1957
7. Jessie (female) b. October 23, 1887 m. Adley Hogan, January 18, 1906

McCracken Family Record: (Walter-Dollie)
Walter son of Jesse T. m. September 1, 1909 Dollie Brown 2. December 24, 1916 Maud Hill
McCracken Children -

1. Mildred m. Merle Crossley
2. Wilson m. 1. June Tolson 2. Katherine Dye
3. Lawrence m. Marion R. Ruth
4. Laurene m. Herbert Needham
5. Donald Ray b. 1923 (mother Maud) m. Katherine Ford

McCracken Family Record: (James A.- Nancy)
James A. son of Henry and Rebecca m. 1. October 13, 1867 Nancy Wilson 2. Betsy
McCracken Children -

1. John H. b. 1869 (mother Nancy)
2. Mary A. b. 1876 (mother Betsy)
3. Addie B. b. 1882

McCracken Family Record: (Richmond W.)
Richmond son of Henry and Rebecca
McCracken Children -

1. Eliza b. 1893
2. Ida May b. 1899

McCracken Family Record: (John B.-Fannie)
John B. son of Henry and Rebecca m. October

29, 1857 Fanny Minerva Mabry b. April 5, 1834 d. March 12, 1901

McCracken Children -

1. William b. 1859 d. in infancy
2. Jackson Leonidas b. September 25, 1858 d. April 20, 1934 m. Nancy Darthula Hampton September 5, 1886
3. Henry Love b. April 5, 1860 d. August 30, 1939 m. Sally McCullough Rose May 2, 1887

McCracken Family Record: (Jackson-Nancy)
Son of John B. and Fannie m. September 5, 1886 Nancy Darthula Hampton b. April 10, 1860 d. 1946
McCracken Children -

1. Fanny J. b. July 21, 1887 d. December 16, 1951 m. Daniel Coffee Trewhitt b. August 30, 1867 d. May 1, 1950
2. Mary Magdalene b. October 6, 1889 d. September 17, 1955 m. Russell Wamsley
3. James Bartley b. August 16, 1892 d. November 25, 1892
4. Henry James b. October 7, 1893 d. May 19, 1977
5. Martha May b. March 15, 1897 d. June 11, 1898

6. Bertha b. January 22, 1899 d. April 18, 1957
7. Rufus Pledger and Bettie b. April 25, 1901

   Rufus d. March 14, 1902

   Bettie d. June 21, 1975 m. February 21, 1932 James Thomas Brown
8. David Franklin b. August 22, 1904 d. April 15, 1948 m. Ada Hall

McCracken Family Record: (Henry Love-Sally) Son of John B. and Fannie m. May 2, 1887 Sallie M. Rose b. March 20, 1864 d. May 10, 1933

McCracken Children -

1. Charley b. May 30, 1886 d. February 13, 1899
2. H. Bartley b. June 13, 1891 d. January 11, 1892
3. David Isham b. September 21, 1893 d.
4. Sally May b. May 7, 1896 d. June 2, 1982
5. Anna Bell b. September 28, 1898 d. May 22, 1983 m. Paul R. McDaniel

INDEX

Liner 222, 224, 225, 287,

www.ingramcontent.com/pod-product-compliance
Lightning Source LLC
Chambersburg PA
CBHW070715280326
41926CB00087B/2155

9781556135057